Edition Axel Menges

Philip Drew

Real Space

**The Architecture of
MARTORELL
BOHIGAS
MACKAY
PUIGDOMÈNECH**

Wasmuth

© 1993 Ernst Wasmuth Verlag, Tübingen/Berlin
ISBN 3-8030-2803-5

Design: Axel Menges
Layout: Helga Danz

Printed in Korea.

Introduction

Projects 1954–1992

Appendix

An Architecture with Roots

Exchange is only possible where each one preserves his own genius, and that is not possible without liberty.

Simone Weil, 1942

The air is chill. High in the Vall de Boí, in the farthest corner of Catalonia in the Pyrenees, the bell tower of Sant Climent de Taüll[1] looks down on the early twelfth-century Romanesque church huddled at its base. The square tower is a lance buried in the side of the mountain. Its six tiers of arches mount upwards in a ladder of grey masonry that interrupts the outline of the encircling mountains and punctures the deep blue of the sky.

Just what makes the architecture of one country, and of a single region, different from that of another is never easy to define. Often, it is the cumulative effect of minor differences and seemingly insignificant departures, the contribution of a decorative scheme, and subtle inflections which betray the presence of an entirely new personality at work in the architecture. In a Catalonia exposed to influences from Spain, France, and other countries bordering the Mediterranean, the subtle nuances of the Catalan spirit lend a peculiar, and unmistakeable, piquancy to the culture of the region.

The independence of the tower from the church is typical of the genius of Catalonia[2]. The tower is an adjunct rather than the climax of the whole. Instead of one artistic unit, two distinct characters co-exist side by side in an easygoing manner that seems indelibly Catalan; an attitude which encompasses both the tower and the church, both the dragon and St George, both Montserrat, the serrated »dragon« mountain and its Abbey, both Catalonia the land and Barcelona its capital, both *rauxa* and *seny*[3]. In reality, there are two distinct characters: *seny* which translates as good sense, prudence, soundness of mind, and *rauxa*, which designates spontaneity, outburst, rage, fury. *Rauxa* is opposed to *seny* as the tower is to the church. The two dispositions: one earthbound and sensible, practical and realistic; the other, extravagant, intense, a symptom of the need to escape the routine and humdrum.

These two characters have their counterparts in Catalan architecture in the combination of realism with sensuousness[4], and a certain eccentric extremism arising from the architect's intense absorption in the sculptural manipulation of his forms.

Outsiders may question this contradiction, and admittedly, there is much that is contradictory in the culture of Catalonia. Nonetheless, the existence of divergent and opposed qualities, of opposition within the culture, is one of its distinguishing peculiarities - its many-sidedness. What this reveals is that over the centuries Catalans found ways to accommodate complexity. This accommodation of contradiction suggests a larger accommodation with life itself and partly explains the richness and inconsistency of much of the art and architecture of the region.

Viewed from the mountainside at Taüll, the qualities of sobriety, endurance, work, prayer, which sustained this early Christian community against the Moors, do not seem remote, any more than the characteristics of Sant Climent, simplicity, gravity and restraint[5], appear unconnected with present-day architecture of Barcelona. Most of all, it is the ability to make the most of meagre resources, an inventiveness and imagination, that is most compelling. A certain simplicity and sobriety animated by a vividness of imagination.

This unlikely combination of industriousness and sobriety with an extravagance of spirit bordering at times on madness, which is really a product of intensity, results in a culture that is simultaneously inward looking, and aware of outside developments, both provincial and cosmopolitan. Catalan development is an instance of Simone Weil's assertion that openness and readiness to learn from other cultures in an exchange of influences is only possible where a society has preserved its genius and is secure in its identity[6]. Catalonia illustrates a successful outcome for a provincial culture dependent on the creative centres of European civilization, able to take from them and benefit without threatening its own autonomous identity.

Josep Martorell and Oriol Bohigas, together with José Antonio Coderch, dominated Barcelona architecture after 1950. No other firm has made so great, or so broad, a contri-

bution to the appearance of the city over the past forty years. Spain lost many of its leading modernists, such as Josep Lluís Sert who emigrated to the United States in 1939, as a direct consequence of the Civil War. In the early 1950s, there was a widely felt need to re-establish ties with the severed thread of Modern architecture. The architecture of MBM is defiantly Catalonian, with roots that extend deep into the cultural soil. There is not one but many roots.

Oriol Bohigas' father was a noted journalist and intellectual who served as secretary of the Escola d'Art Dramatic[7]. The elder Bohigas was horrified by the destruction in July 1936 by the revolutionaries of the churches in Barcelona and their repositories of art and this led him to act to preserve what remained through the Junta de Museus during the Civil War period and thereafter.

Such an involvement in the general culture is something which Oriol Bohigas continues, and although an architect and planner, he has written histories of Modernisme and the Rational Modern architecture of the Republican period[8], as well as contributing to Catalan literature as Chairman of the Board of Directors of Edicions 62 which defiantly continued to publish in Catalan at a time when this was difficult. In 1971 he became a professor at the Escola Tècnica Superior d'Arquitectura de Barcelona, and its director in 1977. He injected new life and vigour into the by then stale curriculum. Bohigas served as a President of the Fundació Joan Miró, and in 1981 he was appointed to establish and head a new urban design group within Barcelona's Planning Department to give direction to the city's development in the lead up to the 1992 Olympic Games.

In 1991, as an independent, he was elected in the Municipal elections as councillor in the city government of the socialist mayor Pasqual Maragall, and was appointed as the political head of Cultural Affairs.

These are many and varied roles, but they had the advantage that they thrust the architect into the central arena of the community, putting Bohigas in touch with all that was happening and informing him of the spirit permeating the institutions and life of Barcelona. Bohigas' Catalan roots have their origin in his family and extend out into the community, in his varied political, educational and artistic, as well as professional roles. The architect in Barcelona has historically assumed a much larger place in giving cultural leadership in the wider spheres of politics[9] and urban development, conserving the cultural heritage, as a friend and ally of the artist, and as someone deeply committed to supporting and encouraging creativity.

2. Josep Martorell, Oriol Bohigas, David Mackay, Albert Piugdomènech.
3. Antoni Gaudí, Casa Milá, Barcelona, 1905-11.

Where architecture and society are organically related, the individual shares the characteristics of the society. Oriol Bohigas and Josep Martorell personify the two complementary facets of the Catalan temperament – perhaps that explains why their partnership has lasted so long and has been so productive.

Bohigas is the tower, the bell ringing out across the valley, Martorell the church bringing many hands and minds together to focus on the common task. The two are so unalike. Both physically, and in their personal make-up, they are very different people. Bohigas is outgoing, extroverted, assertive: a large talkative man with wavy hair and an oval mobile face and active hands. While, by contrast, Martorell is thin and wiry, a small reflective man given to introspection.[10]

Both were born in Barcelona in 1925 and graduated in the same year from the Barcelona School of Architecture. Both are energetic and always on the go. Martorell's parents were teachers and this shows in his dealings with other architects which is a mixture of patience and suggestion, gradually defining and recognizing the important issues at stake in a design. Martorell knew from the beginning that he wanted to be an architect; Bohigas was inclined to follow the path of the historian but changed his mind after talking to Martorell.

David Mackay (the third member of the team) is English-Irish. He was born in Eastbourne, Sussex, and came to Barcelona in 1958 on graduating from the North London Polytechnic. Mackay is an excellent critic and proselyte. He became a partner with Martorell and Bohigas in 1961. He supervises the day-to-day running of projects.

Albert Puigdomènech joined MBM as a full partner shortly after 1985 following their collaboration on the design of the Olympic Village.

The architecture of MBM is a mixture of Catalan realism and fantasy: it is decidedly rational, sometimes rigidly so, but for all that, it is given to sculptural gestures for their own sake and an intense identification with the region. In its mixture of the international and the traditional, its blending of rationalism with regionalism, the architecture of MBM exhibits a typically Catalan flexibility, an ability to combine two mutually opposed tendencies. MBM gave this a name: they called it realistic architecture. MBM's buildings, to varying degrees, are international and eclectic, drawing on such local architectural traditions as the patio and terrace and the filtering of light.

The continuity of architectural traditions was nowhere more evident than in the teaching at the School of Architecture in Barcelona where Josep Maria Jujol was a professor. Jujol was famous for his distinctive »calligraphic« style[11] both as a leading assistant of Antoni Gaudí and in his own right. Jujol contributed the flowing seaweed forms to the wrought iron balconies and plaster ceilings of the Casa Milà (1905-11) and the famous serpentine bench-cum-parapet of the mirador of Gaudí's Park Güell (1900-14).[12] He also made alterations to the cathedral at Palma, Mallorca. Through Jujol, Martorell and Bohigas, as students in the 1940s, were introduced to what is, without question, the greatest phase of architectural creativity in Barcelona's history, that of Modernisme from 1890 to 1914, which besides freely taking over the results of Art Nouveau, consciously set about transforming it into a local style in the quest to give a specific shape to the Catalan identity.

Jujol illustrates the Catalan fascination with conflict in his repeated juxtaposition of different geometrical systems, in, for example, the Casa Planells (1924) in which five cylinders are reconciled with a rectilinear organization behind the curvilinear façade.[13] Such things as the preoccupation with finishing the corners off, with the diagonal and geometry, can be traced back to the influence of Jujol. The evolution of Catalan architecture is a case study in the successful assertion of a regional identity in architecture and art, and in the general culture, whose success was assisted by the possession of a Catalan tongue which increased awareness of the differences that existed between Catalans and other peoples, but an identity which was fiercely fought over and contested at the same time.

Besides Jujol, there was Adolf Florensa[14] who approached a Mediterranean idiom through the Italian Renaissance. Florensa taught wood and stone construction, but his approach was very different from the way it is taught today without any reference to the stylistic and cultural context. For Florensa, construction was part and parcel of art history, the necessary method for achieving the design conception, and therefore something to be learnt in partnership with an understanding of the history of style. It was only in the final year that Modern architecture was touched on and this was done, more by way of completeness, to inform students that such a thing existed, rather than as a means of introducing a vital new departure which they ought to investigate as directly impinging upon their concerns as contemporary designers.[15]

Lifting the Fog

Modern architecture reached Spain at the beginning of the 1930s. Before long it was identified with the Republic and was generally associated as the style of the political left.

In May 1928, Josep Lluís Sert intercepted Le Corbusier on his way to Madrid,[16] and subsequently from 1929 to 1931, the architect worked under Le Corbusier in Paris. The early Modern Spanish buildings are remarkable for their mature application of Modernist principles, but, more surprisingly, given the early date, there was a deliberate adjustment of the Modern forms to accord with local sensibilities and practices that stamp the work as both Modern and Spanish. Joaquim Lloret's Barraquer Clinic (1936-39) is a minor masterpiece, while Sert's apartment block in Carrer Muntaner (1930/31) is the equal of anything then being designed anywhere in Europe. In terms of the rapid assimilation of Modern architecture, Sert's weekend houses at Garraf (1935), with their Catalan vaults set on a rubble stone base, are as good an indication as any of the speed with which Modernism acquired a Catalan intonation. The formation of GATCPAC[17] by a group of Barcelona architects, included in which was Sert, in 1929, as a Spanish arm of CIAM, shows how alive Barcelona architects were to new developments at the centre of Modernism.

The Civil War interrupted the evolution of Modern architecture. Sert went into exile, and the Franco Government which succeeded the Republic quickly demonstrated that it had little sympathy for Modernism. Martorell and Bohigas both graduated in 1951. In the same year they reacted to the anti-Modernism around them by joining in the formation of Grup R, a decision which was to have a lasting effect on their later development. This was an attempt to renew contact with the earlier phase of Modern architecture in Barcelona. Besides seeking to revive the ideals and principles of Modern architecture, Grup R endeavoured to foster discussion of recent work and facilitate external contacts with other architects and theorists such as Alvar Aalto, Bruno Zevi, Gio Ponti, Alberto Sartoris, and Nikolaus Pevsner, in order to enlarge the scope of their own ideas.

The initial members of the Grup R were Joaquim Gili, Josep Pratsmarsó, Josep M. Sostres, Antoni de Moragas, José Antonio Coderch, Manuel Valls, Oriol Bohigas, and Josep Martorell. Alvar Aalto proved to be the closest and the most beneficial in terms of his contribution to the fledgling group.

4. Members of Grup R with Nikolaus Pevsner in 1952. From left to right around the table: Nikolaus Pevsner, Joaquim Gili, Josep M. Sostres, Oriol Bohigas, Josep Martorell, Joaquim Mascaró, Antoni de Moragas.
5. Joaquim Lloret, Barraquer Clinic, Barcelona, 1936 to 1939.
6. José Antonio Coderch, block of flats on Carrer J. S. Bach, Barcelona, 1958.

Grup R met regularly once a week at a member's office, though less frequently in the last two or three years of its existence. A member would present and explain his latest work, frequently this was followed by a site visit to the work and discussion, which on occasion could become stridently critical. The procedure was continued until 1961 when it was replaced by a series of twice yearly »little congresses«, expanded to include Madrid and Basque architects as well as colleagues from other parts of Spain.

It is not clear whether the »R« in the group's name stood for Rationalism or Realism or Revolution.[18] The intention behind the formation of the group was to stimulate debate and assist in clarifying issues so as to form a distinct viewpoint which was later recognized as the Barcelona School. This openness was an advantage. The notion of Realism is important under the circumstances because it suggests an acceptance of, and accommodation with, the given realities of the situation. Realism in architecture finds a parallel in the Neo-Realism of the Italian cinema in the late 1940s[19] by the likes of Roberto Rossellini, Vittorio De Sica, Giuseppe De Santis, Luchino Visconti and others, which projected a moral and an aesthetic dimension[20], to the extent that there was a clear commitment to portraying contemporary social subjects, as well as deriving the cinematic look by shooting the world as it appears outside the studio using real locations and non-professional actors. Architectural Realism implied several things: it meant picking up where thirties Modernism had left off; expressing the reality of construction in details, and where appropriate, adopting or adapting traditional methods. Just as Realism in philosophy applied to whatever is regarded as having an existence in fact, so Realism in architecture required that space be treated as concrete and not merely existing in thought or language.

Real space dealt with the unique qualities of each place. It was specific in character, not universal, concrete rather than abstract.

Real space resulted from Realism. Above all, real space implied the creation of distinct spatial identities within the city whose unique forms were predicated on the consideration of contingent and existential realities – the given urban facts. As with its cinematic counterpart, there was a strong feeling that architecture must serve a social end. Many years later, when Bohigas came to consider the planning of Barcelona, Realism was interpreted as demanding the reinforcement and continuation of the existing morphology of the city.

Later, one of the members of Grup R, José Antonio Coderch, distanced himself without actually disagreeing, in order to establish a more independent position for himself.[21] By 1968, new works by a younger generation, which included Lluís Domènech and PER, ended the Barcelona School whose cause Grup R had once championed.[22] The self-conscious defence of the Catalan identity was weakening to be replaced by a much more international and eclectic outlook. The commitment to Regionalism and Catalan identity in architecture is confined to the two decades after 1950.

Coderch led the way. His architecture was an attractive marriage of Modern style with regionalism and the Mediterranean vernacular. The Pescadores Housing Block, Barceloneta (1951), was contained within a double façade which acted as a climatic filter surrounding a complicated deep plan with splayed walls inside, the whole disguised within a deceptively simple envelope. The Pescadores block announced a number of new themes which were to occupy the attention of Grup R members throughout the 1950s. The choice of organic materials such as tile, brick and timber was one.

The block of flats on Carrer J.S. Bach (1958) is Coderch's masterpiece. The design is one of enormous subtlety and simplicity. Once again, Coderch employed the double façade of louvred screens in front of the galeria, but on this occasion, there are two angled balconies symmetrically placed on either side of the street façade which causes a sliding diagonal movement beneath the outer sheath of louvres. The plan is of the deep plan variety with patios serving the inner rooms.

Similar ideas are present in buildings by Martorell and Bohigas, but they were not alone, as evidenced by Federico Correa and Antoni de Moragas. The Casa Guardiola, Argentona (1954/55), with its pair of open-ended cubes separated by a stair and elevated on a recessed ground storey accommodating the daytime living areas, assisted at each end by slim steel cruciform columns, is more strongly identified with Modern prototypes such as the Barcelona Pavilion, at least in the composition of the ground floor plan as a series of juxtaposed vertical plane elements. The executed scheme is more Mediterranean with its louvred screens protecting the living room and grille block balcony ends, than the sketch design which indicated a Constructivist arrangement of orange vertical panels behind white slab balconies and metal grille glazing to the recessed lower storey.

In the case of MBM there was an early realization that, while the industrialization of the building process was desirable, this was far off in Spain, and the architect had of necessity to come to terms with a much less developed situation. The advent of the New Brutalism complemented MBM's singular determination to express, in as honest a way as possible, the use of materials such as brick and timber.

The early 1950s work reveals an eager re-examination of the elements of Modernism which resulted in, on occasion, a cubic additive form, which in the example of the staggered classrooms of the Timbaler del Bruc Elementary School, Barcelona (1957/58), is more than a little reminiscent of the cubic expression of Coderch. The variety of commissions at that time prevented this from becoming the dominant note; hence the concrete frame of the Escorial Apartments, Barcelona (1955-62), designed at the same time as the Timbaler del Bruc school, is treated as a grid work of open balconies with the fenestration and blinds exploited to soften and vary the severity of the structure.

By 1958 the didactic Modern orientation gave way to a more thoughtful regional stance and accommodation with local motifs as in the Pallars Housing, Barcelona (1958/59), and the Meridiana Apartments, Barcelona (1959-65), with their projecting trapezoidal-shaped window bays that break up what otherwise would have been a very dull multi-storeyed façade overlooking the Avinguda Meridiana (one of the main traffic arteries of the city), at the same time creating a strongly sculptural effect.

Translating Tradition

The commitment of MBM to Modern architecture, to establishing a rational basis for design did not cease all of a sudden in the 1960s, to be replaced overnight by regionalism. There was a gradual shift and assimilation of regional themes depending on the job, and there were buildings in the 1960s which were substantially Modern in conception and execution such as the Piher-Badalona Factory and the offices for La Vanguardia. Quite simply, MBM never thought of Modern architecture as exclusively international, and therefore incapable of being given a regional interpretation. That problem never existed for them because Modern architecture, from its initial introduction in the 1930s quickly acquired a Spanish intonation. This accounts for their interest in Alvar Aalto. After all, had not Le Corbusier borrowed the Catalan vault for the Jaoul House, Neuilly-sur-Seine (1952-56), and the much earlier weekend house at St Cloud (1934/35) designed when Sert and Bonet were working with him?

Traditions are neither good nor bad per se, sometimes they are beneficial, at other times harmful. It really depends on the tradition in question and the situation in which the individual or community finds itself. At times of rapid change traditions offer reassurance and continuity as something to fall back on. In architecture, traditional methods of doing things can also represent an outmoded construction and a thing not to be repeated. What makes these traditional forms so valuable is that the identity of a community, its sense of itself as unique and separate, and continuity of its special relationship to the past, is frequently dependent on the re-expression (even in a modified form) of these inherited motifs.

For the Catalans, the possession of their own language has been an important factor in maintaining a sense of cultural identity. The plastic arts and architecture also made an important contribution that should not be deprecated. It is not surprising to find revivified traditional motifs throughout MBM's work. Such things as: the street; the terrace or *terrassa*; the patio; sunscreens, whether as *gelosia* or draped *persianas*; the double façade such as one encounters in Gaudí's work; cubic Mediterranean form; and the exploitation of a variety of effects of light in buildings all integrated within an essentially Modern mode.

The diagonal is a puzzle. It is difficult to pin down in terms of tradition. There are so many possibilities, from the Avinguda Diagonal running east-west across Barcelona which must be a part of every citizen's subconscious, to the diagonal cut-offs at each corner on Cerdà's plan. Whatever its origin, the diagonal is a persistent theme. The stepped façade may be seen as a variation of this, a way of disguising the underlying diagonal structure, as in the Navas de Tolosa (1960-63) and the Casa del Pati Apartments (1961-64) on chamfered corner blocks.

Kenneth John Conant singled out the treatment of light as something which distinguished Spanish Romanesque, he detected a »traditional skill in exploiting effects of sun and shadow; simpler bulks and the indefinable play of relationships between the buildings and their austere surroundings or background...«[23], which he thought contributed a decidedly Spanish imprint to the new Romanesque.

Besides the strong modelling of the building face to exploit the brilliant sunlight – the light is filtered, broken down so it is softer and less intense as it enters the room – there are other habits, more cultural, social and religious in nature, which combine to distance the outside from the interior and establish an interval. Sometimes, a thick layer of space is wrapped around the rooms, and this establishes a greater psychological as it were, as well as physical isolation.

On the other hand, Spanish people love the outdoors. The mildness of the climate beside the Mediterranean is an invitation to move the living space outside and this encouraged a number of innovations such as the *terrassa, pati, balcó, galeria, pèrgola, corredor, tribuna, mirador,* etc., which are really Mediterranean as much as Catalan or Spanish, which effectively extended the living space beyond the wall boundary. The window bays of the Meridiana Apartment Block (1959-65), which is aligned north-south, were conceived as light catchers specially shaped to trap and reflect the morning and afternoon sunlight. At Meridiana MBM exploited the tilted façade to filter and reflect the light in a manner which recalled the effect of openings in the thick stone walls of farmhouses.

It is not necessary to go back very far to discover examples of this play with sunlight. When the Catalan civil engineer Ildefons Cerdà drew up his plan for Barcelona in 1859 he tilted the 133 m square grid at forty-five degrees to the meridian to obtain the maximum exposure to sunlight.[24] The game of catching sunlight began with the city plan. The elaborate shuttered baywindow at the rear of the Palau Güell (1885-89) is one of many such instances, which demonstrate the ingenuity of Gaudí in filtering light to the interior spaces of his buildings via an intermediate space. The Palau Güell street façade is also an early illustration of the double layered façade, in which the conflict between interior and exterior needs was mediated by splitting the façade into two planes, an inner plane to deal with the internal demands, and an external plane to respond to the formal requirements of the street in terms of fenestration. MBM have reiterated this technique for example in their houses for Serras at Canovelles and Escarrer at Son Vida.

The *pati* or patio is a recurring motif in MBM schemes. The Barcelona patio was borrowed from Naples in the fifteenth century.[25] The Palau de la Generalitat in the Gothic quarter has a patio of orange trees on the first floor which is visible from the gallery of the front courtyard whilst the Gothic palace in which the Picasso Museum is housed on carrer Montcada also has a patio. The Gothic patio provided a mediating space between the street and the dwelling that shut out the noise and bustle allowing light to reach inside the rooms. It was customary to locate the main stair leading to the upper rooms in this fore-patio.[26] An early example of its use by MBM is the Casa del Pati Apartment Block at Ronda del Guinardó, completed in 1964, which had a small fountain and was surrounded on the upper levels by access galleries. The Secretari Coloma Apartment Block (1960-65) contained several small service light-wells in conjunction with a larger landscaped patio behind the main block which admitted light to the entry, and this is repeated with variations in the Xaudiera (1964-70), Mestres, Pineda (1967-69), and Jericó (1974 to 1978) Apartments. In later large scale housing schemes comprising several blocks, the patio was combined with the internal street, usually there are two blocks, sometimes parallel to one another, sometimes a little askew, which share common lift and stair access with the leftover space forming a patio light-well between the blocks such as occurs in the La Salut Apartment Group (1969-73).

A more intimate and distinctly human expression of the patio prevails in private dwellings, notably the Casa Martí (1972-74), in which the patio roof and wall on the outside were enclosed by a small mesh steel grillwork to filter the sunlight and capture any breezes. Sandwiched between the bedrooms the patios provided an indirect means of connecting the rooms with the outdoors. In summer, the cool shady patio becomes a refuge from the hot sun. The palatial Villa Escarrer on Mallorca has a remarkable patio adjoining the southern bedroom wing which was enclosed overhead by a brilliantly conceived octagonal grille of timber protected by a glass pyramid to give the space an open feeling.

The *balcó* or balcony is everywhere. It provides ventilation and light to the rooms behind, a means of cleaning upper windows and an escape from the claustrophobia of the apartment in a city where buildings are densely packed together. Around the interior of the courtyards of the older nineteenth-century blocks the *balcó* is replaced by a glazed *galeria*. Sometimes these *galerias* are found on the corners of the front façades of buildings, often as rounded or circular turret-like projections offering a warm protected environment in winter. The veranda is hardly ever seen.[27] Indeed, Catalans prefer the term ›terrassa‹ in place of ›veranda‹.

Le Corbusier incorporated a veranda in his 1931 holiday house for Hélène de Mandrot outside Toulon[28] to exploit the vista. In the Casa Canovelles at Granollers (1977-81), the house was established on a raised terraced platform, and the equivalent of a veranda was then formed on either side of the main living area by the serpentine alignment of the glazed wall. The solution is reminiscent of the Casa Malaparte by Adalberto Libera on Capri (1940), in which the rooms of the villa were subsumed within a stepped podium springing abruptly from its rocky promontory.[29] In MBM's design the living areas are placed on the podium which contains the bedrooms and service spaces. Though on a much grander scale, the Villa Escarrer also adopts a similar strategy, but in this latter

instance the extension of the living areas outside is much more clearly a case of the terrace having an overhanging roof over part of it.

MBM gave a new meaning to the traditional terrace or *terrassa*. The terrace is treated playfully to produce a succession of levels, often intricately related in a sculptural sequence. This informal sculptured terrain may occur on the roof of a school, or within the dwelling as a manipulation of the floor plane to form a sunken kiva, but sometimes it is taken outside and applied to the ground directly in a park. The Sant Jordi School, Pineda (1967-69), has a remarkable playground on its roof whose ups and downs are ingeniously regulated to form highlights that admit daylight to the main assembly space. The Garbí School (1962-78) has a similarly complex roof terrain that breaks down into a series of smaller scaled intimate areas. These are really enlarged unprotected terraces which sometimes act as miradors. The encircling first floor terraces of the house at Can Bordoi (1962-65), outside Barcelona in the country, are much closer to the conventional definition of the veranda as an open gallery protected by a roof.

In medieval houses, in Barcelona and Palma on Mallorca, it was common for the living area of the house to be located on the topmost floor and left open as a *porxo* or porch not unlike the Italian Renaissance *loggia*. The Can Bordoi verandas resemble an updated version of the medieval Catalan ›porch‹. The walls comprise sliding glass doors and timber louvred screens which allowed the living space to be extended out into the veranda. This inner façade is supplemented by sliding screens which provide further shelter and screening around the terrace edge.

In the Thau School (1972-74), the terraced terrain was taken outside and applied to the space separating the two blocks in the form of a Greek amphitheatre and meeting place for students to take advantage of the natural fall of the ground.

Of course, there were more recent precedents than the *porxo*: Le Corbusier and Jeanneret treated the roof of the Villa Savoie, Poissy (1929-31), as an extension of the living area and his Unité d'Habitation at Marseilles (1947-52) had a running track, children's swimming pool etc., on the roof, so the idea of using the roof in this way was hardly new.

The street is an extension of the dwelling in Barcelona. This is understandable in one of Europe's densest cities. The awareness of the importance of the street in social terms represented a discovery of its former historical role before the advent of the motor car which had been neglected. It took a Herman Hertzberger[30] and Team 10 to once more bring this discovery to the fore. Cerdà's decision to slice the corners off his square city blocks at forty-five degrees in order to provide for steam trams turning had the unforeseen consequence of transforming each intersection into a potential plaza or square. Important avenues, such as the Passeig de Gràcia, with its central strips for people, were a further reminder in Barcelona, as if one was needed, of the importance of the street.

9. Balconies on a nineteenth-century house in Barcelona.
10. MBM, Sant Jordi School, Pineda, 1967-69. Roof terrace.
11. MBM, Thau School, Barcelona, 1972-74. Terraced terrain between the two blocks.

In MBM schools and housing, the corridor and the street become a social focus for communal activities, intended to encourage social interaction and a sharing of experiences. The corridor was obliterated in their schools to be replaced by a learning space and a social mixing area. This produced open interconnections between spaces and an opening up of the classroom. The dining hall in the Garbí and Thau Schools, and the corridor of the Catalunya School (1981-88) were both conceived in this way and an importance and heightened expression attached to them in recognition of their significance as a communal focus. The quality of the space was further enriched by covering the space of the Catalunya School with a double layered translucent roof.

The reform of the corridor and its newly found educational function in the school reflected an altered attitude to education in the 1970s which placed an increasing emphasis on unstructured and informal learning and sought to create opportunities for the kinds of spontaneous exchanges which spark off creative development of the individual. In the larger housing projects the street was internalized within the block to remove it from exposure to traffic, and frequently galleries were provided to connect apartments which were designed so as to provide opportunities for neighbours to meet and develop an identification with their immediate neighbourhood.

One aspect of this was the creation of indeterminate spaces whose limits are only grasped imperfectly. The idea behind this was to avoid firm boundaries to spaces. The inspiration for this was the enduring concern to filter the inside from the outside which originated in tempering the climate in Barcelona, though something not dissimilar also results in Le Corbusier from his technique of joining unequal spaces by bending partitions to escape the module.

The problem had been tackled by architects before, indeed the idea of the *galeria* and the balcony with *persiana* awning draped over the balcony balustrade to form a shaded outside alcove provided ready-made models for the double layered façade. Had not Gaudí simply hung the bush-hammered stone façade of the Casa Milà on a steel frame inside to avoid the restrictions of normal load-bearing walls and free up the planning! The traditional habit of introducing the *gelosia* (Spanish *celosia*) or lattice, originally an Arab device[31] which filtered sunlight and created internal privacy without restricting air flow, further increased the blurring of spatial boundaries. The confessional screen is also called a *gelosia*, which adds to the sense of its pertaining to things which are hidden.

One of the most obvious applications of the traditional *gelosia* occurs around the main stair of the Can Bordoi House as a screen to the upper bedroom gallery, but a similar

12. MBM, Can Bordoi House, Llinars del Vallès, 1962 to 1965. Living room and screened bedroom balcony.
13. MBM, Martí House, Sant Jordi d'Alfama, 1972 to 1974. Metal *gelosia* over a patio.
14. MBM, Heredero House, Tredòs, Vall d'Aràn. 1967/68. *Gelosia* screen over windows.
15. MBM, Can Summaro Library, L'Hospitalet de Llobregat, 1882-84. Porch.

detail occurs in the square grid masonry-and-glass entrance screen of the Catalunya School and the triangular concrete tile screens of the Canyamars Children's Vacation Housing beside the covered walks. In many MBM buildings, notably the Casa Heredero, Vall d'Aràn (1967/68), and the Bonanova Apartment Group (1970-73), a small square mesh steel *gelosia* screen is applied to the outside over windows and services. The Casa Martí, (1972-74) has a metal *gelosia* enclosing its patios.

The double roof of the Catalunya School repeats a theme enunciated on the steel truss supported roof of the gymnasium swimming pool of the Garbí School (1962-78), in which the trusses were aligned diagonally so they brace one another.

The history of Catalonia, especially in the fifteenth century, reveals the importance of the Mediterranean to Catalan trade and affairs.[32] It has been said that Barcelona faces towards the sea, not towards Spain. In the 1960s the main influence on MBM came from Italy and this accords with the historical orientation of Barcelona as belonging more to the Mediterranean cultural sphere.[33] The Rationalism espoused by MBM carries the imprint of Giuseppe Terragni which reveals itself in small ways as in the cylindrical expression of the columns in the hallway of the Casa Martí and the porch of the Can Sumarro Library (1982-84). This Rationalism frequently shows itself in formal gestures such as the diagonal cut to the façade of the La Costa Apartments, Barcelona (1974-77) following the slope of the hill.

Mediterraneanism manifested itself in a preference for cubic forms arranged in informal expressive sculptural groups suggestive of anonymous village housing and a concern for the sun shading of openings. Le Corbusier's adoption of vernacular forms and the Catalan vault after 1935 supplied a precedent for a series of houses such as Casa Luján (1959-62) and the Europalma Houses, Mallorca (1963-65), which, to some extent, imitate Le Corbusier. In the Europalma Houses on Costa de la Calma, the Mediterranean idiom is a mature mixture of vernacular and the Corbusian idiom of rough stone walls and informal

placement of the buildings, to coincide with the site conditions. An early testing of the idiom occurred in the vacation housing for children at Canyamars (1961-65) in which the Corbusian inspiration is more visible, especially in the strong expressive forms of the southern dormitory wing. The Santa Agueda Apartments, Benicassim (1966/67) on the coast north of València, are pure examples of Mediterraneanism in practice. So too are the Pals Golf Houses (1971-73). Not surprisingly, it was the holiday housing in the sixties and early seventies, for which Mediterraneanism was most favoured. These relatively traditional forms give a more relaxed impression. They are the result of a deliberate effort to be Mediterranean, to enhance contrast in recognition of the stronger sunshine and blue skies. The Mediterranean is a constant in the sub-conscious, an inescapable dimension. The Santa Agueda Apartments were a protest against the bland slab blocks then springing up along the coast. In the Jericó Apartments, Barcelona (1974-78), there is a deliberate manipulation of the brickwork for sculptural effect to avoid monotony and to increase interest, but it is gentler and less exaggerated, when compared with the Santa Agueda Apartments.

One of the sources of a Mediterranean atmosphere is the shading of windows and openings. This is not by any means confined to housing. The Santa Agueda Apartments are the most interesting because they adopt the traditional draped *persiana* awning supported on a metal framework which originated in medieval times. Examples of coir mats draped over balconies can be seen in Palma, Mallorca, to this day.

All the apartments in Benicassim have wide balconies, each with its own metal armatures, and extendable green plastic awnings. These were designed so that the owners of each apartment could unfurl the awnings however far they wished, depending on the season and the weather conditions. When fully extended, the awnings create intimate shaded outdoor rooms outside the apartment living space pierced by streaks of light in places, combined with tantalising sideways glimpses of the sea and neighbouring balconies. The thick timber batten balustrade, reminiscent of the pre-cast concrete battens of the Can Bordoi House terraces (inspired by classical balusters), was yet another casual reference to the traditional *gelosia*.

The Sant Jordi School was provided with orange adjustable canvas sun awnings, while the Gama Apartments, Badalona (1964/65), had vertical louvres mounted in an external track, a solution also adopted in the Alegre de Dalt Apartments and the Thau School. The reliance on such simple and effective sun controls reflected MBM's philosophy of Realism,

of favouring solutions that were convenient and practical. They also recognized that in Spain, unlike the United States, society cannot afford high energy solutions to climate control. In retrospect, this was fortunate because the buildings which resulted are all that much more expressive and interesting.

Looking in more than one Direction

The architecture of MBM defies simplistic analysis which seeks to apply to it a single all-embracing criterion. One is confronted by an architecture that exhibits a variety of themes, changing viewpoints, and attitudes. Recently, David Mackay acknowledged that »architecture must embrace eclecticism to a certain extent«. He went on to add, »It is also about buildings which have to be built, and depends on its materials and how they are combined and put together (the ›joints‹ as Louis Kahn used to express it). Its social, economic and user aspects make up its basic programme. But this programme must be mellowed by local climatic conditions and be imbued with a sense of place – approaching but r ot consuming Kenneth Frampton's Regionalism.«[34] It is difficult to imagine a clearer and more precise definition of »Realism« applied to architecture.

Realism means, among other things, looking in more than one direction, having more than one strategy to deal with any given situation. This does not imply the abandonment of Rationalism, rather, it introduces a note of caution. In practice, MBM led the way in the reform and modification of Modern architecture in the 1950s with the aim of avoiding a pedantic unthinking application of its Rationalist tenets, without first checking their appropriateness, in what was then a poorly industrialized country.

Frequently, in place of some universal and inviolable principle, the critic is presented with recurring patterns, an established manner of dealing with typical problems which the architect meets again and again. The stepped façade is one such recurring pattern. Stepping satisfied the desire to look in more than one direction, to provide alternative views from a room. In Barcelona, Cerdà's cut-off blocks led to problems which increased if the room was small – a conflict between the plan and the plane of the façade. One way of resolving the conflict was to replace the diagonal face by smaller stepped corner-projections. The first application of stepping occurred in the Navas de Tolosa Apartments (1960–63), and it recurs in the Xaudiera Apartment Block (1964–70). Stepping minimized

the perceived bulk and introduced an element of sculptural play which was absent from straight façades. The contradictions of the corner were finally resolved in the Casp Apartments (1966-69) with their straight façade, with balconies interspersed between the corner-rooms. The long Roca Apartment Block, Tarrassa (1967-72), was stepped back to fit it onto an L-shaped lot.

Stepped forms occur in other building types. This is best illustrated by reference to the Garbí and Sant Jordi Schools.

The diagonal is a *sine qua non* of MBM; so often, and so unexpectedly, does it make its appearance in their architecture. At once dynamic and economical, in addition to being the shortest distance, the diagonal is more interesting than an exclusively orthogonal geometry. It sometimes disguises itself as a diamond prism projecting from a plane face, as occurs in the Meridiana Apartments façade, or, as in the gymnasium *terrassa* partially embedded in the elevation of the Catalunya School, where its roof makes a terrace for student activities.

The angled entrance screen is yet another example. The splayed façades of the early Pallars Housing divided what was an overlong façade into four acceptably sized units. Likewise, the splayed ends of the Piher-Badalona Factory, completed in 1959, the same year as the Pallars Housing, have a similar geometry.

The La Costa Apartments façade was sliced by a diagonal trace which is unusual, since the diagonal is normally confined to the plan. The most effective use of the diagonal occurs in the Bonanova Apartment Group (1970-73), where it performs a number of duties: in this example, diagonal balconies are echoed by the diagonal balconies of neighbouring towers thereby relating tower to tower; but the diagonal also directs the view between the buildings.

The diagonal balconies are less of a disruption to the envelope and make each tower appear more integrated. At a much smaller scale, diagonals were introduced in the eastern wall of the main floor of the Can Bordoi House, ten years previously, to enlarge the *terrassa* and increase the inside exposure.

Another MBM mannerism is the corner. Here the diagonal came to the aid of the architects. The sharp wedge is a favourite device for terminating a corner as demonstrated by the apartment blocks at La Salut, Sant Feliu de Llobregat (1969-73), and the Nestlé Office Building at Esplugues de Llobregat (1983-87), where it added greatly to the dramatic

effect of the building's ends. At La Salut, the housing was accommodated in two rings (double layering on a very large scale), an inner square diaphragm of housing surrounded by a trapezoid of two L-shaped blocks leaving triangular interspaces between them. Diagonal lines slice through the corners of the two inner blocks.

The diagonal dominates the Villa Escarrer composition, to the extent, that the square *parti* on which the plan was based is barely discernible. Indeed, the entire building form seems to converge at a single point at the apex of the triangular podium. From the east side, the villa resembles a ship with its bow plunging into the lawn. For anyone standing near this eastern apex at the intersection of the two diagonals, this is the most powerful place of all – the point where the form culminates. This was recognized by positioning the main bedroom on the upper floor so that it confronts the converging sides of the triangle.

Another mannerism is the serpentine wall, which if it is less in evidence, remains a friendly device, much like the casual wave of the hand, it relaxes the severity of the linear. Wavy curved walls are a reminder of nature and an escape from total artificiality. The undulating curved wall was inspired by the Finnish architect Alvar Aalto. It is found in such famous works as the timber ceiling of the Viipuri Library and the Finnish Pavilion at the 1938/39 New York World's Fair.

The most arresting application of the serpentine plane occurs in the Xipell Infant School, Ciutadella, Menorca (1975-78). There, two staggered serpentine diaphragms enclose the corridor adjoining the classrooms, and by doing so, increase the feeling of movement, adding to it a quality of being at ease that is absent from the standard rectangular shaped teaching cells. Serpentine effects such as this are infrequent, but in the Casa Canovelles, the flowing line of the glazing sambas its way around the living, sitting, dining and study areas of the main terrace. On the opposite wall, the living room wall inadvertently steps off the edge into space. This has the most energetic appearance of any freely undulating wall before 1981.

The serpentine is really more at home in landscape and park. The central promenade of the Basses de Sant Oleguer Sports and Leisure Park, Sabadell (1983-86), combined with the circle to suggest a fluidity in keeping with the swimming basin function. Similarly, the serpentine road alignment along the waterfront of the Villa Olímpica corresponds to the reformed outline of the coast. It also reduces the monotony of a straight roadway.

The straight stair is something of a preoccupation with MBM. It all started when the architects observed the bunching up of workers at the Piher-Badalona Factory during the change of shift on a dog-leg stair. The straightening out of a stair emphasized its importance, but in addition, it enhanced the spatial continuity and unity of the interior street of the Thau School. The straight stair acquires an architectonic significance when it is attached to and expressed on the outside, as happens in the second Piher Factory at Badalona. Stairs, in general, are a source of interest because they connect spaces vertically and this can lend added excitement to the spatial drama, when, as occurs at the Teachers' Apartments at Pineda (1967-69), a glazed spiral breaks free of the rear façade and cantilevers off the galleries.

True to Type

Nothing old is ever re-born. But it never completely disappears either. And anything that has ever been always re-emerges in a new form. It seems to me that at the moment we are striving towards a whole.

Alvar Aalto, 1921

20. MBM, Navas de Tolosa Housing, Barcelona, 1960 to 1963.
21. MBM, Casp Housing, Barcelona, 1966-69.
22. MBM, Pallars City Block, Barcelona, 1958/59.
23. MBM, Bonanova Flats, Barcelona, 1970-73.
24. MBM, La Salut City Block, Sant Feliu de Llobregat, 1969-73.

The sympathy between MBM and Aalto arose from a shared perception that personal identity was to be found in the familiar and the employment of materials, craftsmanship and iconography, as a source of continuity of values. As with Aalto[35], their typology is both a source of discipline for controlling the programme, and an appeal to memory – a means of individualizing experience.

One typology in particular recurs throughout their work, that of the square divided into four equal smaller squares by two symmetrical axes. Ostensibly, this quadratic *parti* was derived from Palladio, but as Rudolf Wittkower demonstrated in his analysis of the schematized plans of Palladio's villas[36], Palladio preferred either a triadic plan derived from the traditional Venetian house with its central hall running from front to rear, or in an exceptional case such as the Villa Rotonda, symmetry about two axes which allowed too little flexibility.

The quadratic typology was applied to individual houses, but it was also used in the later Garbí School addition of 1978. The Casa Almirall, La Garriga (1975-77), and the Casa Amil, Sant Vicenç de Montalt (1975-78), have a bi-symmetrical order and short stairs radiating from the central chimney core. The exterior is an austere cube with windows and screens inscribed in the façades in such a way as not to disturb the cubic expression of the form. This clean expression was later extended to the Casa Camps-Juaneda, Menorca (1978-85). The square plan of the Casa Otero (1975-77) is bisected by a central entry hallway leading to a stair, however, it was unlike the Almirall and Amil houses, in having a form that is more traditional and Italian in inspiration. The gallery on all four sides is capped by a symmetrical pyramid-shaped roof of tiles.

Occasionally, the quadratic *parti* is surreptitious and rather less obvious. The Casa Heredero (1967/68) was the earliest and by far the most elaborate in its arrangement of the domestic functions on floor decks radiating outwards from a central core lodged between four chimneys and the stairs at the centre of the house. The Can Bordoi House also has a square plan and a loosely symmetrical space, but its symmetry is eroded and disguised to such a degree that it is barely recognizable in practice.

The most ambitious quadratic form, in terms of its scale and elaborateness, is the Villa Escarrer. The *parti* is cleverly masked by superimposing the large square over a triangular podium so the two overlap and fuse. Each of the smaller squares in the corners of the large square is separated by two hallways which occupy the cross axes. The northeast square is omitted entirely, to be replaced by an enclosed orange tree patio. Incompleteness is a source of heightened tension between symmetry and asymmetry. The presence of this tension detracts from the wholeness of the composition.

MBM explained their preference for this particular typology by saying that it imposed a discipline and formal coherence of the parts that was an advantage when organizing each element to satisfy the various functions. The *a priori* imposition of a formal pattern is a tool for organizing and structuring an intractable client brief. It reduces a complex series of demands to a simple easily grasped image. The process is not unrelated to the kind of minimal images produced by the Russian Suprematist artist Kazimir Malevic in his *red square* composition of 1915.

Notwithstanding this, it is also evident that one of the effects of the format's inflexibility is that it frequently leads to undue fragmentation of the form which is most noticeable in the Casa Heredero. Even on a much larger scale, as for instance in the Villa Escarrer, quadratic symmetry results in a feeling of confusion and labyrinthine multiplicity, an impression which weakens the gestalt. The elevation of form over content, which is the ultimate outcome of such a procedure, can only be seen as a version of Mannerism.

Another, less direct inference to be drawn from the use of the quadratic *parti* is an attempt to draw MBM's architecture into the same circle as the Mediterranean Classical tradition, in contradistinction to Northern European sources: a relationship attested to by the Can Bordoi House with its precast balustrade.

Several quadratic plans were expressed three-dimensionally as a helical form that rotates about a central axis. Sometimes a helical form is implied externally, when, as occurs in the Casa Heredero, the reality is far more mundane, with the section rather more conventional. The spiral was a favourite of Frank Lloyd Wright.[37] Wright introduced it in his 1947 proposal for a parking garage at Pittsburg, here, the spiral was used as a ramp for motor vehicles, but at the same time as he was designing the Pittsburg garage Wright also developed the Guggenheim Museum with the same spiral motif.

The spiral proved a resounding commercial success when it was applied to the design of shops with a continuous interior spread over many levels and connected by half stairs, because it removed the traditional barrier between the ground floor and upper floors, thereby encouraging and leading shoppers farther into the retail space. The Serras Shop, Granollers (1968-72), was an early notable example. It reversed the Villa Rotonda's

25. MBM, Amil House, Sant Vincenç de Montalt, 1975-78.
26. MBM, Almirall House, La Garriga, 1975-77.
27. MBM, Otero House, La Garriga, 1975-77.
28. MBM, Iluro Building, Mataró, 1971-74.
29. MBM, Villa Escarrer, Son Vida, Mallorca, 1985 to 1988.

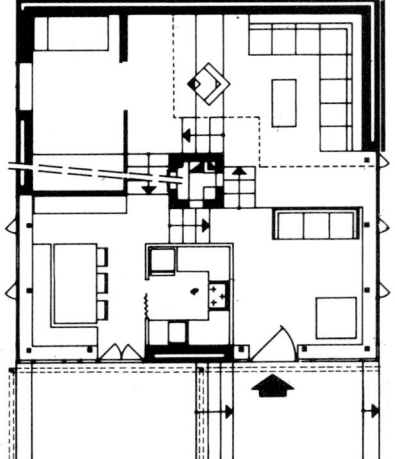

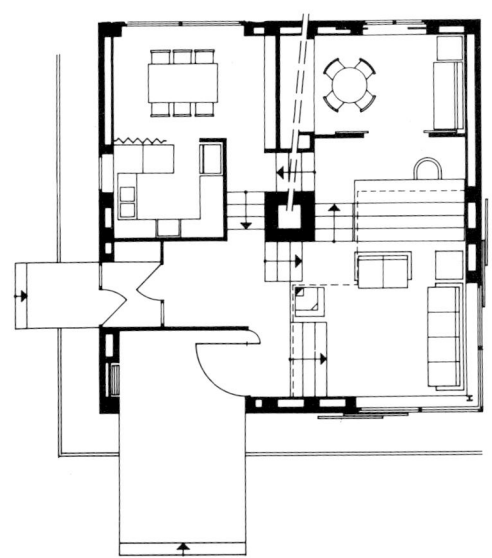

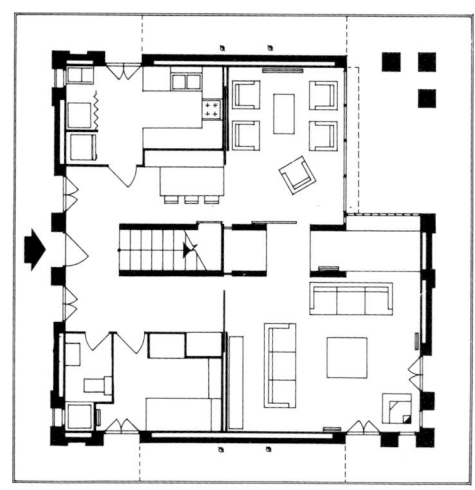

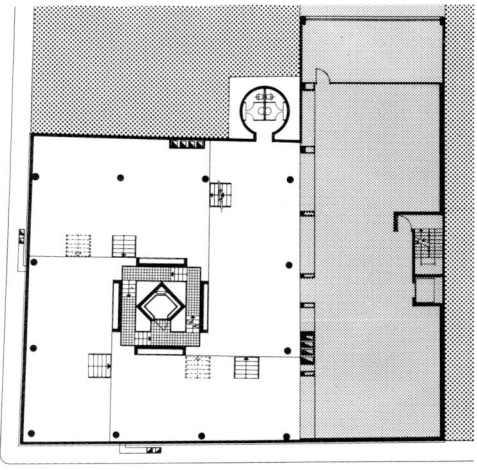

emphasis on a centripetal central space, converting it into a subservient space serving the perimeter living areas thereby reversing the spatial movement to a centrifugal one that played down the central dome as the spatial focus.

The clearest demonstration of helical form structured around a central core was the Iluro Building, Mataró (1971-74). This comprised in plan a square open gallery filled by a diamond-shaped lift shaft serving four centripetal floors, each one a quarter of a floor higher than the preceding floor. The building resembled a giant stair with the floor trays replacing the stair landings. The Casa Almirall, La Garriga (1975-77), and the Casa Amil, Sant Vicenç de Montalt (1975-78), the Casa Camps-Juaneda, Menorca (1978-85) and the Harbourmaster's House, Olympic Port (1989-91), applied this helical motif of four spiral floor decks within a square plan with great tenacity. Indeed, the four houses are a remarkable demonstration of the a *priori* design procedure. The location of the window openings in each wall supplies a clue to the helical internal structure of the floors, but this only be-comes fully apparent once the observer is inside the house.

After Franco

No dictatorship is ever truly benevolent, but Franco's was more endurable than most, only intruding in the lives of citizens when matters directly concerning the continuation of his rule were at stake. There was, it must be admitted, a preference for a vacuous Neo-Classical monumentality, the restriction of the Catalan language, and the discrimination against Catalonia in the distribution of governmental largesse. Fifteen years after Franco's departure, the distorting effects of centralism can still be observed.

It is always tempting to oversimplify a situation, to automatically assume that the architecture created under the aegis of a dictatorship such as Franco's must inevitably project the same political values. This was not the case.

The reality was more complex, and the explanation for this is that many of the architects who supported Franco politically, approached their task as designers quite differently, indeed, there was a noticeable discrepancy between the new order proposed by such buildings and the existing political order.[38] This divergence illustrates something which was noticed by Barbara Lane in her study of architecture under the Nazis, to wit, that the Nazi regime did not succeed to any marked extent in extending »totalitarian« control over architectural style. Franco was even less successful than the Nazis in this regard.[39]

The end of Franco's political rule removed some of the pressure on Catalan society and lessened the need to defend the Catalan cultural identity. The importance attached to Catalan identity was intensified in proportion to the perceived threat; the diminution of the threat with the end of the Franco regime in 1975 removed much of the pressure on the Catalan identity, and so its defence was seen as less urgent.[40]

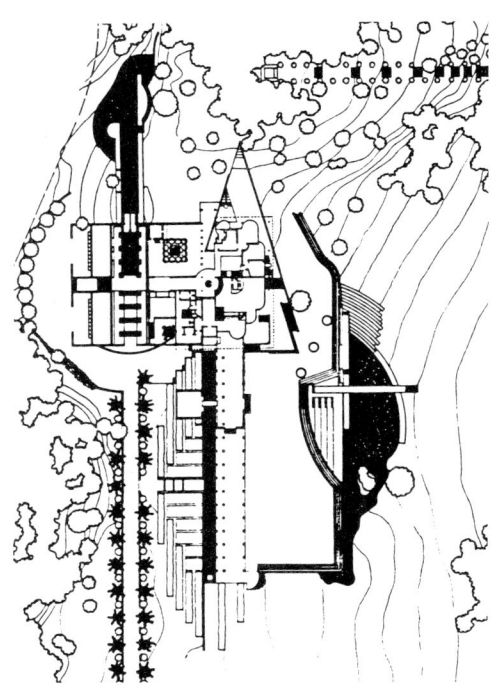

It is worth recalling that Barcelona architects were already beginning to seek a more open and less nationalistic stance by the 1970s, five years before Franco's death. It can be confidently stated that by the early 1970s, Catalan architects were coming increasingly to share the same preoccupations as the rest of their colleagues in Europe. Their sense of isolation and their attachment to a distinct regional architectural identity, separate from Spain and Europe, began to wane in proportion with the relaxation of Franco's perceived threat to Catalan identity. This, in its turn, was replaced by an increasing consciousness of Europe-wide tendencies in which the architect began increasingly to share a supranational European culture.

By the 1960s the Neo-Fascists had accepted a commercialised version of the International Style, but, by then, many Catalan architects including MBM were already well advanced in the regional adaptation of Modern architecture, using local materials in an honest and often highly expressive manner. The differences that existed between Catalonia and Spain were not so much concerned with the rejection of Spain, Catalan architects being, in the main, ahead of the country in assimilating new trends, and in having developed ties with Modern architecture as early as the 1930s. Charles Jencks is not correct when he states that »Catalonian architecture will be anything rather than Spanish...«, for the facts show that this was not the case at all. The truth is that Catalonia, as a separate society, is much more independent in making its choices, and more exposed and receptive to influences emanating from Europe, especially Milan and northern Italy, including Switzerland.

This openness ensured that Barcelona architects were well informed, so when Franco did go, they were prepared. They had a carefully formulated programme of urban reconstruction waiting to be implemented for overcoming the neglect experienced under Franco. One of the important features of this period of opposition was the close ties forged between key architects such as Oriol Bohigas and the intellectuals who used their years in opposition to consult the community about its needs and to formulate priorities so that when the time came for them to assume power, they had a comprehensive grass roots political programme, the details of which included architectural and planning objectives. Such things as public housing, new schools and library facilities, the repair of Barcelona through concrete projects that could be readily implemented, rather than grandiose abstract planning schemes directed at the 21st century were determined beforehand.

The new Catalan policies were not hasty, or opportunistic last minute afterthoughts, but direct and sensible political responses to the needs expressed by the community. Thus, the large number of housing and school buildings are a direct consequence of MBM's involvement in carrying out the new Barcelona Government programme. As too is the creation of new parks within the city. Following the recession of 1975, and the subsequent slow-down in economic activity, Barcelona once more began to expand rapidly in the 1980s, and this momentum continued unabated, and even gathered momentum in the lead up to staging the 1992 Barcelona Olympic Games and the World Fair at Seville.

In 1968, Oriol Bohigas stated that avant-garde Realism required, on the one hand, the production of an open work whose codes could be read by all, and on the other, the breaking of orthodox conventions. For Bohigas, the essence of Realism could be summed up in one word – pessimism.[41] By pessimism he meant the acceptance of the world, not as one might wish it to be, but as it actually presents itself to us. Thus, pessimism entailed a taste for the critical, contemporary, and ambiguous. All this was thought of as included in the will to Realism.

Realism, Bohigas maintained, arose from the mental outlook of the Catalan people: in a certain vitality and energy, sensuousness and plasticity of form and a fondness for the intense focus on detail. One of the most striking aspects of Grup R, compared with other similar avant-garde architectural tendencies elsewhere, is the degree to which architecture is aligned with contemporary culture and politics. Realism implies something more than the willingness to conform to the reality of the task, and a willing acceptance of whatever technologies present themselves to the architect. Bohigas contended that the character of Catalan architecture – its burdens – takes its origin from the nature of the Catalan middle class which he considered as quite distinct and unlike the bureaucrats making up the official bourgeoisie in Madrid.

By the 1970s, the Barcelona School was losing its coherence, and some of its members, such as Federico Correa, Alfons Milà, Oscar Tusquets, Lluís Clotet, Cristian Cirici, Pep Bonet, Ricardo Bofill, Lluís Domènech, Ramón Puig, Laureà Sabater, Lluís Cantallops, many of whom were becoming increasingly busy, began quite understandably to undertake larger commercial projects in keeping with the new economic circumstances and to further elaborate and refine their individual approaches. This hastened the decline of the Barcelona School which was replaced by a wider diversity of ideas and an emphasis on the realities of practice to the detriment of theory.[42]

Rejuvenating Barcelona

New ideas need to be expressed using familiar language, in terms that people readily understand. This is how Oriol Bohigas envisaged the repair of Barcelona in the 1980s. As he saw it: »If you are to say things which everyone can understand you must use familiar words to say whatever it is you wish to say, always employing traditional grammar and syntax.«[43]

The city should possess a distinct memorable image. It needs to be legible – easily read by the people who live in and use it. Furthermore, the actual form of a city should genuinely express the society and activities of individual people so that they are encouraged to form an attachment with their urban surroundings. The idea was simple enough.

Most Post-Modern architects prefer historical styles with their accompanying superficial interpretation and trivialization of history, and locate their buildings in the city with little genuine understanding or sympathy for its traditional morphology. Oriol Bohigas advocated the opposite approach: he argued for the retention of recently devised and efficient building types integrated with the traditional city pattern. In his own words, »Historical styled buildings do not make a historical city«.[44] Bohigas called for the return of the street, avenue, square, and urban park, of traditional urban structures – to reinforce the existing historic morphology.[45] At the same time, Bohigas considered that the old building types were outmoded, less convenient, and suggested that people would be better served by the new types from the twentieth century. It was a policy of fitting modern building types into traditional city patterns without disturbing the traditional forms.

This was the strategy Bohigas suggested to Narcís Serra, when the new mayor of Barcelona approached him for advice in 1980 on policy for the repair of public space. The Nova Icària extension of the city, over 46.7 ha in area, which included the 1992 Olympic Games athletes' village, suggested itself as a major test of that strategy.

The Bohigas programme rejected the earlier grandiose utopian ideas of city planners which he sought to replace with specific plans founded on the district. The idea was to identify crucial nodes with which to stimulate the redevelopment of old decaying quarters drawing on private resources, but stimulated by the repair of such strategic public sites, a pathfinder approach, directed by the city at first, but with the clear intention that these improvements would form a catalyst for the wider regeneration of the quarter. This method has been described as metastasis, using the organic analogy of the transfer of a bodily function, pain or disease, originally well established in one part or organ, to another.[46] The idea, quite simply, was that by repairing selected public spaces in key locations within each district, this would, in due course, lead to the general improvement of the entire district, the process of civic enhancement gradually spreading throughout the surrounding urban tissue.

This approach, with its emphasis on the district, followed much the same lines advanced by the American urban theorist Kevin Lynch in 1959.[47] Lynch held that the imageability of the city depends on reinforcing the identity of distinct districts having well defined edges or boundaries, and systems of paths leading to nodes whose location is confirmed by important landmarks.

Pasqual Maragall, who succeeded Serra as mayor, is an unusual politician in as much as he appears to relish controversy if he senses it is likely to advance the culture. What he wished, above all, was to avoid the mediocre, something which is most likely where art is required to conform. As well as launching Barcelona internationally and restoring dignity to its urban landscape, Maragall regarded the new concrete projects as fostering »... an atmosphere of controversy and discussion in a Catalan society threatened by conformism, ideological uniformity, and the fear of confrontation«.[48] Robert Hughes described the sculpture-and-park programme as the most ambitious of its kind that any government of a twentieth-century city had carried out, and correctly observed, that Barcelona would have the largest and most varied sampling of major late Modernist sculpture designed for public urban sites, some old and some newly created, in the world.[49]

It was soon discovered that few of the younger architects had much experience at all in producing a real architecture for public spaces. This proved a serious handicap to the realization of the plan. Many of them had only ever worked on small private domestic commissions. This difficulty was exacerbated by the changes then going on which increasingly affected the outlook of Spanish architects after 1975, inasmuch as they were swayed by the prevailing mood of Post-Modern eclecticism with its superficial view of historical style. The architectural historian Ignasi de Solà-Morales observed acidly that a good many of the completed projects were of only minor interest »...because, in themselves, they offer nothing more than the use of a certain architectural method, which they have definitely not invented, and a firework display of cultivated references to Noucentisme and Hoffmann, which do not get them much further than pure self-satisfaction at their own erudite and surprising resonances«.[50]

Fortunately, there were exceptions. The renovation of the square facing the Església de la Mercè enables the visitor to the square to appreciate the architecture of the church's façade for the first time without the irritation of buildings obstructing the view or the distraction of urban flotsam and jetsam in the square. Many of the projects involved little more than replacing the existing paving and the addition of planting and furniture. Most of which involved nothing more than the elaboration of nineteenth-century urban modes. The Plaça Reial is a illustration of what may be achieved by such economical interventions.

A good many of these civic improvements relied almost entirely on sculpture. At the Horta Velodrome (by Esteve Bonell and Francesc Rius) the poet Joan Brossa treats the public to a wickedly humorous comment on the decay of language, or is it art? Who çan tell? A giant letter »A« sculpture crumbles then tumbles down the grassy hillside. El Parc de l'Escorxador (by Antoni Solanas, Màrius Quintana, Beth Galí and Andreu Arriola), located on the site of the old Barcelona slaughterhouse at the intersection of Carrer Tarragona and Carrer Aragó, has an elevated square with a reflecting pool for Joan Miró's colourful blue red green and yellow tiled statue *Woman and Bird*. Nearby, the square is surrounded by a Mediterranean woodland.

The bold character of the Parque de l'Espanya Industrial (by Luis Peña Ganchegui) is quickly established by the Surreal torch-shaped light stands and the playful curved snake-like edges of the lake and its immediate surroundings. The park is sculpture on a large scale in which people intrude as strangers, and certainly they don't appear to bear any meaningful relationship to its scenic effects.

Part sculpture, part architecture, the exceedingly minimal structures that give the Plaça dels Països Catalans (by Helio Piñón and Albert Viaplana) outside the Sants Station a measure of identity (a kind of metaphor for the minimal city), sum up Spanish architectural achievements in the 1980s. The great shapeless expanse of the square is surrounded by a quantity of buildings that are inconsistent and lacking in design. Into this has been inserted an elegant minimal shade *pèrgola* supported by sixteen slender metal columns and stretched out beside it there is a long low undulating *pèrgola* running from the direction of the station constructed of the same materials. Scattered about are balls, tilted posts and convex mesh screens. This helps to establish a nucleus for the square which otherwise would lack any focus or point of concentration. Abstract and minimal, a mixture of sculpture and architecture, the Placa dels Països Catalans is important for what it reveals about the current condition of Barcelona architecture.[51] It reveals, first of all, a conscious topographic inflection, second, an explicit articulation of a constructional poetic throughout the work, and thirdly, it is driven by the desire to create a minimalist dynamic spatial form. One thing is missing: an appreciation of the human dimension, meanings that are accessible, or any interest in spaces where people may feel welcome and at ease.

If the Plaça dels Països Catalans is adrift and diffuse, the Fossar de la Pedrera, on Montjuïc, conceived by Beth Galí, is a moving memorial to patriotic Catalans executed in 1939. Here, a circular lake, impounded on one side by the rough stone wall of the old quarry, provides a suitably calm focus.

The firm of MBM was asked to design the Parque de la Creueta del Coll. The swimming basin and its surrounds have been completed with the intention of planting a much larger area of the park formed by the hill itself and its adjoining slopes with trees.

Assessments of the success, or otherwise, of the individual projects will necessarily vary. This is to be expected. And inevitably, the strengths and limitations of the artists, sculptors, and architects stand revealed in the works themselves. But, for sheer diversity, richness of content and scale, the projects taken altogether are unrivalled anywhere in the world this century as an enduring enrichment to a modern city.

The 1992 Horizon

1992, much like 1888 and 1929, was seen as a dominant horizon. Barcelona was a city in waiting.

It is a measure of Catalan pride that Barcelona's citizens should voluntarily set about cleaning the city's face – all the numerous handsome building façades begrimed by years of filth – at the request of mayor Maragall. The Olympic Games is merely a pretext, an opportune historic occasion in the life of the city which was consciously seized upon as a goal for the further repair and embellishment of Barcelona.

In the past, exhibitions have served as an excuse for filling-in missing pieces and extending Barcelona: there was the Universal Exhibition of 1888 which resulted in the reconstruction of the old citadel, formerly the site of a military fortress; while the International Exhibition of 1929, rather than satisfying a purely local role, spearheaded a new phase of growth with the construction of the first Metro line, and the extension of Cerdà's two great avenues, the Gran Via and the Diagonal.[52]

Some peoples see themselves as the victims of history, as subject to historic influences they are unable to control, let alone escape. One needs only to remember the Civil War, to be reminded that Catalans know as well as any other people what it means to be victims, but they are also a people determined to use their knowledge of the past to shape their future. That is an aspect of the Catalan identity – their's is not a passive consciousness of history and its patterns, but an active determination to make history work for them, to be its master rather than its victim. The Olympic Games in 1992 are a stage, and an important one, in the positive direction of history.

1992 is also an important chronological marker for MBM, not only because of their involvement in the planning aspects of the Nova Icària zone, and their work on the Olympic Village in partnership with Albert Puigdomènech, but also because they are the architects (with Peter Rice) for the Pavilion of the Future at Expo Seville '92. Seville's World Expo is Spain's answer to the Olympics at Barcelona. Such is the rivalry between Barcelona and Madrid that one success demanded its immediate riposte. The Pavilion of the Future is devoted to communications on the earth and the new satellite and telecommunication space technologies. The ostensive inspiration for Seville's exhibition is Christopher Columbus' unintended discovery of the Bahama islands.

The Cerdà plan gave Barcelona a clear memorable image. This has survived in spite of the fact that speculative development in later years compromised Cerdà's conception of a city comprised of octagonal square blocks with two parallel buildings on each, and a garden in-between, interlaced by pedestrian paths, independent of the street network, across the middle.[53] The redevelopment of the old industrial area along the waterfront separating the city from the sea, now known as Nova Icària, which contains the Olympic Village, took as its starting point the extension of this cellular pattern based on the Cerdà plan.

In 1986, the municipality of Barcelona had some 1,752,627 inhabitants crammed into a metropolitan region of 97.62 square kilometres. Within the greater metropolitan area of 477.33 square kilometres there were some 3,096,748 people.[54] Much of the formless expansion of the city beyond the central area is recent and added to the problems of the existing city. The additional population numbers highlighted the urgency of the task of improving the efficiency of the city. Traffic which passed through it needed to be diverted to a ring road around the city to provide some relief from congestion and noise, whilst the newer suburbs on the periphery desperately needed the addition of significant urban foci to give them a structure and identity.

Four areas on the edge of the city were selected for reconstruction, and it was here that the Olympic facilities required to stage the Games were located. The Olympic Games

31. Lluis Peña Ganchegui, Parque de l'Espanya Industrial, Barcelona, 1982-85.
32. Helio Piñón and Albert Viaplana, Plaça dels Països Catalans, Barcelona, 1981-83.
33. Beth Galí, Fossar de la Pedrera, Barcelona, 1983 to 1986.
34. MBM, Parque de la Creueta del Coll, Barcelona, 1981-87.

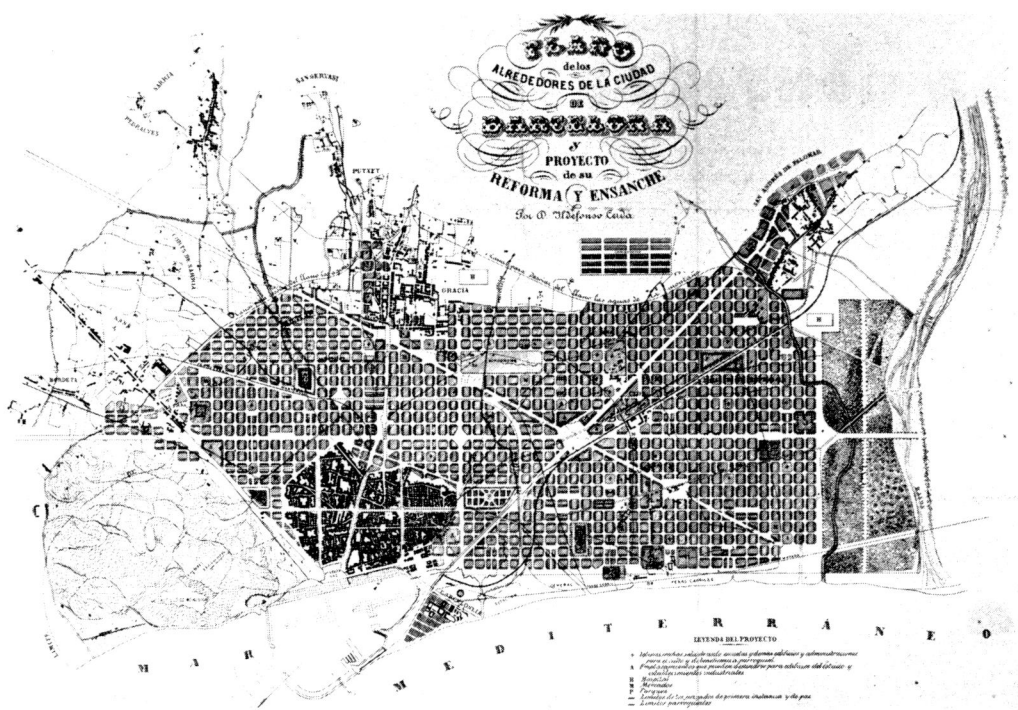

established a timetable for the attainment of these objectives. The four areas selected were Montjuïc (the site of the principal athletics facilities and the main stadium, indoor stadium or Sports Centre, the Press Centre and swimming facilities), Diagonal, Vall D'Hebrón and Nova Icària (the site of the Olympic Village adjoining the newly developed seafront).[55] The Olympic facilities were intended to serve the long-term needs of the city. The Olympic Village will provide a nucleus of housing in this newly created district on the eastern edge next to the extended Ciutadella Park.

MBM and A. Puigdomènech were responsible for the plan of the Nova Icària zone and the coordination of the work of individual project architects, together with the design of the housing and facilities of superunit 6 below Avinguda d'Icària facing Avinguda del Litoral, and the coastal zone containing the ring road and parks together with the harbour and its architectural amenities.

One of the principal aims of the proposed construction was to establish a new relationship between Barcelona and the sea, between a city isolated from its seafront by a nineteenth-century industrial zone which had run down over the years.

The architect, in this instance, resembles a humble fisherman repairing a damaged net who reinstates each torn mesh, neatly replacing each missing mesh with a new one, until the damaged section is indistinguishable, except for its newness, from the surrounding net. In the new Nova Icària district, MBM and Puigdomènech enlarged the Cerdà urban mesh of the closed city block and superimposed it on the original street pattern. The existing urban morphology was retained and extended, but not in its original unaltered state, instead a number of subtle reforms were introduced, the Cerdà block became a superblock, the original streets were allowed to penetrate the cell walls, and the inside was left more open. The idea of a green central area reserved for pedestrians was updated, and the buildings themselves were updated from the nineteenth century to Modern types.

The architects explained the new urban structure this way: »This entire zone is at present structured according to the orthogonal pattern of Ildefons Cerdà's 1859 eixample. This grid and the urban morphology it has produced – the closed city block and the corridor street – is the most representative image of what today constitutes the real central expanse of the city. For obvious reasons this fundamental pattern must be retained and the urban form and its image respected as far as possible. In other words it is necessary to accept the ambiguous form of the ›almost closed city block‹ and ›almost corridor street‹ as the framework in which an interesting dialectic between permanence and transformation takes place. Accordingly, all the orthogonal eixample streets are to be maintained, together with those others which do not detract from the overall appearance, such as

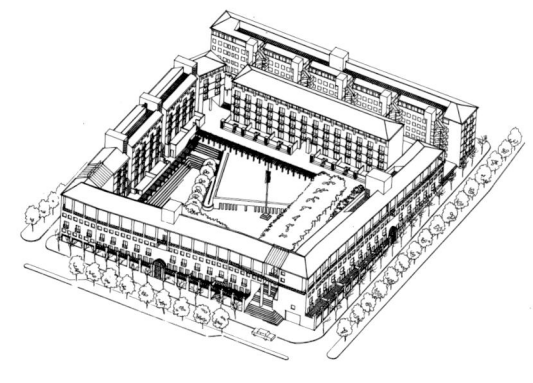

Avinguda d'Icària. The Avinguda del Bogatell, because of its anomalous diagonal direction, plays no structural part and as a result can be downgraded to become a pedestrian route.«[56]

A precedent for the change in scale of the urban blocks exists in the proposals of Le Corbusier, and more particularly, the »Plan Macià« for Barcelona by the architects of GATCPAC worked out in collaboration with him. David Mackay noted a fundamental difference. In the »Ville Verte«, the change of scale was accompanied by a change in the form of the streets which attempted to neutralize its structural intervention, at the same time that architecture was required to relinquish its role as a definer of urban spaces. The change in scale, Mackay contended, was necessary, »... precisely in order to maintain a traditional configuration while using a new structure together with new typologies generated by the great social and cultural changes since 1859«.[57]

In making this point, MBM were drawing on their very considerable experience in working within the confines of the Cerdà eixample. A great many of their Mansana apartment developments were shoe-horned into the traditional Barcelona-sized block, and this resulted, all too frequently, in the central space left over being insufficient to permit the introduction of the kind of support amenities and open space provisions which were considered necessary. The Mollet Mansana illustrates the thinking behind the Olympic Village. It was conceived as one element in a much larger neighbourhood. It also represents a sort of prototype of the mixture of traditional morphology and new building typology advo-

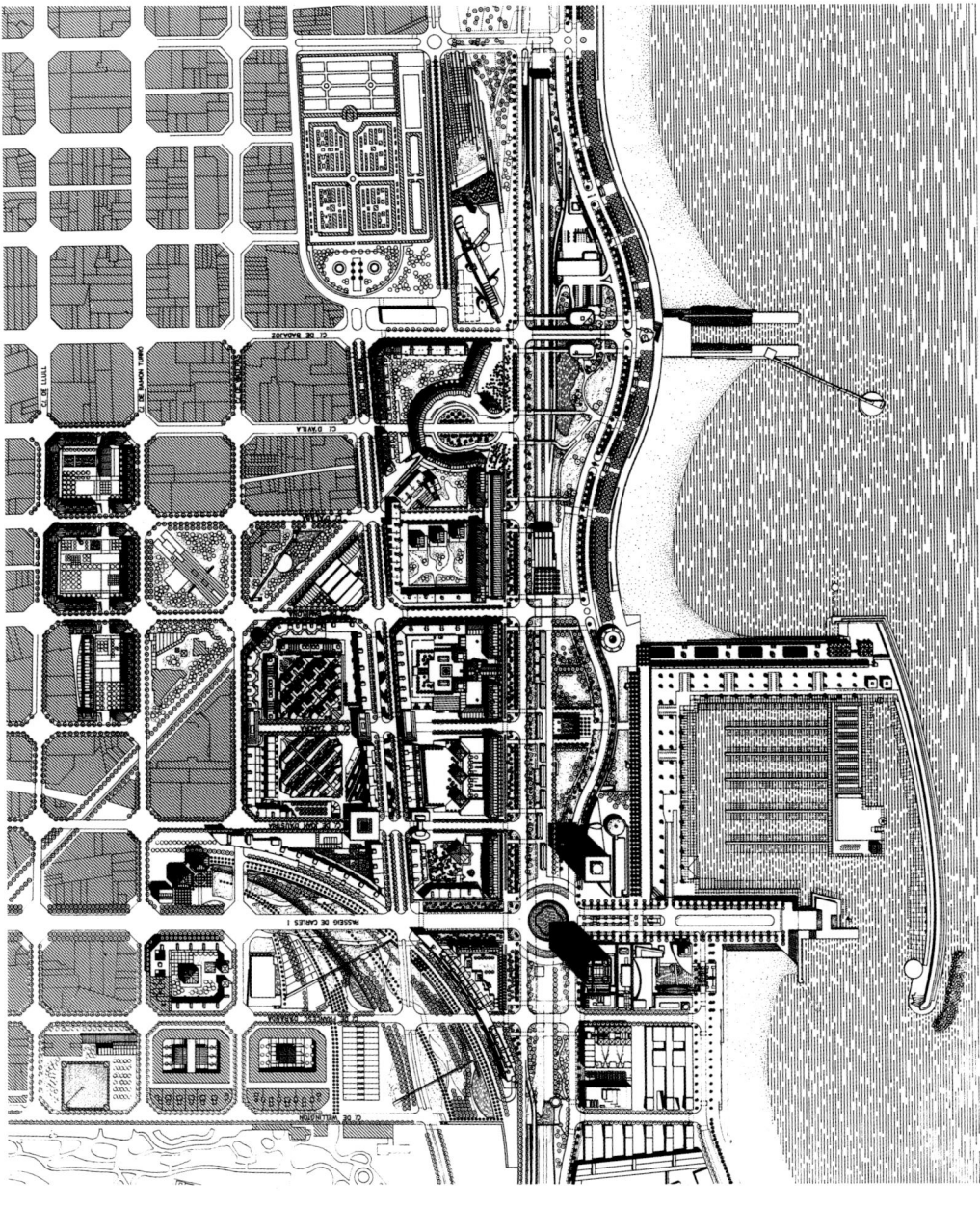

35. Ildefonso Cerdà, plan for the expansion of Barcelona, 1859.
36. MBM, Mollet City Block, Mollet, 1983-87.
37, 38. MBM, Nova Icària, Olympic Village, Barcelona, 1985-92.

cated by Oriol Bohigas. It is simply constructed in a warm orange brick and tile roofs, and accessed by an elevated gallery on the two uppermost storeys. The architectural treatment is traditional Mediterranean with a strong Italian inflection which results in a reassuringly familiar, easily comprehended style. Gateways open the internal court to the street, and what was intended as a shopping centre/supermarket under the square, has been developed as an undercover car park for the residents. The interior space is partly private and partly public – it belongs to the housing.

In the Olympic Village inside the courts, pairs of diamond towers and low pavilions overlook a serene garden which is sensibly insulated from the noise and fumes of the motor traffic outside. The deliberately neutral expression given these buildings – to free for later development – meant that there was little that was especially revolutionary or startling about them. They shape and define the urban spaces, acting as neutral shepherds almost, that move back and forth, driving the spaces this way and that, so a quality of urbanity emerges quite imperceptibly to remind one that this is indeed a great city.

The qualities of light and enclosure, of the street and square, the patio, and the avenue, have been extended to the Olympic Village so it comes across, not as some special privileged enclave, set apart and different from the rest of the city, but as an integral part of the older city. The Olympic athletes will live in the city and not in some satellite suburb. That is what this exercise has been about.

Between the Mediterranean and the Village lies a newly constructed park bordered by the main ring road motor circulation route which has been buried and hidden, and, in some parts, placed completely below the surface in a tunnel, in order that the city may be connected directly with its seafront. As if to affirm this, the Passeig de Carles I was driven through between twin hotel/business towers and thrusts out into the sea forming a broad jetty on one side of the new Olympic Port. This is the site for the Olympic sailing events. A marina is located here. The Nova Icària is a seaside district bordered by a superb belt of parkland for public use along the new edge of the city. At the Harbour Basin, low buildings and the municipal sailing school with its tall skylights looking reminiscent of the kitchen chimneys of the Topkapi Saray in Istanbul, gather in and surround the open expanse of the Olympic Harbour and form an »aquatic square«.

The serpentine alignment of the Passeig Marítim which mimics the sinuous curve of the beaches at a slightly higher level, is a reminder of nature brushing against the edge of the city. At Seville, in the Pavilion of the Future, similar stately curves roll like the great Atlantic swells that bore Christopher Columbus onwards, five hundred years earlier, to his landfall at San Salvador in the Bahamas, gather themselves and break against a necklace-of-stone knit by tensile cables into a Neo-Gothic colonnade. The form of the Pavilion, despite its considerable size, is really very simple. One is reminded of Robert Venturi's Football Hall of Fame, inasmuch as the Pavilion is a billboard with a shed behind it. But this is a distinctly Spanish, not to mention Catalan billboard. The rolling roof separates into leaves like slices of orange peel, so formed that the two adjacent strips produce a highlight in the gap between the two profiles. The bent truss beams that support the roof rise from the canal edge on the west to the stone scaffold of the colonnade which frames Seville Expo '92's Park of Guadalquivir.

Thirty years before, Peter Rice was an engineer with Ove Arup working on Jørn Utzon's Sydney Opera House. There, the shells were really a series of precast concrete vertebrae threaded onto post-tensioning cables to form continuous vaults.[58] The Pavilion colonnade is in some respects similar, but here, the precast concrete units of the structure have been replaced by stone. Because the wall is a plane structure, it has had to be strengthened laterally, and this is achieved by a system of outrigger guys on the outside face. This creates a certain permeability of the wall opening it to the park.

It is an ambiguous gesture – this colonnade. On one hand, it suggests an ancient Roman aqueduct of which Spain has several splendid examples at Tarragona and Segovia, yet it is both engineering and sculpture in a way that is almost a tradition in Spain. One has only to recall Eduardo Torroja and Santiago Calatrava, or Gaudí's ingenious vaults for the Church of the Colònia Güell (1898-1915) to be reminded that structure is at once an expression of the Spanish sense of economy and something sensuous and beautiful in its own right.

39. MBM, Pavilion of the Future, Expo '92, Sevilla, 1988-92.
40. MBM, egress canopy of the Sanctuary of the Virgin of Montserrat, Montserrat Monastery, 1980 to 1983.

It has been remarked[59] that Catalonia is similar to a dry stone wall which is repeatedly washed away by floods, following which it is rebuilt. With each rebuilding, the stones are fitted more snugly, the gaps between close, and the wall becomes more compact and stronger. The renunciation of the reconquest of the peninsula by the Aragonese crown in the twelfth century resulted in the containment of Catalan interests in the succeeding centuries and a more intense inward focus in Catalan society. Repairing the dry stone wall, society rebuilding itself, has its advantages. This is tradition, self-knowledge, and the discipline that this imposes.

Just as a tree whose root system is prevented from spreading forces its roots deeper and deeper into the surrounding soil, so a society unable to spread itself grows deeper within its culture. Tradition encompasses this sense of being deeply rooted in one place. The roots become dense and concentrated as they search for all the available nutriments in the confined space. As such, tradition represents an accumulation of history and learning which has been encoded within the culture, some of it meaningful, some of it useless in present circumstances, but all of it constituting a part of the Catalan identity.

Acquiring an identity is not an end. Rather, it is a beginning. A strong identity, one such as Catalans share, provides an assurance, a guarantee almost, that enables the society to remain open and capable of absorbing new influences without the attendant anxiety or fear that it will be swamped.

The architecture of MBM shares in that Catalan identity. Their architecture is a sturdy branch of the Catalan tree. Trees do not thrive if they lack wide spreading branches and leaves to sustain them. The Catalan tree leans over its fence into Europe. It is a European and Catalan tree. This is mirrored in the architecture of MBM.

Since 1986, MBM have designed projects for Bonn and Berlin in Germany, for Naples, Torino, and Siena in Italy, for Aix-en-Provence, La Ciotat, Nîmes, Le Creusot and Paris in France, and to a lesser extent, in other parts of Spain. That is a reflection of the firm's increasing prestige and recognition both within and outside Spain. Much of this arises from the perception that MBM have made a significant contribution to contemporary urbanism in terms of resolving the contradiction between continuing the traditional morphology of the city, but marrying it to Modern building types, producing in the process an urbanism that is reconciled to the past, and to human experiences and values that were once lost, without diminishing or detracting from the Modern architectural culture of the twentieth century.

Theirs is an architecture rooted in Catalan history and tradition, but an architecture that is also international, and to that extent, eclectic in its search for the best ideas and alliances with architectures outside Barcelona. The spirit of the Catalan people, and by extension, of Spain, is a part of what MBM do as architects. The stimulus of economic growth in the 1980s, of which the 1992 Olympics are but a telling climax, parallels the myth of the phoenix bird renewing itself and rising from the ashes of the past. It is an achievement made possible by a strong, confident, cultural identity.

To visit Barcelona is to observe regionalism at work and to see the conception of a regional expression vindicated, not as some dry academic polemic, but in terms of a vital architectural culture, satisfying the needs and enriching the society it is bound to serve. Spain's land may be parched, its mineral deposits worked out, or nearly so, its many landscapes often harsh and hostile, but there remains one great resource – its people. Their character is so rich and unquenchable as to invest everything which happens. Architecture too is affected, for architecture, after all, is not something separate, but a living part of the culture and the society it is meant to serve.

It was George Orwell who remarked on the essential decency and, above all, the straightforwardness and generosity of the Catalans, noting that if you ask a Catalan for a cigarette he will force a whole packet upon you. Orwell found in Catalonia a »real largeness of spirit«, which he met again and again in the most unpromising circumstances. It is no exaggeration to say that Catalan architecture, and this is well illustrated by the forty years of work by MBM, possesses a similar largeness of spirit which far outweighs any shortcomings it may have.

It is an architecture which takes hold of the imagination, which stays in the mind long after one has left Spain, which beckons from afar like a friendly smile in a crowd.

Single Houses

Surprisingly, in a country where apartment living is the rule, and Barcelona must rate as one of the most densely developed cities in Europe, MBM have been responsible for a good many private houses. There are several reasons for this. During summer the city is unbearable: the pollution from motor cars, already a critical health problem, worsens considerable compared with the winter months; the temperature rises, and with it, the humidity; then there is the austere dusty countryside, a mixture of the Mediterranean, southern California and Arizona, to tempt people out of the city.

Spain is blessed with a rich diversity of landscape types so it is little wonder that the middle classes escape whenever the opportunity avails itself to the Balearic Islands, to the south of Barcelona, or to any one of the many burgeoning resorts on the coast. The holiday house, the house as an escape from the overcrowding and hectic pace of city life, is almost a necessity for many. For others it becomes a religion.

Enjoyment of life, the enjoyment to be had in such simple pleasures as eating, drinking and relaxing in the sun, or some shady terrace close by the water, these are things which Spanish people have developed into an acute art form. The house in the country, or beside the sea, is an indispensable instrument for their pursuit. This capacity to enjoy simple activities, to make the most of life's experiences, lends a sensuousness to the mundane, a sensuousness and delight in simple things which finds its counterpart in the art and architecture of the Catalan people.

MBM's houses can be found at a variety of locations: in the high Pyrenees at Vall d'Aràn, beside the Mediterranean, at the Baix Ebre, in the hill country north of Barcelona around Llinars del Vallès, or on the magnificent island of Mallorca. Not all the houses are in the open countryside, some, such as the Casas Guardiola, Otero, Almirall, and Amil, are in lesser towns, and some, for instance the Casa Max Cahner, are in Barcelona.

The houses after 1954 are essays in the Corbusian Purist vocabulary, however, in addition to the simple cubic expression and acceptance of the bi-nuclear plan, there is a clearly manifested concern to take the Catalan dimension implicit in Le Corbusier further, and to develop it to the point where it is transformed. The Casa Luján (1962), Max Cahner (1962), and the Europalma Group (1965) illustrate this regional translation of Le Corbusier.

In the Canovelles House, Italian inspiration is paramount. Its influence can be seen at work in the traditional form of the Can Bordoi House with its perimeter *terrassa* and Classical precast concrete balustrade. The encircling balcony of the Otero House was based on Karl Friedrich Schinkel's Charlottenhof pavilion. Ultimately, this led to a full-blown Neo-Mannerism in the extraordinary Villa Escarrer, but it is a vein of Mannerism that returns sentimentally to the decorative splendours of the Modernisme period before the First World War, to a period of architectural greatness in Barcelona's artistic and architectural history which is a part of every architect's psyche.

The Casa Guardiola is very much a student exercise, but a very confident and accomplished performance in spite of that. Already, at this very early stage, Martorell and Bohigas display a fascination for pure geometry and simple cubic forms.

The Can Bordoi House completes an attractive older nineteenth-century farm group arranged around a large square. Nearby the site, on the ridge of a steep hill, was a castle used as a hunting lodge, which was destroyed by an earthquake in 1428. The traditional character of the new house is in deference to the qualities of the existing farm buildings and a rather splendid house with a remarkable glazed *galeria* which faces southeast. The living areas are elevated above the ground-floor garage and store to make the most of the elevated hill prospect. The bedroom sleeping accommodation is on the level above the living area grouped around a large hall-like space screened by beautiful timber *gelosia* screens to shield the upper private zone.

The perimeter terraces, really an extensive system of verandas, is integrated into the living space using sliding screens and doors opening inwards which allow the dining and lounge spaces to be merged with the terrace. The overall simplicity and strengthened horizontal treatment of the form has been carefully calculated to blend with the tile and brick of the existing buildings, one of which has been converted into a museum for the metal and pottery remains found at the castle ruin.

Only very rarely is the architect presented with the challenge of designing a house on so exposed and magnificent a location as the Casa Heredero. Built for a successful chemist who later became an industrialist, and conceived both as a family home and place of entertainment, the house is sited in Spain's premier skiing area. It is a mountain dwelling. The mountain peaks are all around it. The roof offers shelter and protection, its shape is a subtle parody of the scenery, with its profile mimicking that of a neighbouring mountain.

Chimneys are a feature of the roofscape of Barcelona, something which George Orwell marvelled at on his stay there in 1937: »From the little windows in the observatory you could see for miles around – vista after vista of tall slender buildings, glass domes and fantastic curly roofs with brilliant green and copper tiles...«[61] It was Gaudí who transformed chimneys into wonderfully evocative sculptures and human apparitions. The roof of the Casa Heredero culminates in a cluster of four chimneys grouped about the central core of the house. They are symbols of man's defiance of nature in choosing to live here, and a miniature village crowning the mountain-roof top.

For all its outward simplicity, the Casa Heredero is a spatially complex and involved work with many linked levels and unexpected hidden corners. It is a house crowded with surprises and intimate nooks. Warm and inviting, the forms shield the house's occupants from the harsh elements outside.

It is essentially a very simple plan, as well as being a harbinger of the later series of quadratic *parti* houses. It is based on four floating rectangles, two smaller squares at the centre forming a stack and bathroom core, superimposed over a larger square, the four squares being staggered and separated to accommodate the central stair system, a modern version of Leonardo da Vinci's spiral stair at Chambord in the sixteenth century, which provides access to a multiplicity of floors on three principal levels.

All this has resulted in a house which gives the impression, when first encountered, of undue complexity and fragmentation. It is impossible to form a clear idea of the interior, rather it seems to consist of a proliferation of small and often, as it turns out, delightful spaces that wrap around and envelop the individual. The terraces, protected by movable screens, offer an unrivalled view of the mountains.

Externally, the simple envelope (an idea MBM developed when designing factories) has had large chunks removed to produce the outdoor terraces, but on closer examination, what appears to be a complex strongly expressed form is seen to be a simple cube mounted on stone walls with bits and pieces removed from it.

The Casa Almirall, La Garriga (1977), is typical of the series of houses based on the square *parti*, divided into four smaller squares at the corners internally, with the stair and circulation areas radiating from a central core, which naturally is also a square. The adjoining swimming pool and outdoor terrace occupy a second square, staggered and displaced to one side, and separated from the house cube by the entry. Windows and openings are suppressed within the planes of the overall cube which is extended vertically by a timber lattice screen on the roof for added privacy.

Mies van der Rohe's 1922 project for a glass skyscraper exercised a special fascination on Barcelona architects; José Antonio Coderch was the first to use it for his 1969 Trade Building Group in Barcelona, and MBM subsequently adapted it for their 1977 Casa Canovelles scheme, realized in 1981. Possibly, it was the freedom implicit in Mies' transparent glass towers, a certain sensuous sculptural play that attracted so much notice, but there may also have been a feeling that Mies van der Rohe was in some way Spanish, because of his earlier 1929 Barcelona Pavilion.[62]

Whatever the reasons, there can be little doubt about either the origin of the Canovelles glazed form, or the result. The Mies tower had two circular elevator and stair cores with the transparent glass skin expressed in faceted vertical planes which swayed in-and-out as they sidled around the cores on an irregular-shaped base. The Canovelles glass walls follow a similar but far from identical profile as they expand and contract to sketch in the boundaries of the living and dining spaces. This movement is carefully calculated so as to leave a usable terrace outside, with a smaller enclave next to the dining table. At one point the wall follows the profile of a grand piano, so perhaps the form is a kind of musical analogy, a musical composition, as it were, frozen in glass.

The glass effusion is restrained between two solid bookends, the main bedroom and its en suite and the kitchen, pantry, laundry annex beside the main entry. Downstairs, hidden in the platform which provides a base for the upper living spaces, is first of all the double garage, followed by a series of bedrooms. The bedroom openings on the long southeast face of this platform are double layered: the regular rhythm outside coincides with the formal needs of the exterior composition, whilst on the inside, set back from it, the openings are arranged to suit the internal subdivision.

Compared with the Heredero House, the Casa Canovelles appears to lack a roof. Two series of slim steel I-beams run the total length of the platform overshooting it at the ends. These columns support four beams but little else. On this framework, an artificial shade net has been stretched to fend off the sun. The roof itself has been suppressed. The effect of this is to convert the house into a kind of twentieth-century tabernacle[63], a desert tent pitched on an elevated base.

The rows of I-beams pay homage to the necessity for order. The tent-like erection that shelters the main floor of the dwelling is a statement about the anticipation of sophisticated architectural forms in the primitive archetype. There is something peculiarly Spanish, not to mention Catalan, in all this recalling the *toldo* sunshade.

The expression of the Casa Canovelles is marked by contrast: the contrast of the platform as solid and earth-hugging, and the upper level as voluptuous and abandoned in its light tent-like transparency. This lifts the house towards the sky. The immediate environment is unattractive. Consequently, it is a relief to have the house float upwards so it merges with the deep blue of the sky.

Modern architects have conditioned themselves to think in terms of a minimal aesthetic. The Villa Escarrer, Palma, Mallorca (finished in 1988), is the very opposite, a lavish architectural banquet intended by its owner to serve as a showpiece. There is also the matter of consistency. How is one to relate such an extravagant work to the socially responsible urban housing which for so long was the hallmark of the MBM practice?

There is a straightforward answer to these criticisms. There was always a Neo-Mannerist side to MBM's architecture, but in the Villa Escarrer, this tendency is elevated in importance so it controls the form. It should also be remembered that Gaudí did work which was extremely costly in its day, but these buildings are now admired because they are thought of as beautiful, or in some way as offering a special and unique architectural experience. The ultimate criteria must be aesthetic.

The Villa Escarrer commission was unique. It provided freedom to try out new lighting ideas, new materials and details, and to integrate the work into a grand landscape. It offered the same artistic opportunities as, say, the design of a Renaissance villa.

Simply because the house is so very large (it is about 3,000 square metres), it would have been easy for the building to emerge without any clearly defined shape, as a chaotic disassembly of rooms. There was a clear challenge to order in the complexity and elaborateness of the building brief. The imposition of the square-on-triangle *parti* provided the necessary discipline.

Mannerism is anti-classical: it prefers many images to one image, inconsistency and contradiction to unity, fragmentation and incompleteness to wholeness, and rich surfaces to organic form. Some art historians argue that Mannerism is concerned with facility[64], others contend that it expresses alienation and the collapse of certainty[65]. Whatever its social and historic causes, the Villa Escarrer is a perfect demonstration of the Mannerist response.

The interior is an assembly of rooms, each exquisite in its own right, yet there is hardly any effort to ensure that the same ambience is extended throughout the edifice. Each space is designed as a separate work. The interior breaks down into a sequence of different and unique spaces.

At the geometric centre of the house, thin slabs of translucent marble fixed in square metal frames create a Hoffmann-like effect. The sides of a hall directly below have been painted by the artist Albert Ràfols-Casamada to evoke an undersea atmosphere of Monet blues, candy-coloured tropical fish, interspersed amongst swirls of lolling seaweed.

Alvar Aalto has been honoured in the wavy white timber ceiling of the indoor swimming pool along with Edwin Lutyens, while Louis Kahn has not been forgotten either in the triangular-shaped coffered main roof over the open southwest-facing living space. The interiors are unashamedly eclectic.

Self-consciously Mannerist touches have been invoked in such things as the discontinuation of the horizontal blue ceramic bands on the outside of the service wing, and the positive-negative joke of the irregular-shaped template cut out of and removed from the corridor screen of the lower bedroom wing and deposited on the ground outside in the triangular sunken court. The beautifully displaced circles in the polished marble floor of the patio are another instance of the delight in mannered effects.

Mannerism is an acquired taste. Not everyone finds it to their liking. The Villa Escarrer is an important work which illustrates both the sensuous side of Catalan taste, a love of excess taken to extremes, a delight in filtering and managing light, the use of materials and textures, which was a feature of Modernisme, but one that has been largely forgotten, and an eclectic taste which is undeniably American in inspiration.

Guardiola House, Argentona
1954/55

This family weekend house for an uncle is located nearby the existing village of Argentona in a new suburb north of the industrial town of Mataró. Argentona is one of a number of small commercial and industrial villages and towns north of Barcelona which are strung out between the Mediterranean and low hills that also double as ports. In addition, Maresme is a rich horticultural district; farther inland, elevated villages amongst the hills make convenient summer or weekend retreats readily accessible from Barcelona.

At the time of the Guardiola House Martorell and Bohigas were heavily involved in Grup R. They and other members of this small group of architects set about re-establishing a connection with the architectural ideals of the Spanish Republic before the Civil War which effectively ruptured links with the Modern Movement. Hence the cubic forms and primary colours of the Guardiola House should be read as making an important symbolic statement and affirmation of Modernism. Structurally, the house is a mixture of load-bearing walls, concrete beams and exposed steel columns. Purity of construction has been subordinated to the rhetorical gesture.

Perfectly preserved, today the house is inhabited by the original family. It is situated on a flat site on a typical subdivision. The street is on the north side with the garden on the south. All the rooms enjoy a sunny outlook to the south. The upper floor is divided into two parts to provide for the different needs of the family. On one side there are bedrooms for the owners and their guests, and on the other side, separated by a staircase, are bedrooms for the children and grandchildren. Below on the ground floor, the space opens to the outside. Flowing forms and a strong visual connection help to unite the interior with the garden. Living and dining rooms, and porch are here. Screened from the western afternoon sun, the kitchen and service rooms form an insulating buffer to the street.

1. View from the east.

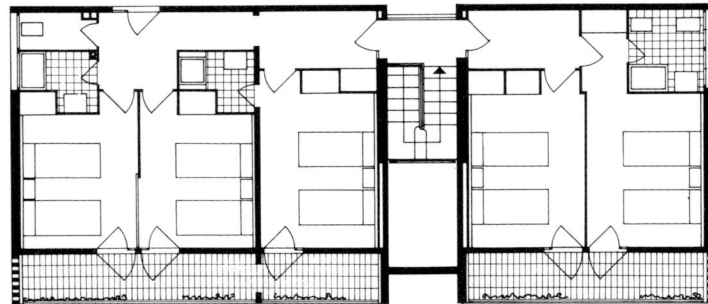

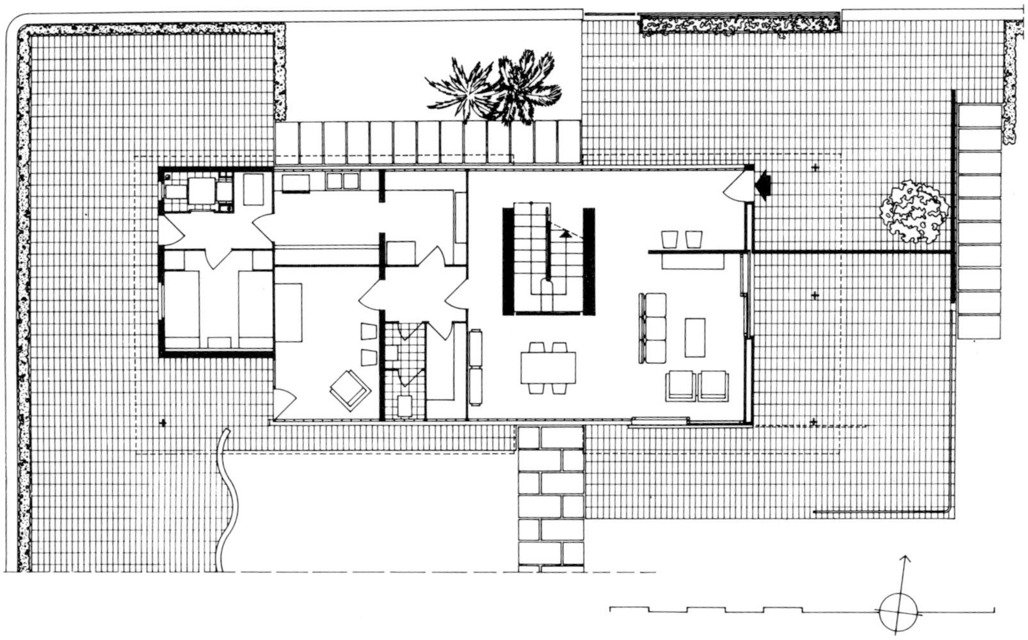

2. Plans (ground floor and 1st floor).
3. View from the garden. The cubic forms make an important symbolic statement and affirmation of the Modern Movement.
4. View from the south.

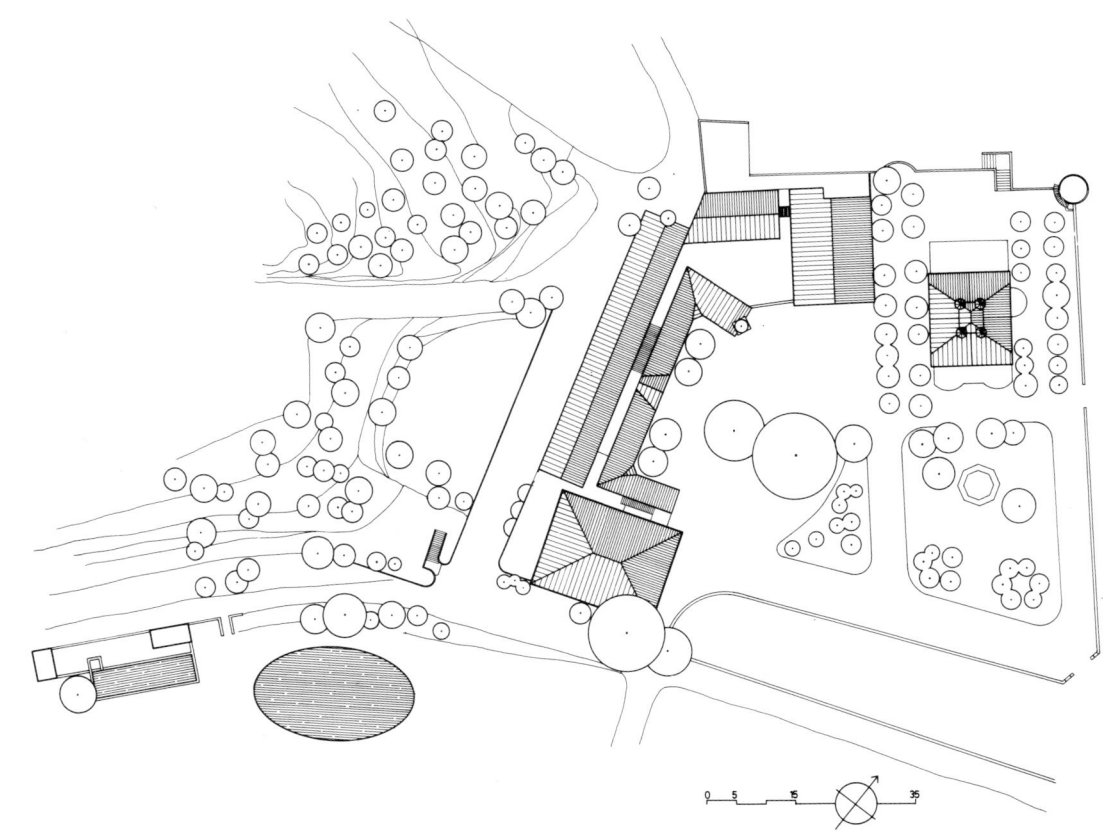

Can Bordoi House, Llinars del Vallès
1962–65

The form of this house harmonizes in its scale with the existing farmhouse, stables and nineteenth-century »manor house«, which together surrounded a courtyard and so formed a compact nucleus of buildings. The intention was to promote a relaxed and welcoming atmosphere for visitors and guests, at the same time inviting an »open-air« meeting of building with the immediate countryside appropriate in a combined weekend-cum-summerhouse. A pavilion type was chosen having a large simple envelope to match the existing buildings. Surrounding the house by a veranda had the intended effect of making it receded and partially disappear as if the house was placed within another, thereby creating an ambiguous inside-outside filter that softens the spatial interaction between building and landscape.

The house is set on a wooded hillside parallel to the sea, a distance north of Barcelona. It faces north at one end of a U-shaped group comprising stables and a nineteenth-century »manor house« in a defensive arrangement dating back to medieval times.

The owners required new accommodation suitable for family living on weekends and during the summer in which to receive friends and entertain visiting groups. These groups sometimes held meetings and study sessions. Young people also needed a base for walks in the countryside.

Initially the client had thought of the house as separate from and independent of the existing buildings, but he welcomed the chance to renovate the old buildings and improve the social life that existed within them, going so far as to agree to demolition of a wing of one of the farm buildings. The combination of a low pitched tiled roof supported by a light steel frame, of natural finished timber windows and louvred screens with precast concrete balustrading was calculated to give the house a character that is at once modern and traditional.

1. General view showing the relation of the house to the existing farm buildings.
2. Site plan.
3. The main approach to the house from the east.

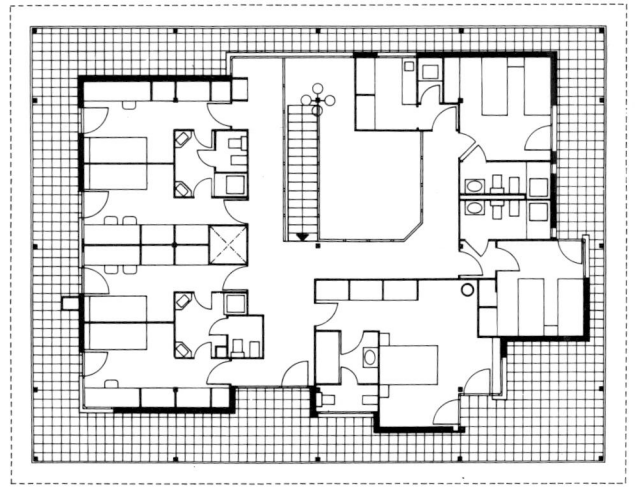

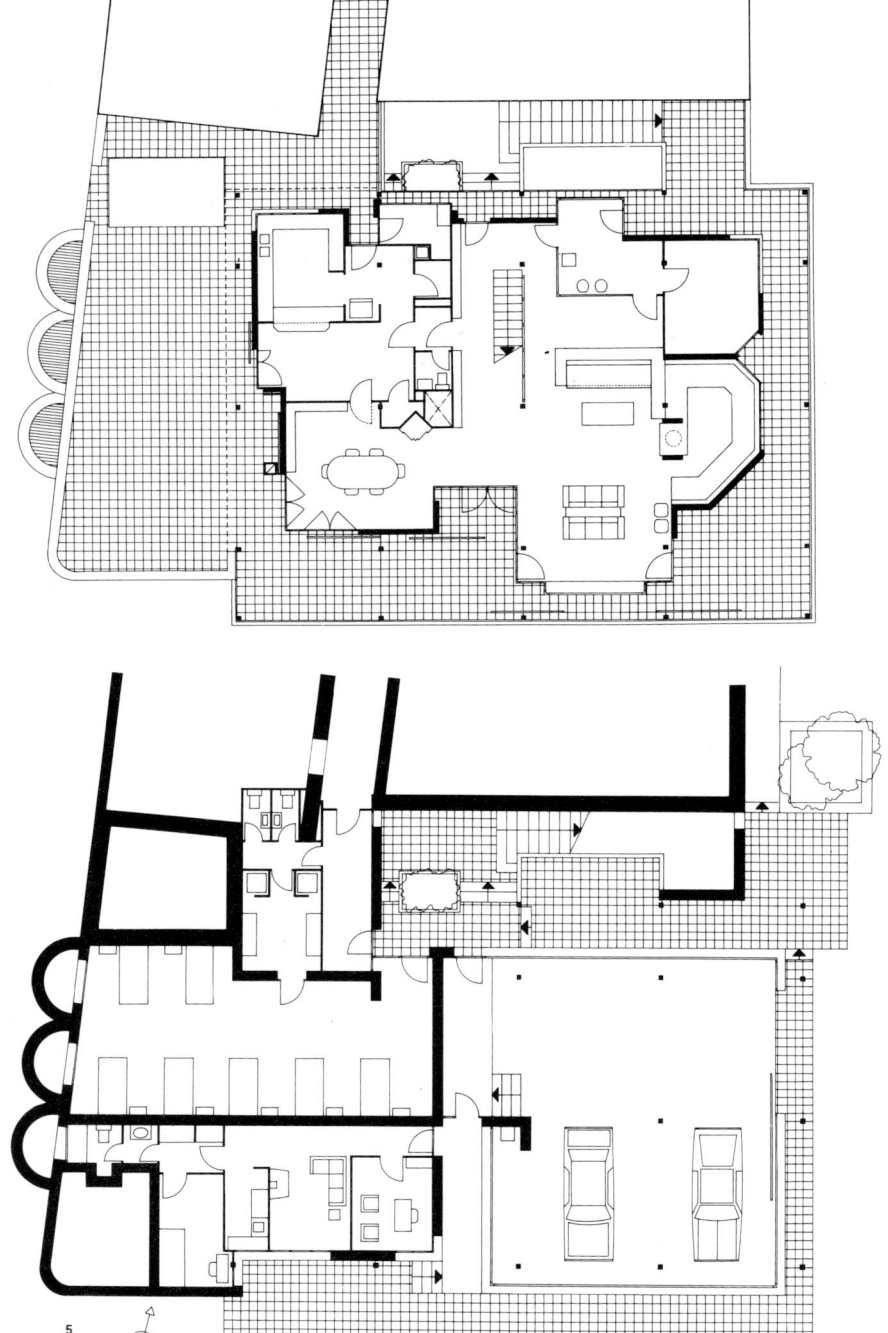

4. Plans (ground floor, 1st floor, 2nd floor).
5. View of the main hall showing the ambiguous effect of the perforated wooden screens.

Europalma Houses, Costa de la Calma, Mallorca
1963-65

Basking in the sun, the island of Mallorca is a popular haven for tens of thousands of Europeans seeking a break away from their normal routines.

Although a Mediterranean character was obviously expected, a more inventive and less predictable approach was chosen in preference to the traditional Spanish-Ibizan Colonial style of red tiled roofs set on white walls with arched porches. The programme called for nine detached houses, each individual and different. There was no end user as such who could be consulted to advise on planning. Sert's 1930s weekend houses at Garraf south of Barcelona (these had already entered history because of their influence on Le Corbusier) suggested themselves as a model. MBM had already used them in their 1959-62 Luján House at Palau de Plegamans, north of Barcelona. A basic module consisting of a low tiled Catalan vault supported on rough stone walls was adopted for the Costa de la Calma houses.

As well as merging the houses with the dry sun-baked slopes and shallow valley floors the stone walls helped to disguise the irregular site boundaries. In place of the popular image of the semi-circular white arch typical of Spanish holiday architecture that exists only on the outside, the profile of MBM's vaults extended from the outside into the interior spaces of the dwelling. Reinforced concrete tie-beams above each vault were introduced instead of the customary tie-rods to permit an uninterrupted interior space and so avoid any difficulties from arising in the internal subdivision of the houses.

1. General view from the south-east.
2. View of the second house in the west.
3. View from the house in the north-east to the south.

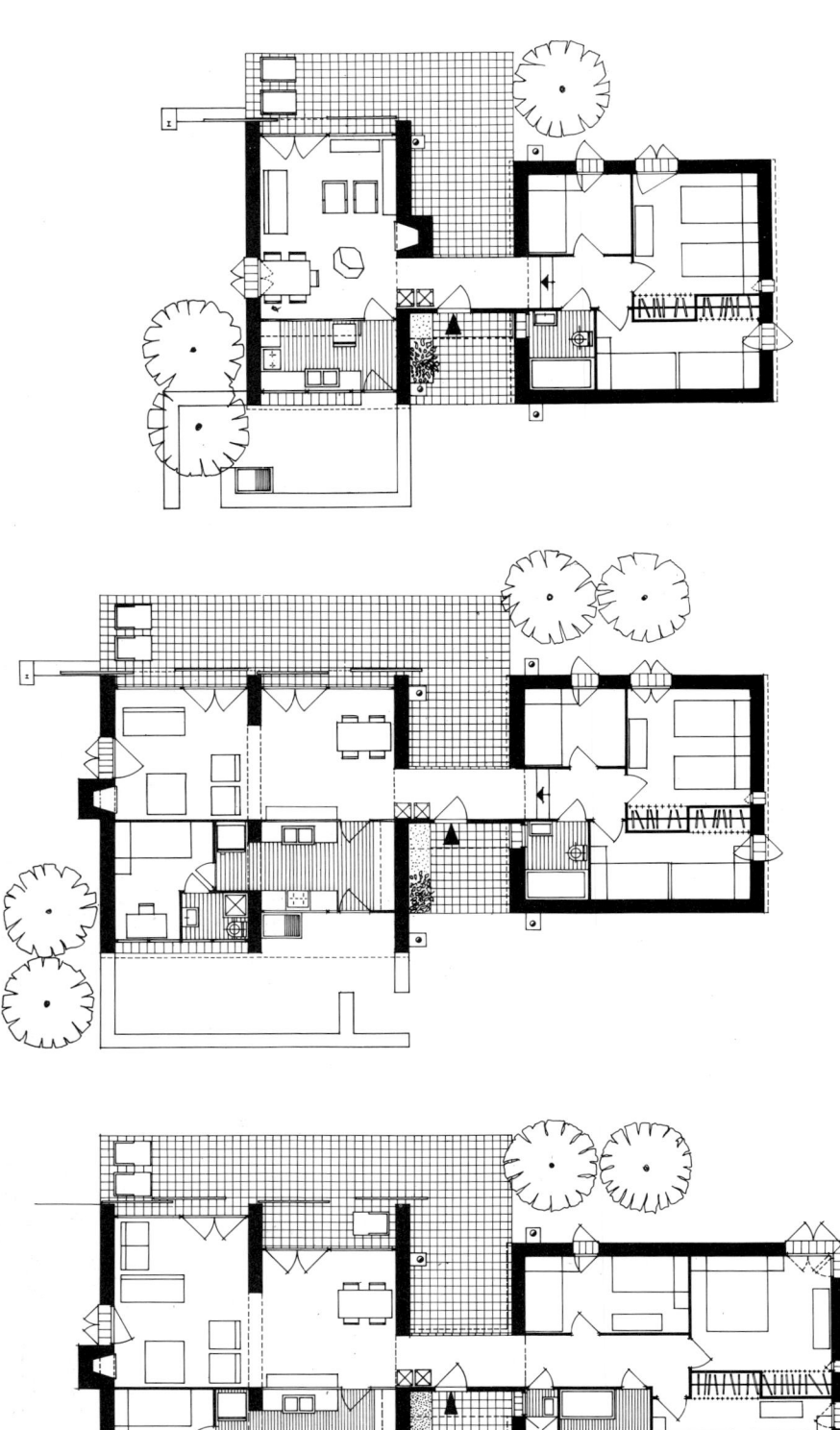

4. Plans (large four-bedroom house, small four-bedroom house, three-bedroom house).
5. Site plan.
6. View of the house west of the access road showing the continuity of the architecturally defined exterior spaces.

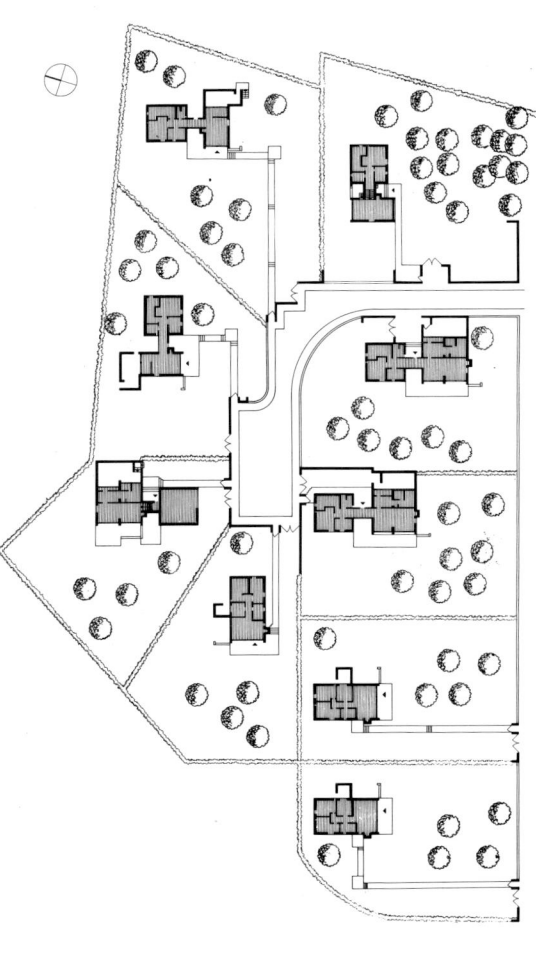

Heredero House, Tredós, Vall d'Aràn
1967/68

1. Axonometric view of the central core of the house.
2. View from the north-east.
3. View from the south-east.

Near the village of Tredós in the Pyrenees, perched on the steep mountainside above the main road and facing south, the Heredero House is less imposing than its 500 m² might otherwise suggest. The sheer size and extent of the mountains dwarfs the buildings, their vastness individualizing and isolating objects so they are assimilated in the grandeur of the scene. There is a curious contradictory phenomenon, for the mountains, at once so huge, appear so close, even the acoustics are foreshortened. Distant sounds are easily heard. The mountains come forward, there is a peculiar nearness, even a sense of intimacy, that personalizes, that gives the vastness of the scene an unexpected intimate quality.

The Heredero House took its cue from the scale and shapes of the neighbouring barns in the valley. It is meant to be read in isolation unlike village houses which read as members of a group. The design avoids the popular image of the Swiss chalet. Without renouncing modern architecture, the house is constructed using an appropriate vocabulary that not only answers the severe climatic problems but is at ease amongst the vernacular buildings of the Vall d'Aràn.

The severe weather here forces people to spend much of their time indoors, especially during the long evenings. In a house containing three generations of family and their friends it was a vital necessity to provide independent though related areas. A kitchen and breakfast room was provided as a common area for the family; on the floor below is the caretaker's apartment for the couple who look after the house when the family is away.

Climate played a leading role in thinking about the form of the house: a compact volume with all the water services located in a central core minimized the exterior wall surfaces while using the rooms as thermal insulation wrapping around the core. Around this core containing the staircase, services, and chimneys, the volume of the house was divided into four »wings« which expand independently to accommodate the varied family needs. All this is assembled beneath an all-embracing pyramid-shaped roof, an artificial miniature mountain that echoes the profile of surrounding peaks. The outside is finished in red granite chip render with flush aluminium windows and grille railings to strengthen the volumetric interplay of the surfaces. The house sits on a stone base which was extended horizontally to fasten the house into the mountainside. Extended retaining walls are almost a geological reference to the mountain and mimic the road below the house.

Because of the severe winter conditions, the house was designed with a steel frame which was prefabricated in Barcelona, transported to the site and erected in under six months.

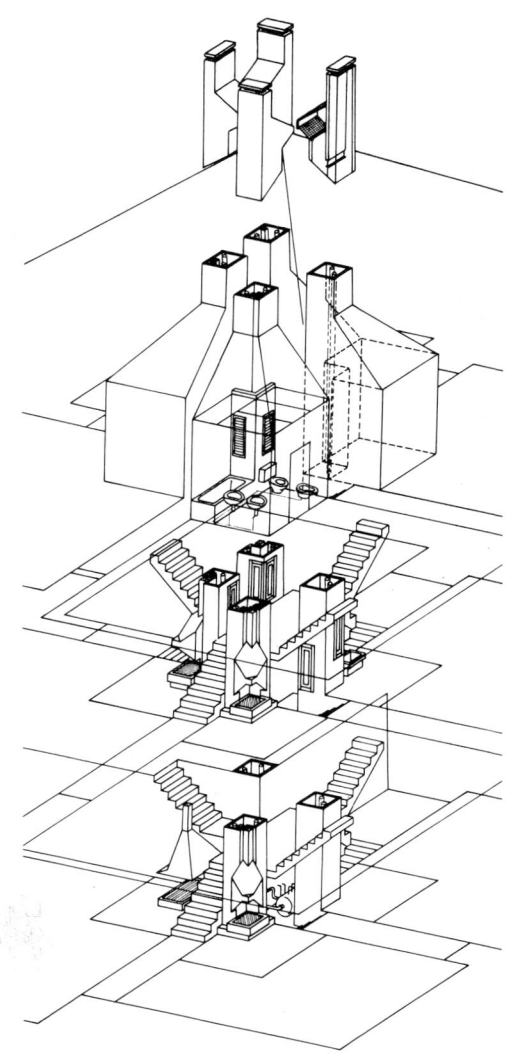

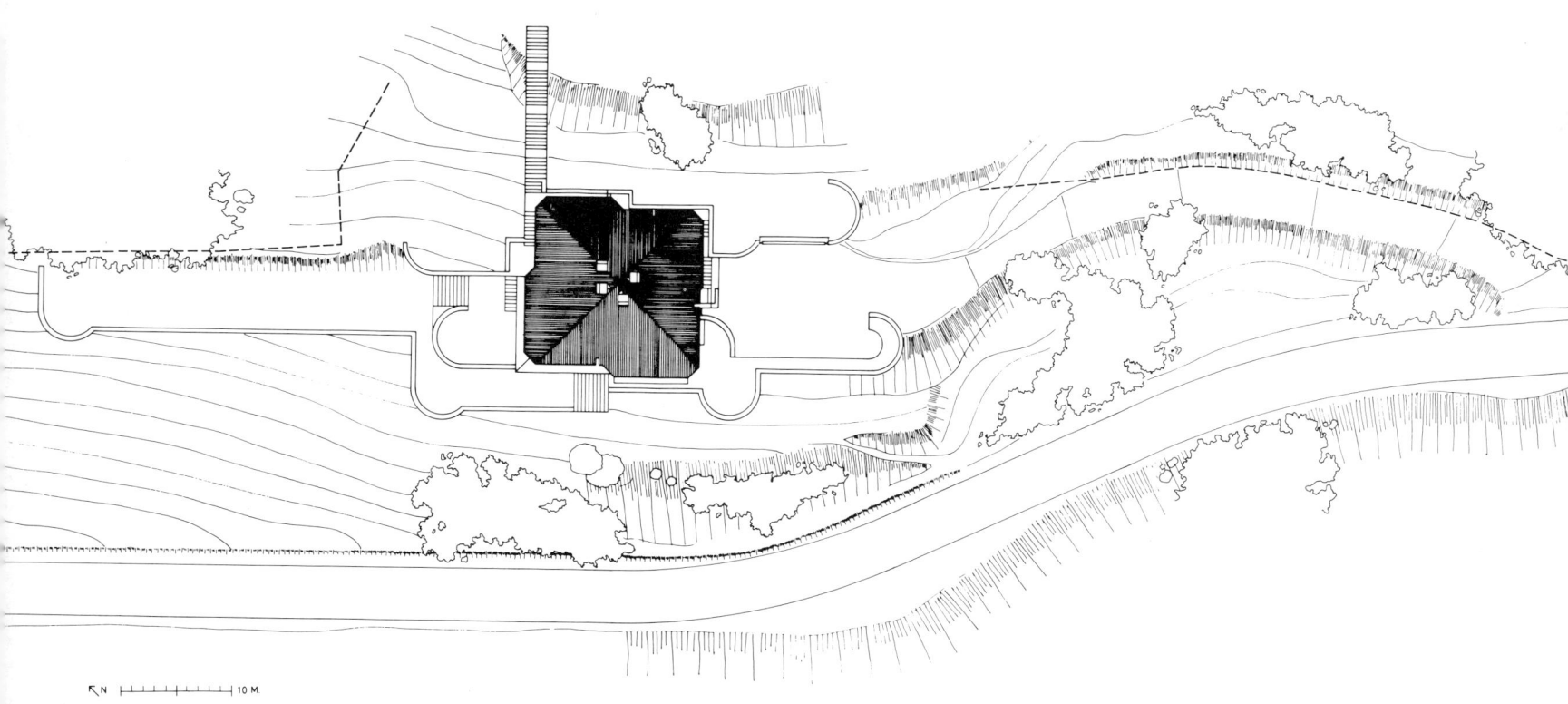

N ├─┼─┼─┼─┼─┤ 10 M.

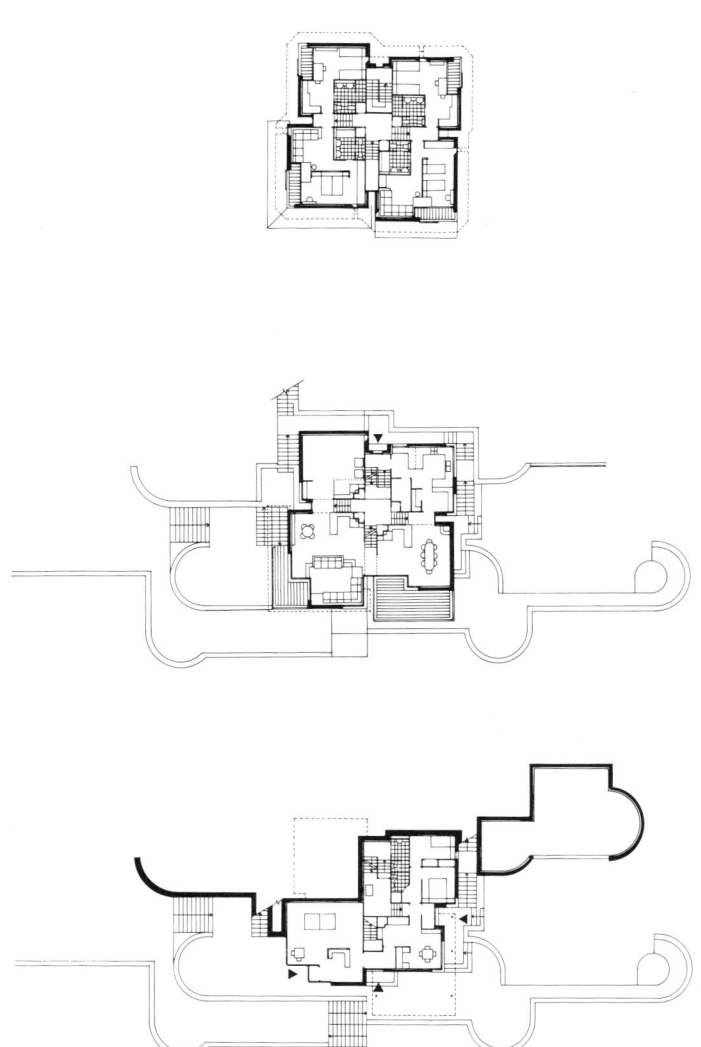

4. Site plan.
5. Plans (basement, main floor, 1st floor).
6. Façade detail.

Martí House, Sant Jordi d'Alfama, L'Ametlla de Mar
1972-74
Interior design: I.D.P.

One hundred kilometres southwest of Barcelona on the coast, the arid Tarragona heath-land is protected by coastal pine woods. The Martí House was planned to be the first of a group of four or five dwellings occupied by the parents and their married children. All were to have a central hall forming a spine to which all the various rooms were attached. These halls were thought of as extending past the ends of each dwelling as paths that cross and unite the buildings with the landscape. As events transpired, only the parents' house was built along these lines.

The corridor scheme was motivated by two concerns: first, the client's programme, and second, the desire on the part of the architects to revivify the corridor which was the foundation of the urban apartment in Barcelona. In part, this was a reaction to modern architecture's championing of open plan which had for so long been a key space concept. In essence, they argued that enclosed space was very useful and just as valid as open space. The Modern Movement needed to be reformed to include enclosed space in its repertoire.

Of equal importance was the client's remarkable collection of pre-Columbian ceramics assembled on frequent visits to South America. Thus, the spine of the house consists of a long corridor space entered at one end and terminating in an apse at the other. The form of the corridor is heightened by the insertion of a double row of closely spaced columns and with light falling from above through a continuous strip skylight. In-between the columns, shelves have been provided to display the archaeological collection. Rooms are attached on either side of this. Enclosed courtyards between the bedrooms filter the wild and somewhat harsh landscape. A clearly defined living area has been extended as a ter-race on the south side to demarcate the boundary between the cultivated and the built. With the passing of time the area of the garden has been increased, without trespassing on or impairing the essential wildness of the surroundings.

1. View from the south.
2. View from the east.
3. The porch and terrace on the south side of the house.

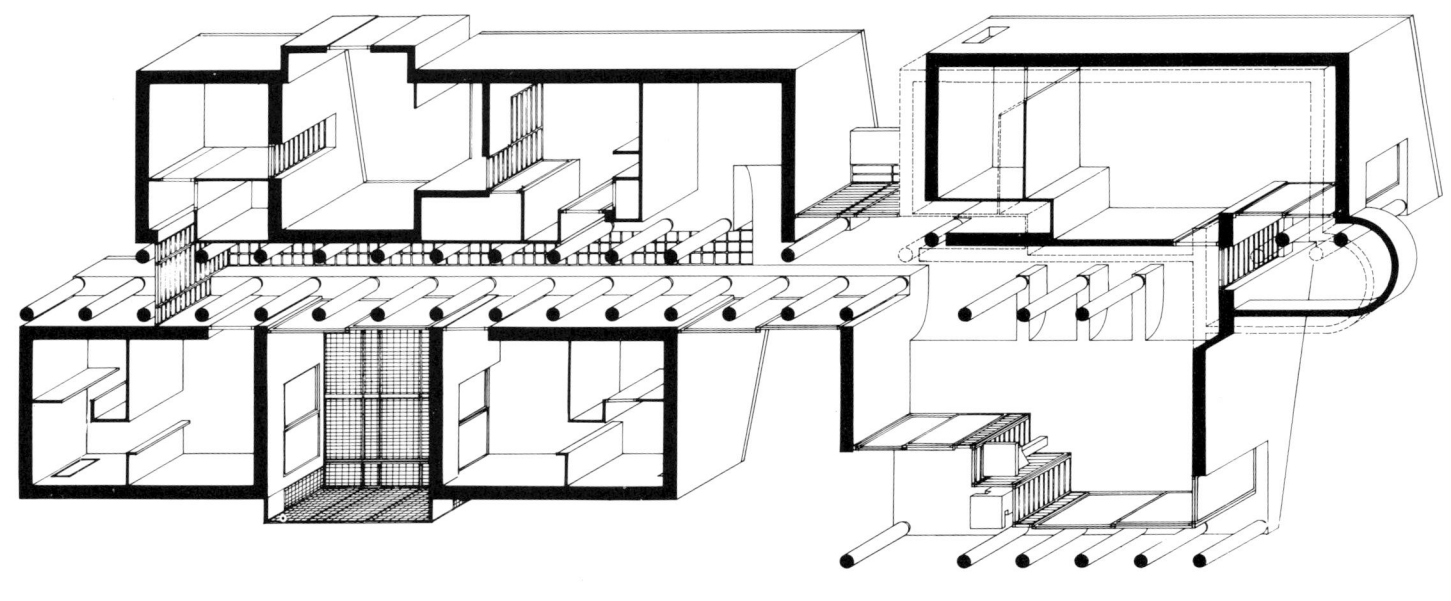

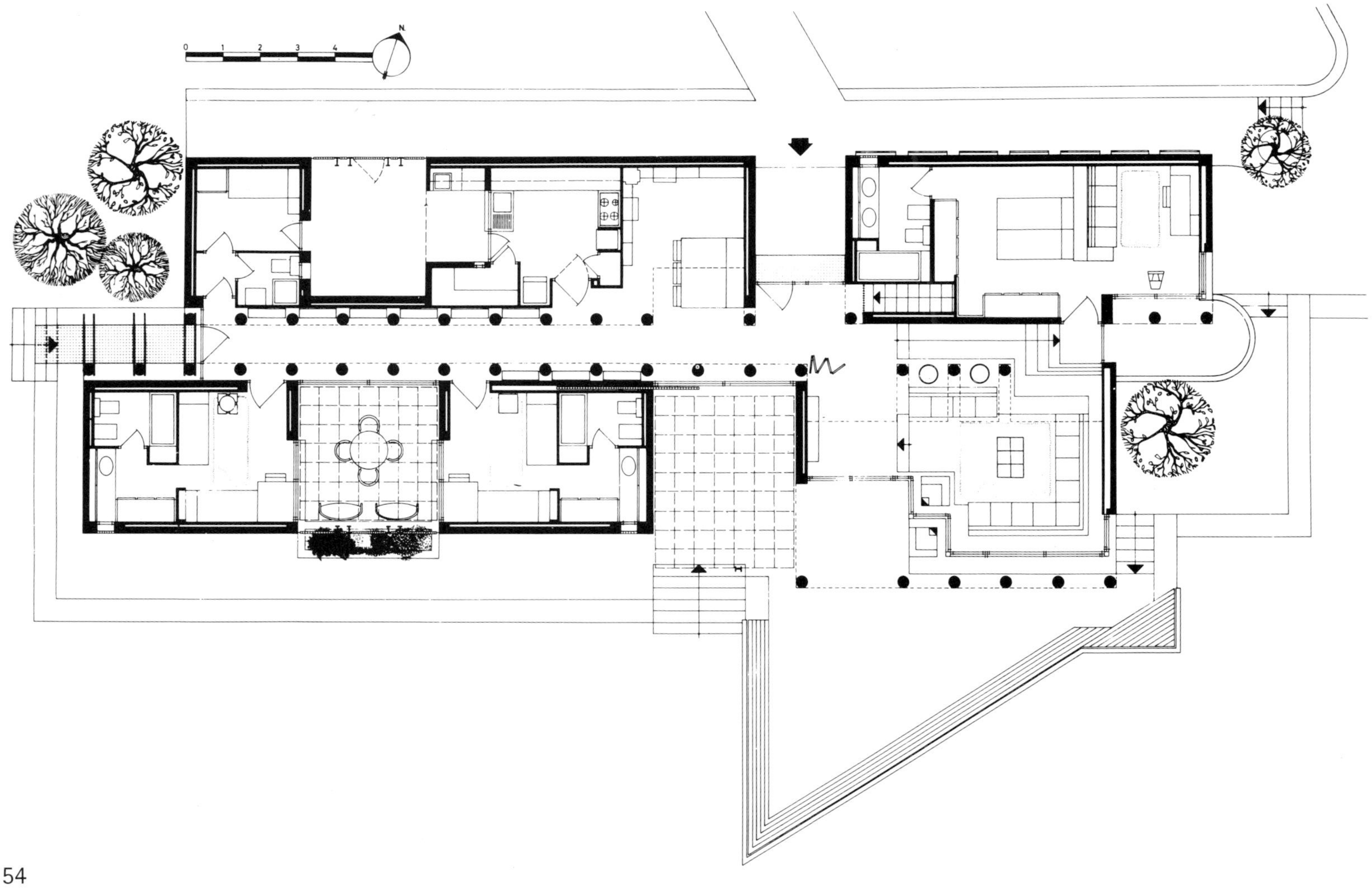

4. Axonometric view.
5. Plan.
6, 7. The corridor spine is emphasized with closely placed columns that articulate closed and open rooms. It is used as a gallery containing the archaeological collection of the owner.

Almirall House, La Garriga
1975-77
Interior design: I.D.P.

This house is one of a series of four similar houses, similar in size (190 m^2) and with much the same typological schema. The basic typology was adjusted to fit each landscape much as a person wears different clothes to suit each social occasion. House form in this instance is independent and autonomous much like traditional barn buildings.

The site was a nineteenth-century garden. The idea of the owners was to subdivide the garden for their children, and it was for one of these that MBM designed a house. A compact form such as a cube was ideal because it conserved as much of the garden as possible. The basic cube was modified by extending it up and over the roof to create a private shaded garden terrace on the top of the house. This also provided thermal insulation overhead from the hot summer sun. The walls outside were painted green and the aluminium windows set flush with the wall to emphasize the simplicity of the basic cube.

The house's rooms are disposed in a spiral configuration around a central core which contains the water and air-conditioning equipment, an arrangement reminiscent of the Heredero House. Each quarter footprint is stepped 80 cm higher than the last so the house resembles a large spiral staircase. The public areas within the house were built in concrete block, which besides its desirable acoustic and textural properties, implied an avant-garde attitude to cheap mass-produced industrial materials. This was a deliberate choice by the clients.

1. View from the south-east.
2. Plans.

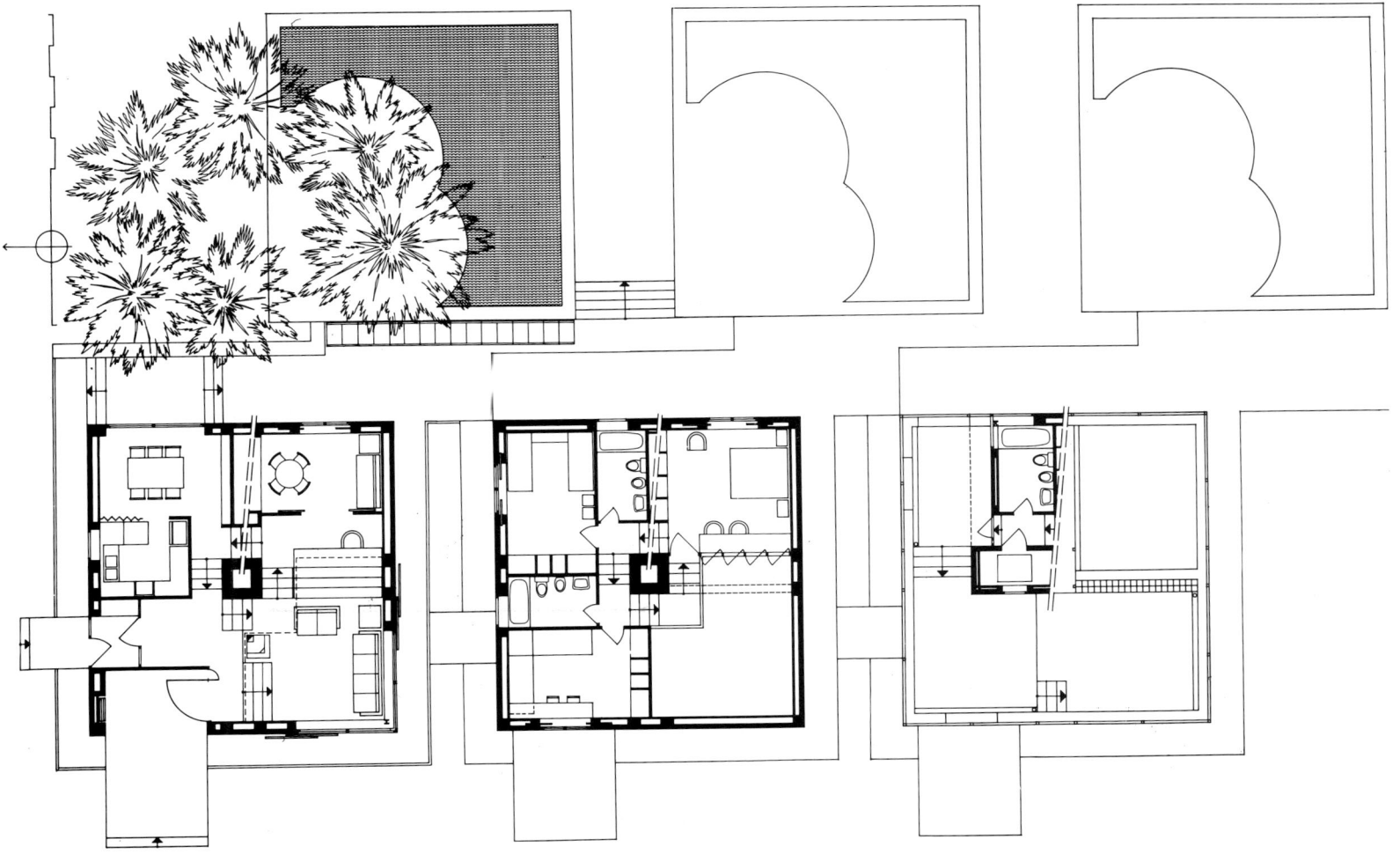

3. View from the west.
4. View from the north with the front door to the right just behind the tree.
5. Interior view showing the spiral configuration around the central core.

Canovelles House, Canovelles, Granollers
1977-81
Interior design: I.D.P.

The Canovelles House sits on the brow of a hill in the countryside by itself overlooking the busy market town of Granollers. It consists of two pairs of parallel steel frames superimposed on two extended rectangular concrete block masses, the northern one higher than its southern counterpart which is stepped stair-like leading down into the garden. To this seemingly simple scheme of a solid basement storey surmounted by linear frames, elements of great complexity have been added, namely the volumes between the frames and the irregular free form glass cage enclosing the living area.

The steel framework lightly sketches in the boundaries of the two parallel units composing the house, giving it a more open feeling, at the same time serving as the supports for a series of vertical and horizontal overhead awnings.

The living area pierces the higher of the two units in what is easily recognized as a scaled-down version of Mies van der Rohe's famous 1922 scheme for the Friedrichstrasse glass skyscraper in Berlin. This free form living area is designed to accommodate a range of family activities simultaneously. The kitchen is closely linked visually to the living area because both clients are keen gourmets.

The terrace basement storey has a double façade to mediate the disparity between inside and outside; outside, the regular composition of openings is related to the steel framing module, while inside, the bedrooms and bathrooms openings strip windows are spaced to suit the individual room functions.

1. View from the east.
2. Axonometric view.

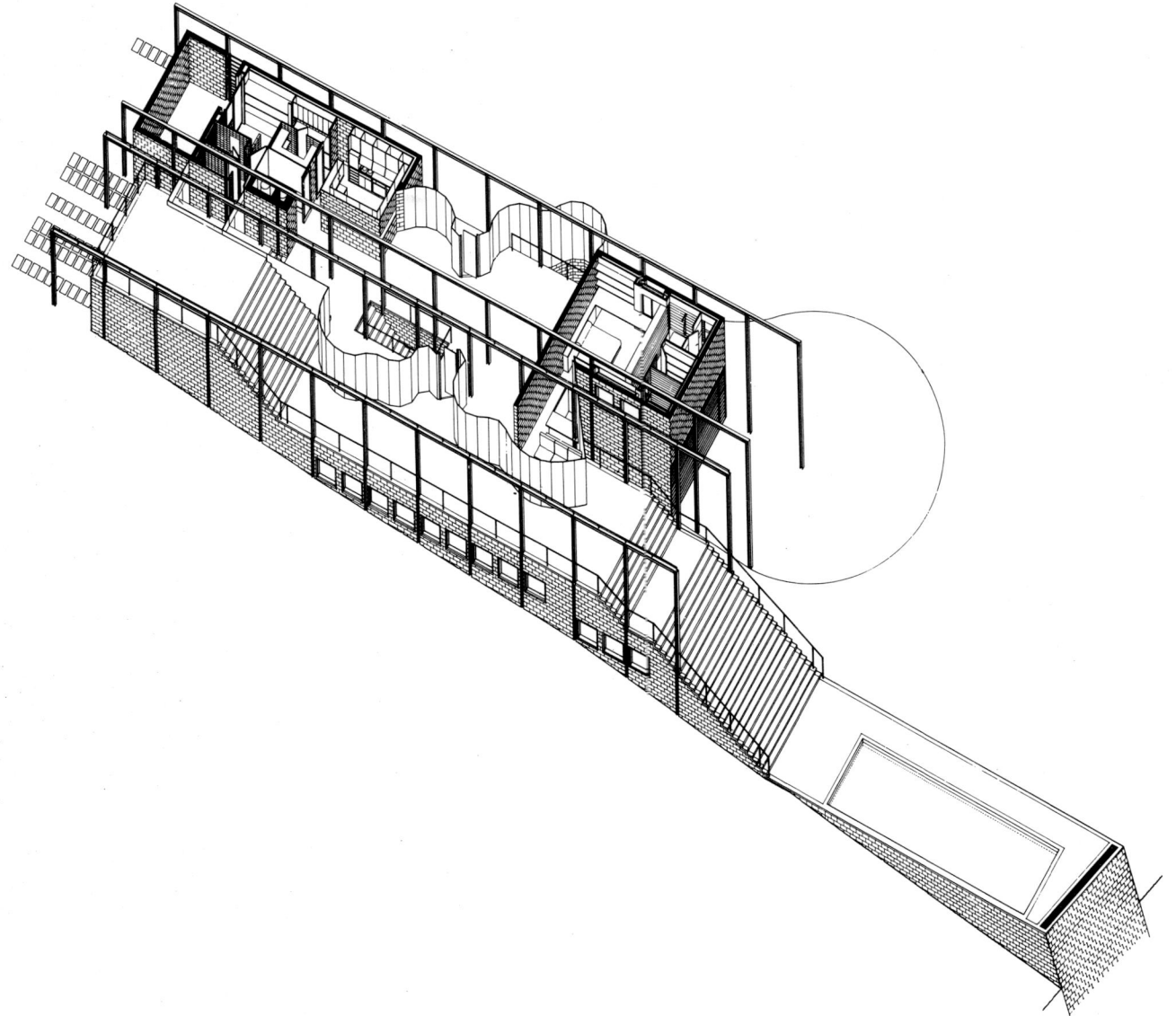

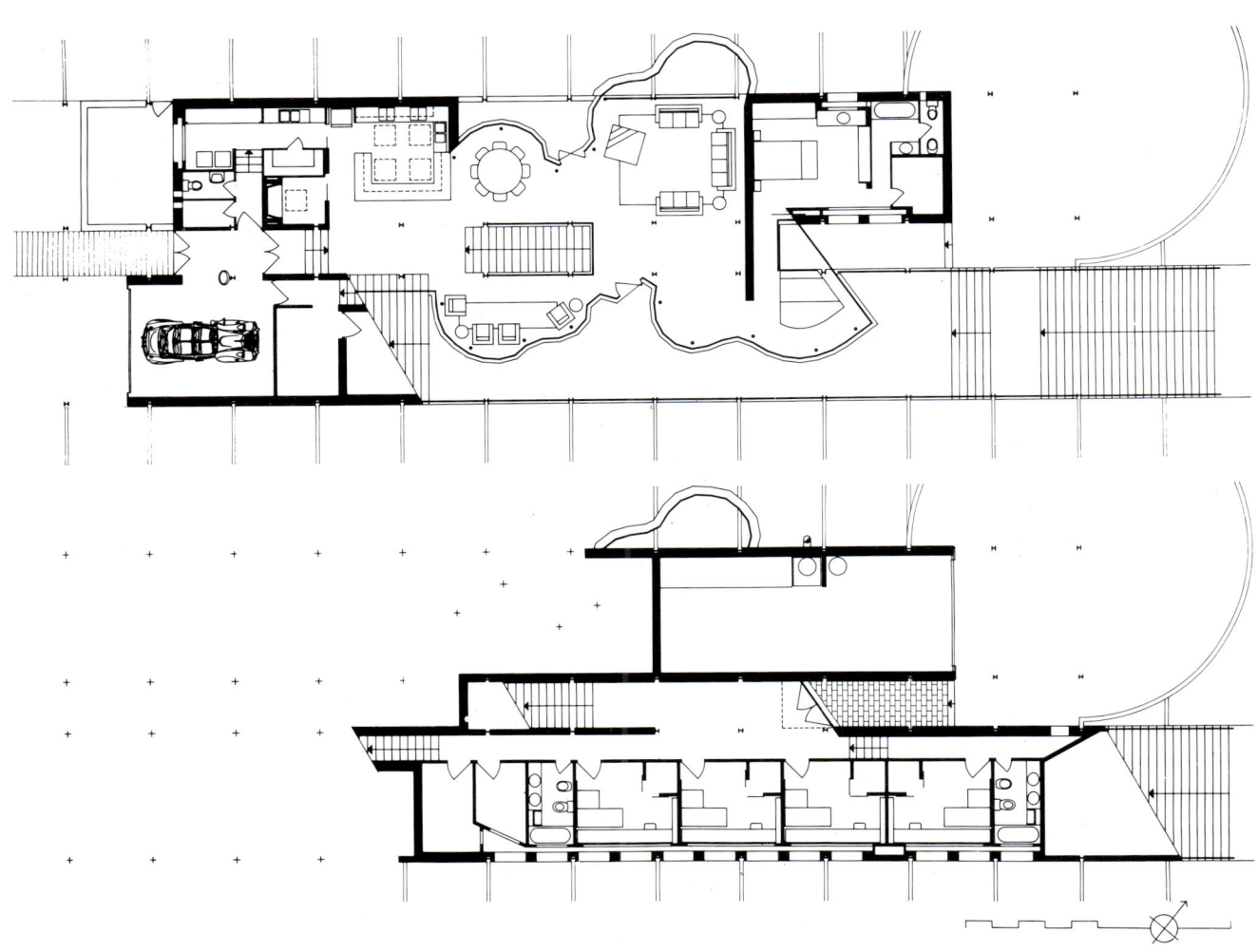

3. The screened terrace.
4. View from the living area towards the dining corner and the small north-west terrace.
5. View from the interior towards the main terrace.
6. Plans (basement and main floor).
7. View from the south.

Villa Escarrer, Son Vida, Palma, Mallorca
1985-88

This large 3000 m² house fulfills the client's wish for a spectacular setting in which to entertain friends and associates. It is a combined residence and business showplace. It resembles a palace more than a house with its large gardens and artificial lake designed in a similar vein to an eighteenth-century park with the water features serving as an extended entertainment area separate from the house itself.

The form is highly geometric, but it is a geometry based on a square divided into four smaller squares by cross axes half its size on which a triangle has been superimposed, the whole then being modified so as to break down the rigidity of this schema. This geometrical framework was maintained throughout the vagaries of the design development with two fundamental changes which were necessary to overcome problems to do with the expansion of the accommodation and adaptation to the local topography.

How this was achieved illustrates the workings of a Realist approach to solving problems. This involves starting out with a pure form but being prepared to modify it where necessary to deal with individual contingencies, but in such a way as to retain the imprint of the pure form. In the Son Vida Villa this was achieved by leaving off one side of the closed square forming it into a »U« so it could be added to. This was expressed externally by leaving the fourth side (containing the garage) and other intermediate walls in a rustic unfinished state and abruptly cutting off the pitched roof with two north facing glass walls instead of the usual dry jointed dressed stone cladding which prevails elsewhere.

The second contingency was the specifics of the site: being on the brow of the hill it was necessary to provide a larger base for the building to permit the development of a terrace with easy access from the living area. This base also contained additional living accommodation, a string of bedroom suites and service areas. These required a somewhat larger area, triangular in shape, than was called for in the rooms of the upper level. It was achieved by displacing the lower storey to deal with the fall of the hill and by angling the bedroom suites to the morning sun.

The design liberates the inside spaces. The rooms are hardly ever complete in themselves, this incompleteness, the tearing down of barriers between inside and outside and between spaces, is used to encourage a movement across the spaces into the distance. Such references as in the blue mural seascape in the long gallery room by the artist Ràfols-Casamada are especially theatrical, provoking memories of external scenes beyond the house. Although the Son Vida House belongs unquestionably to this century, its opulent rhetoric recalls the extravagant Mannerist villas of the sixteenth century.

1. View from the west. The sculpture in the foreground by Miguel Moreno marks the end of the long pergola.
2. Site plan. The house is situated in a vast park with a lake in the southern part.

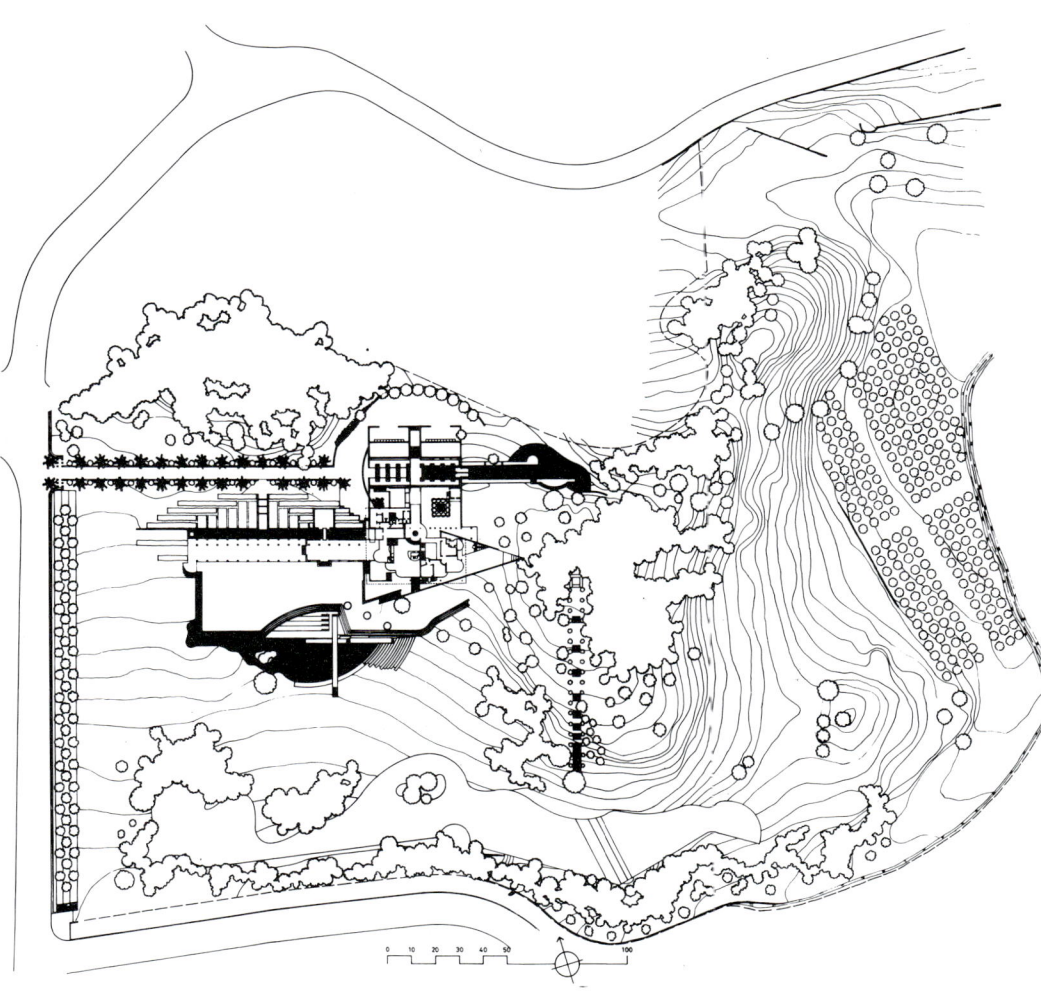

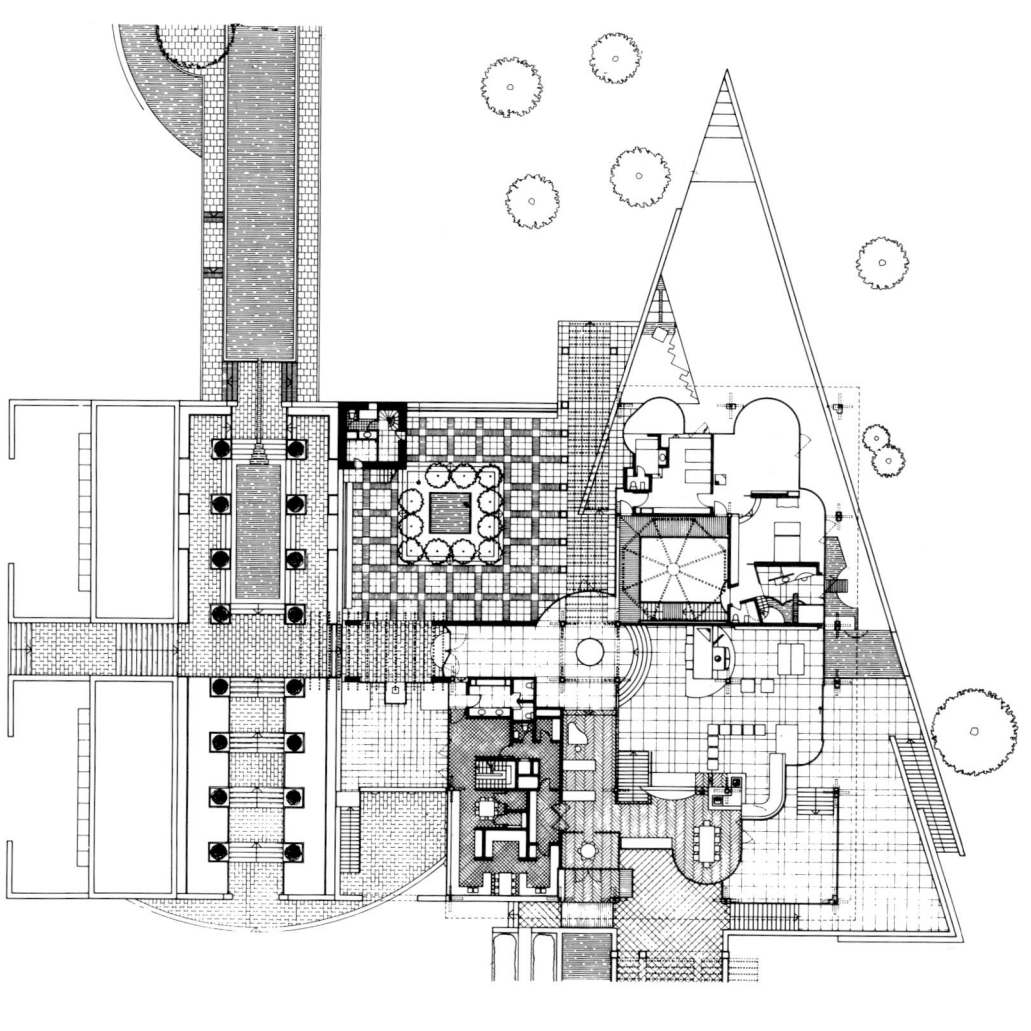

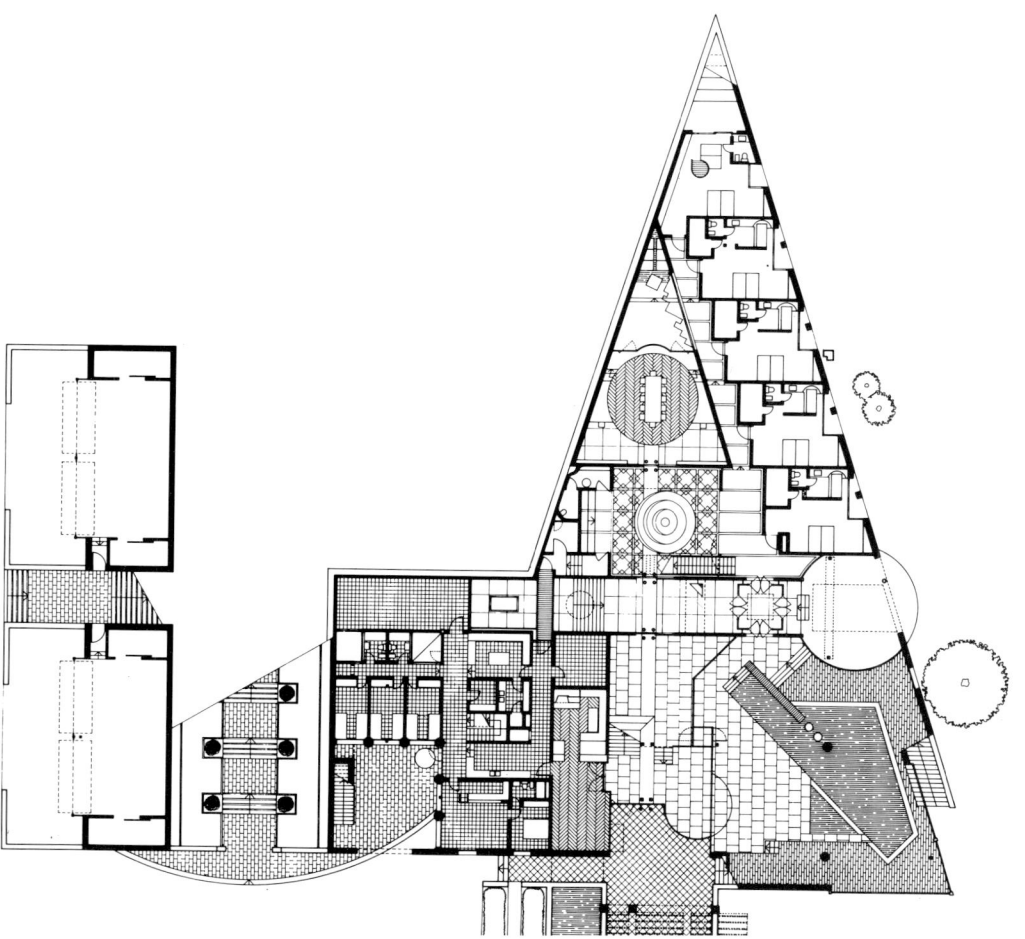

3. Plans (basement, main floor).
4. View from the entrance drive and court beyond with the winged sculpture by Maties Quetglas.
5. View from the south-east showing the base of the building containing the bedrooms that give directly onto the garden.

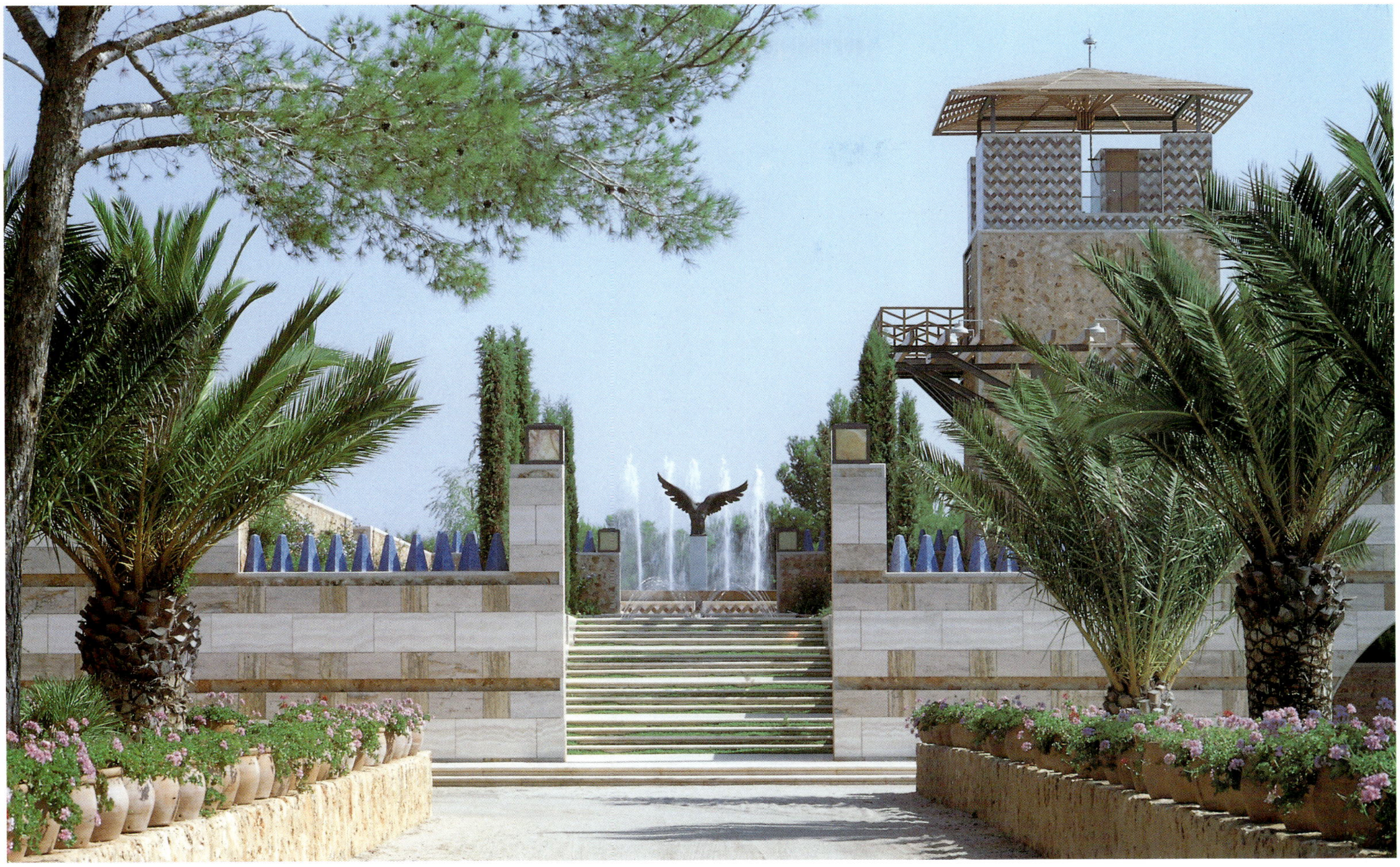

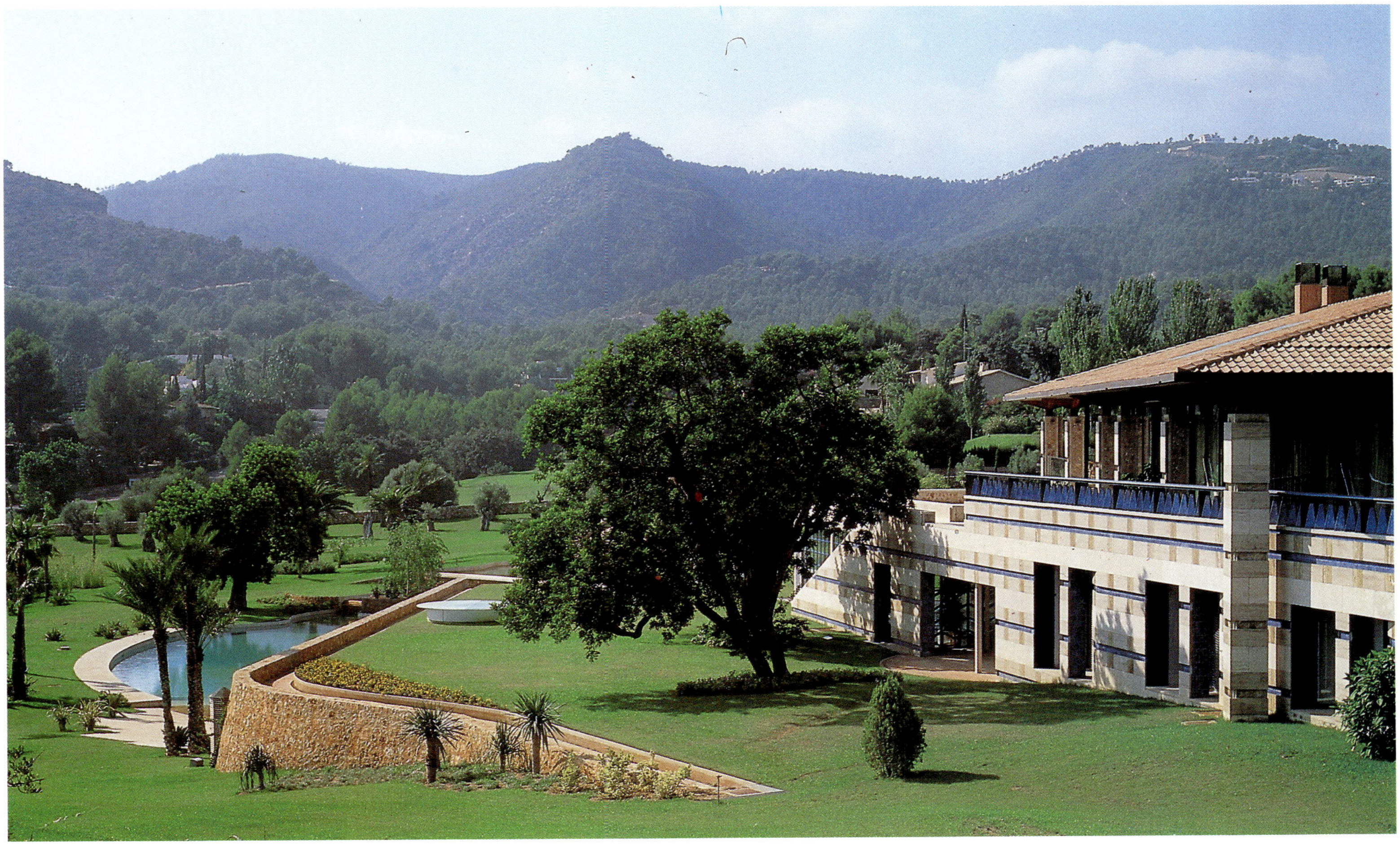

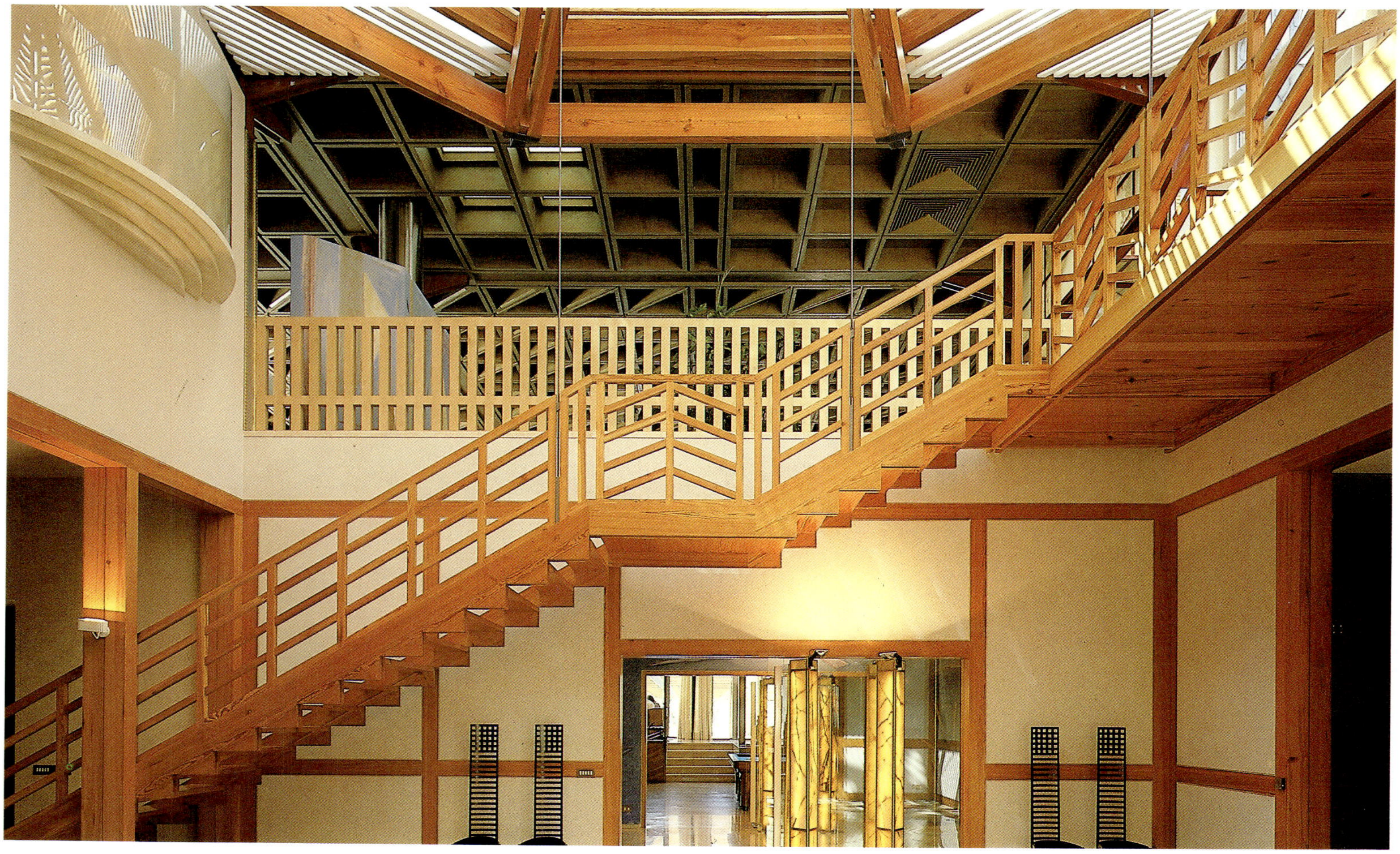

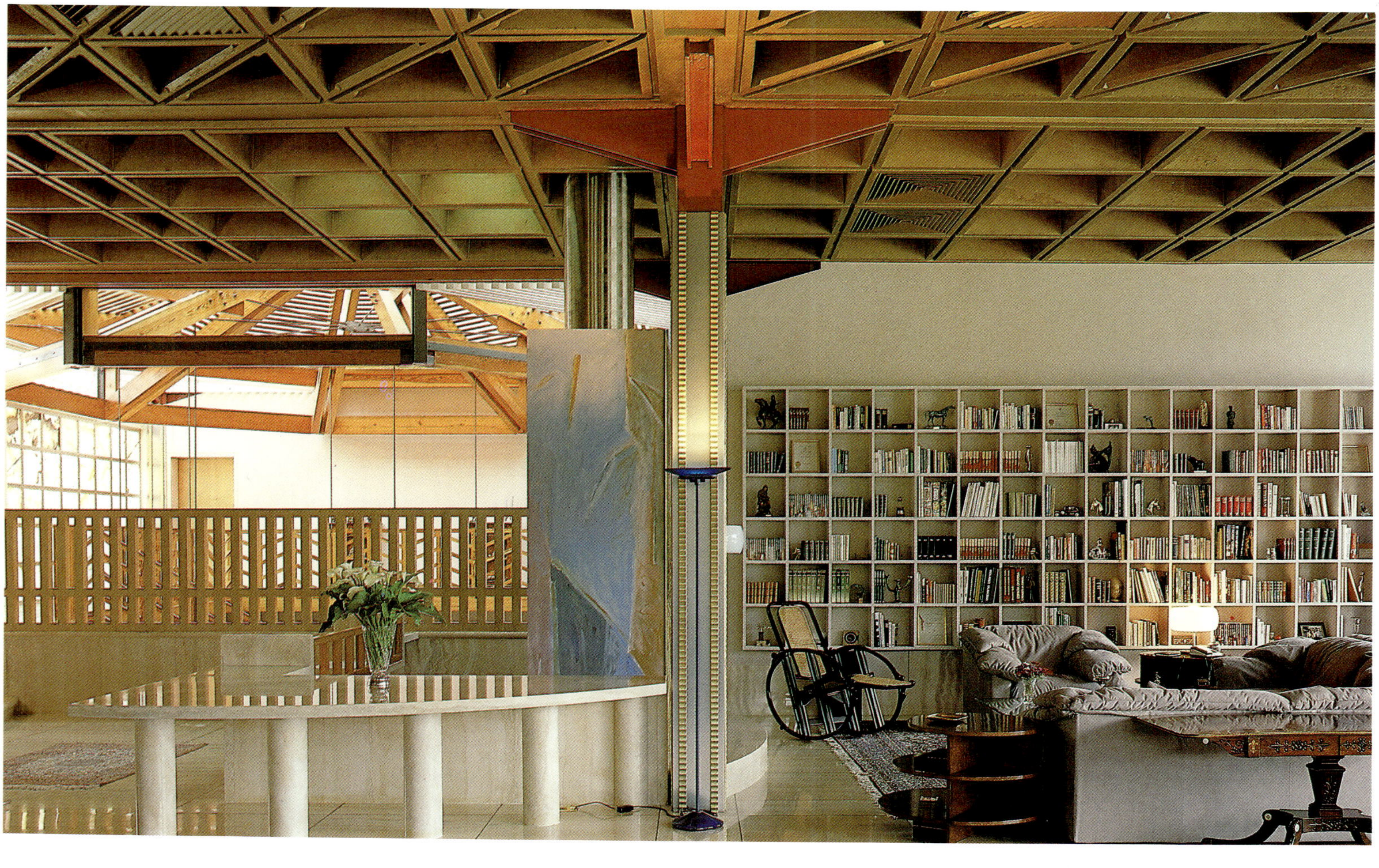

6. The »Gothic« court looking towards the main living area above and the long gallery below with the game rooms beyond.
7. The main living area with the »Gothic« court beyond.
8. View from the west along the canal and the long pergola.
9. The long pergola.

Group Housing

It is in the field of urban group housing that the firm of MBM made its greatest contribution. From the very first, when works such as the Manzana Pallars in 1959 received recognition, the creative thrust of the architectural practice has been to do two things: to improve the architectural quality and amenity of block housing, and to use such projects to develop and enhance qualities of urbanism.

The dominant concern in all of this was the relationship of the city block and the street. Modern architecture, to a considerable extent, had abandoned the street. MBM, following a European-wide trend, reversed this, and used the mass of their housing to define the street as a dignified and socially relevant element of the city morphology.

The Pallars Group, of which only a portion was ever completed, formed a doughnut circling the perimeter of a Barcelona block. Instead of the customary undifferentiated building wall that was customary, MBM subdivided the block into smaller separate buildings two apartments wide and two deep, four to each floor, with a double tower across the splay corner. The stairs were located in-between each six-storey tower to form a gap, and the building face splayed as a further measure to alleviate the uniformity of the street façade.[66]

The Meridiana Apartment Block is famous for its diamond bay-window alcoves. It faced onto two streets which allowed the apartments on either side to be arranged with shared lift and stair accesses, separated by four internal patios for light and ventilation.

The Navas de Tolosa Apartment Block (1963) tackled the problem of the splay corner which is so typical of Barcelona. It proposed the solution of subdividing the splay face into smaller corners looking in two directions. Unfortunately, it was a solution not without its flaws and was much imitated to the architects' sorrow.

Although MBM accepted as a matter of principle the use of traditional materials such as brick, timber, and terra-cotta roof tiles, they were interested in experimenting with industrial materials when the opportunity to do so arose. The Secretari Coloma Apartment Block (1965) adopted a »J« plan configuration with a landscaped court in the hook. The façades were systematized and included a staccato arrangement of timber screens infilled by glass blocks and fibro cement between the balconies. The Via Augusta Apartment Block (1964) is a much more comprehensive experiment in assembling a façade from standard prefabricated panels. It adopted a horizontal expression of alternating spandrels and windows. The top floor has a wide terrace with one of the best views in all Barcelona. The offices for Barcelona's La Vanguardia were similarly based on a strongly expressed panel system using stone which was varied to create an interesting horizontal rhythm of vertical fins between the exposed floor slabs.

As its name suggests, the Casa del Pati Apartments (1964) were arranged around an internal patio which had its own fountain to suggest coolness and withdrawal from the street. This, too, was on a famous splay corner, and met the challenge by fracturing the splay into a number of corner rooms. This theme of traditional form is amplified in the Borrell Apartment Complex (1966) with its hypnotic octagonal light well separating the two principal access stairs and projecting glazed *tribunes* cubes mounted on the street façade. Like the Secretari Coloma façade, it was assembled from timber wall panels.

The solution of the splay corner takes over the form of the Xaudiera Apartment Block which was reduced to a series of steps so that the corner room, which was initially a means of subdividing the splay, in the end dominates the block. The vertical treatment of the stepped form is emphasized by contrasting the glazed and solid steps in the tower profile. In the Casp Apartment Block (1969) the corner solution achieves a synthesis by returning to the flat splay and recessing the corner room behind this face.

Stepping as a device for reducing the impact of large forms became an accepted technique, even when there was no splay corner. In the example of the Roca Apartment Block (1972) the stepping is used to increase the sculptural impact of the brick forms, leading the eye upwards to a climax at each stair tower jutting from its eastern gallery. Brickwork is especially expressive, particularly when its texture is emphasized. To this, the apartment complex on the Crescent de Viladecans added the factor of the crescent, the strongly articulated brick piers sweeping by imperceptible degrees, from a northern to a north-eastern orientation. This was an extensive group. To cope with its size, MBM created two parallel walls of apartments separated by a narrow corridor of open space. This was a solution of layering the groups which was to prove enormously fruitful in the later work.

In 1973, both the La Salut Block and Bonanova Apartment Group were completed. They announce a new sophistication in the treatment of large urban housing blocks. Bonanova, by its seductive use of the diagonal splayed balcony using a Wrightian geometry, and La Salut, by its double ring of housing dispersed around the periphery of the city block, produce a hierarchy of major and minor enclosed spaces, achieving a unified street treatment with shops, but providing for the needs of people living in a very dense settlement.

Both housing groups are architecturally striking, the Bonanova being the most attractive of the two because of the variety of its spaces and smaller scale. The L-shaped Bonanova buildings faced southeast and the splayed face permitted the living room of the apartments to turn towards the southwest, thereby providing a desirable orientation, while avoiding any conflict with the site. Of the original three L-shaped buildings only two were built, and this results in intimate high-quality spaces, numerous changes of level leading to a pleasant terrace with inset swimming pool, and masterful treatment of brick planes, curved and stepped, that draw the pedestrian under and around the housing in a series of small spaces of varied openness and outlook. The garden and landscaping contributed greatly to the final effect.

La Salut is much bigger and this shows. A rectangular ring set within a trapezoidal outer ring, the ends of the housing slabs have been cut into splayed facets like the Bonanova Apartment towers, but on this occasion the treatment is confined to the ends. The central court, formally planted with regular rows of palms, is one of the most successful semi-public spaces designed by MBM. Unlike the earlier group housing projects where the brickwork texture is exaggerated, at La Salut the brickwork is cleanly cut, and openings are precise rectangular voids extracted from the solid of the wall.

The 1960s were a decade of rapid tourist growth for Spain and MBM shared in this, to the extent of designing a number of excellent groups of holiday apartments at Benicassim, Pals, and on Mallorca. The Europalma Holiday Apartments belong to the early 1960s. They are grouped informally facing in different directions according to changes in the site and outlook from their perch on the cliff top to a grand sweep of bay.

Constructed of rough stones with exposed off-form concrete floors and balconies, and with pitched tiled roofs, the architecture of the apartments draws on traditional motifs, as exemplified by the vertical rippled pattern timber balcony balustrades and louvred screens, but it is a restrained and tasteful use of traditional details which carefully distances itself from the kitsch. The Halen Housing Estate, completed in 1961 by Atelier 5, provided an early model for this type of landscape-orientated development.

Whereas the Europalma site sloped steeply, and this added considerably to the interest created by the forms, as well as complicating its realization, the Santa Agueda Apartments, Benicassim (1967), are fitted onto a flat site in such an interesting way that it produces its own hill by stacking the apartments one on top of each other and stepping them back and forth, so they overhang one another in a wavy artificial hill which surrounds the grassed common on two sides. All the apartment terraces face onto the common. The open galleries accessing each apartment are on the outside overlooking the street.

This is a beautifully judged tribute to the vernacular with its *persiana* awnings, metal armatures, heavy timber batten balustrades, and traditional patterned tiled roofs, which evoke an atmosphere of pleasurable surrender to the sun and the sea. The coast at this location is fairly dull, so the architecture offers visual compensation.

The Pals Golf Houses (1973) pursue the same theme, but with far greater control and discipline. Once again, the blocks surround a common landscaped terrace with its mandatory swimming pool, but on this occasion, the apartments were marshalled in thin paired strips of set back terraces, only one of which was built. Narrow shaded pedestrian ways alternate with wider landscaped strips in the corridors left over between each long projected apartment band. Green tile caps on the walls emphasize the stepped motif, and this movement is played up by the deliberate sculptural expression of the chimneys.

The apartments at Pineda (1969) for the teachers at the Sant Jordi School, with their celebrated flying spiral stair, cannot be considered holiday housing, however, their relatively small size hardly fits the scale of urban housing normally encountered by MBM. There are twelve apartments in the block, two on the ground floor, and two levels of five duplexes above. The rear spiral stair was required to connect the gallery serving the upper duplexes to the first floor stair. There is something particularly Italian about the appearance of the block with the canvas awnings and plain faced brickwork and the steel chimneys thrusting through the roof. Possibly, it is the contrast of such a vertical block set in an open field.

The late 1970s marked a new phase in urban group housing, with developments such as the Manzanas Martí l'Humà, Sabadell (1979), Sarrià (1979), Mollet (1987), La Maquinista (1989) in Barcelona, and expanded activities in Berlin with the Friedrichstadt Housing Unit, Berlin (1981) for the IBA. The Villa Olímpica is a fitting climax. By the 1980s, and into the 1990s, MBM were kept busy with urban proposals for Turin, Pamplona, Aix-en-Provence and Paris.

The Martí l'Humà Public Housing contains 145 units of 80 to 120 square metres area in two wings separated by an internal street bent around the corner with the upper floors of the higher outer slab pushed back to comply with height line requirements. The two boomerang-shaped walls of apartments step down towards an internal landscaped garden with a circular swimming pool for use by the residents. The flats are double height with the larger units on the curved corners. Strongly modelled fenestration and seemingly arbitrary cantilevers and recesses add interest to what is otherwise an affectionate tribute to the earlier Rationalism of the Italian Giuseppe Terragni.[67]

The Gateway Houses on Kochstrasse, Berlin (1985-91), comprise three buildings each of which is deeper than the buildings on either side in order to accommodate the higher density of dwellings facing east and west to remove them from the traffic noise on Kochstrasse to the south. Once again MBM have been successful in giving their forms a distinct Berlin feel. This they have done by borrowing such architectural elements from the gable houses near the corner of Friedrichstrasse as the autonomous brick gable set back from the main façade, the glass block tower, the porch set back behind the façade, and the Constructivist upper street gallery.

The gables serve as a leading motif, being repeated in the form of gable walls for the garden houses in order to relate the new to the old. The garden houses stretch in a row from Kochstrasse to Zimmerstrasse in an L-shaped block with private gardens on the west and south. This was done in such a way as to avoid any feeling of isolation on the part of the residents of being next to the Berlin Wall. A small buffer has been inserted between the Wall and the garden houses to reduce the impact of the former. The result is a rich urban collage of early Modern and Constructivist elements which integrate in a quite natural way with the traditional urban qualities and cosmopolitan atmosphere of Berlin as a city.

Barcelona, with a population of 4.6 million, is today one of the leading cities of Europe (and certainly one of the most interesting) in what is undoubtedly one of the fastest growing economies in Europe. Against this background, the provision of adequate, decent housing is a paramount priority. MBM have shown a determination not only to find intelligent and well considered indigenous solutions to meet this challenge, but a regard for a degree of equality which did not consist of a lowering of standards, but the very opposite, a lifting of standards. One of the most reliable indicators of the seriousness of MBM's intentions was their unflagging pursuit of design quality to add to, and enrich, the lives of ordinary people. Good architecture is as essential as providing for basic needs.

Pallars City Block, C. Pallars 299–317, Barcelona
1958/59

In 1958, the time when this group of 130 dwellings was built, the Franco regime was encouraging private industry to provide rental housing for its employees with the offer of tax relief. The minimum dwelling size of such dwellings then was 60 m². In response, an important metallurgical enterprise in the Poblenou Barcelona neighbourhood acquired the entire length of a Cerdà city block with the idea of lining all four street frontages with housing in what was then regarded as a paternal social gesture.

In contrast to the large back-to-front dwellings of the bourgeoisie at the beginning of the twentieth century, MBM's minimum size dwellings resulted in a back-to-back arrangement combined with an enclosed light well which permitted limited cross-ventilation. The depth of such buildings was established within the city plan. The outcome of all this was an extremely economical grouping of four dwellings per floor, each with its own staircase.

The split level access to each of these dwellings from each stair half-landing also results in a symmetrical distribution along the axis between the front and back façades. This has three advantages: it removes the entrance from the corner of each flat and moves it to the centre; it creates a clothes drying area between each façade and the staircase; and finally, the split level increased the privacy of bedroom windows facing onto the light well by avoiding their alignment with the windows of neighbouring bedrooms. It should also be noted, that these light wells serve only bedrooms – the kitchen with its associated noise and odours was placed well away from these quiet areas.

In the familiar Cerdà street the façade expression is affected by different widths of buildings corresponding to smaller property divisions. In the Pallars Housing a different approach was adopted to achieve a similar articulation of the housing form. This consisted of dividing the housing into standard bay widths, each bay having a »V« front to correspond with the pitch of the roof and separated from the adjoining bay unit by a recessed staircase.

The selection of the materials for the project and the choice of façade elements is symptomatic of a critical attitude towards orthodox Modern Movement precepts at a time of Neo-Realism in Italy and the New Brutalism in England. In Barcelona, the recent visit of Alvar Aalto, and the impact of local material stringencies together with cheap labour, encouraged the modification of Modern architecture to accommodate traditional construction techniques and materials.

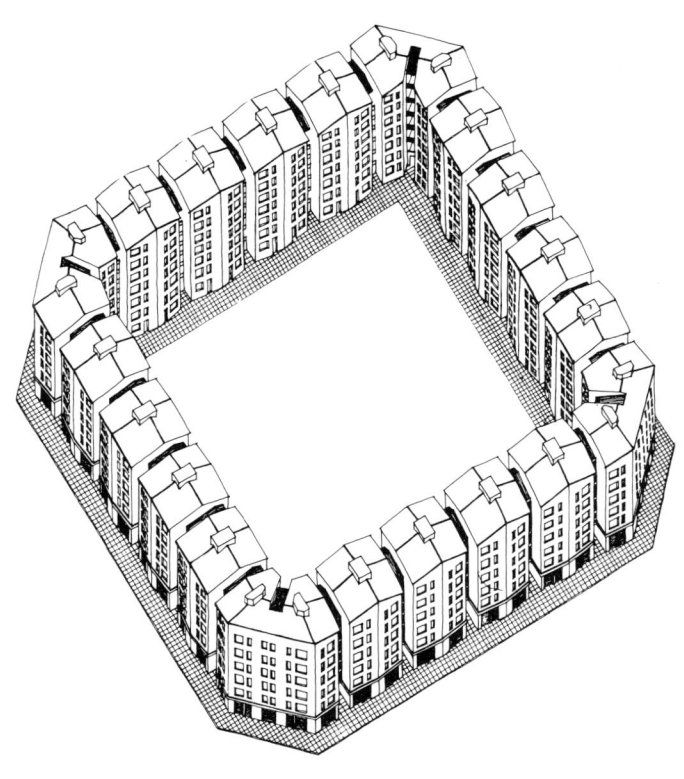

1. Axonometric view of the complete city block.
Only one of the four wings was built.
2. View of the building from the chamfer.

3. The interior of one of the dwellings.
4. Plan of a typical dwelling.
5. Site plan as built.
6. Detail of an entrance door to the building showing the articulation of the bay-system of the street façade.

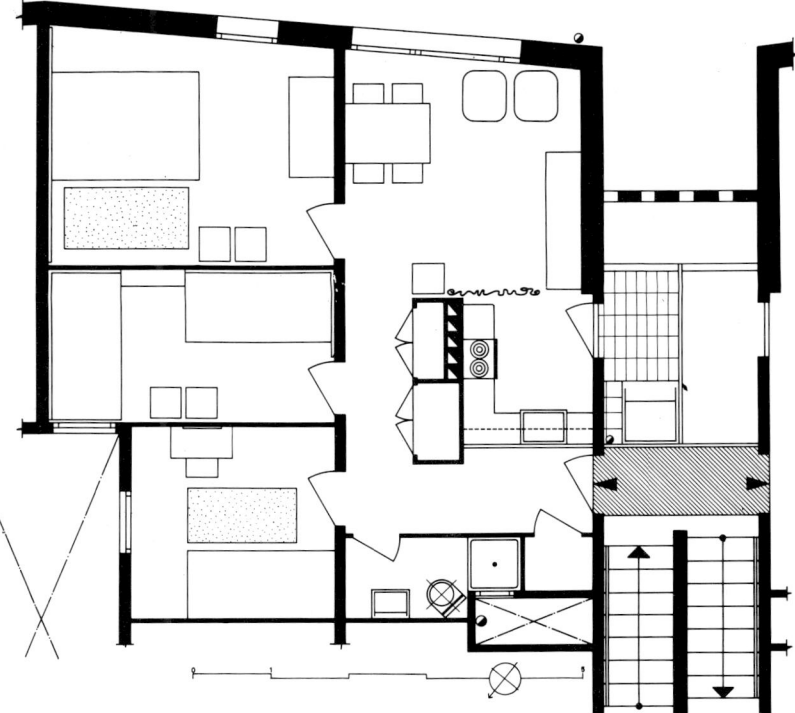

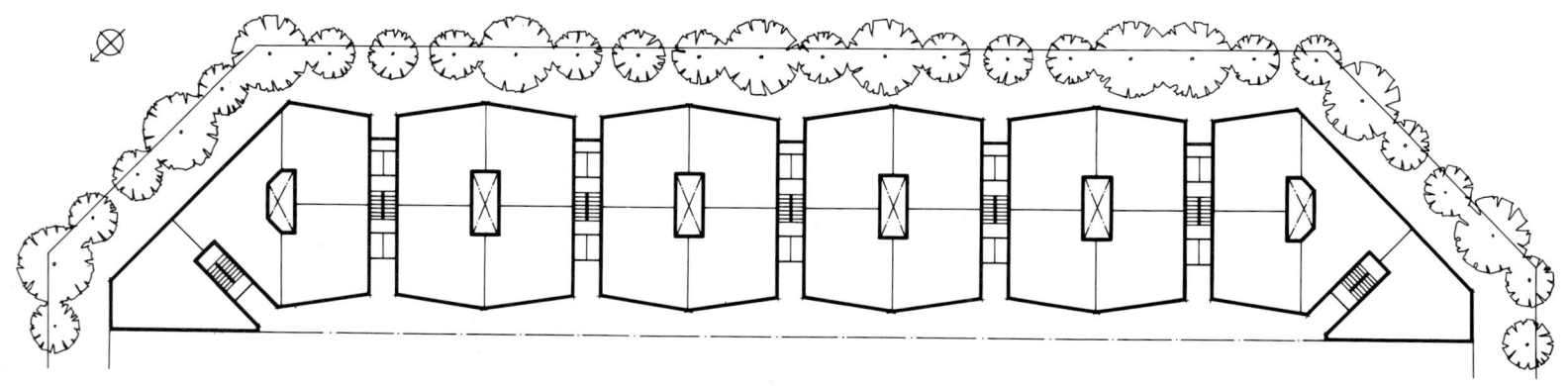

Casa del Pati, Ronda del Guinardó 44, Barcelona
1961-64

The economic boom that occurred all over Europe in the early sixties resulted in an enormous immigration to Barcelona from other parts of Spain. The city's population grew at the rate of 80,000 people annually. This resulted in uncontrolled housing developments by private developers, assisted by state subsidies, who built in the suburbs surrounding the city outside the urban plan.

At the same time, cooperative housing associations were established to beat the relatively high prices engendered by such a housing market and to counter the unimaginative nature of this housing. Frequently, the owners of land who lacked the capital to develop it themselves would agree with a cooperative to give their land in exchange for a specified number of dwelling units. The chamfered corner site known as Ronda del Guinardó is just such a case, being the second venture of its kind by this cooperative society. Rather than an enclosed light well, a three-bedroom scheme, 66 m^2 in area, was decided on which placed the kitchen on the façade. This arrangement proved extremely popular and there was a large demand for this type of flat elsewhere.

The placement of thirty-nine rectangular units like so many stacked dominoes along the two northern and southern façades produced a large interior court. This was treated as a community space somewhat like a village square around which all the entrances are orientated. This further reinforced the spirit of the cooperative association. A fountain was included at the lower level to strengthen the reading of the court as a public space. This composition established a graduated hierarchy between the individual dwelling and the city since the individual dwelling relates first to the space, then is linked to the city beyond. In this fashion, the architecture encourages a neighbourhood identity while it diminishes the sense of anonymity of the city dwelling.

Priority has been given to the interior court over that of the external urban order. The façade is affected and suffers from the orthogonal distribution of the standard dwellings which have the unfortunate effect of breaking up the chamfered corner.

The structure is simple load-bearing brick with reinforced concrete at the street level which was required to support the cantilevered elements.

1. Plan (typical floor).
2. View of the north façade from the Ronda del Guinardó.

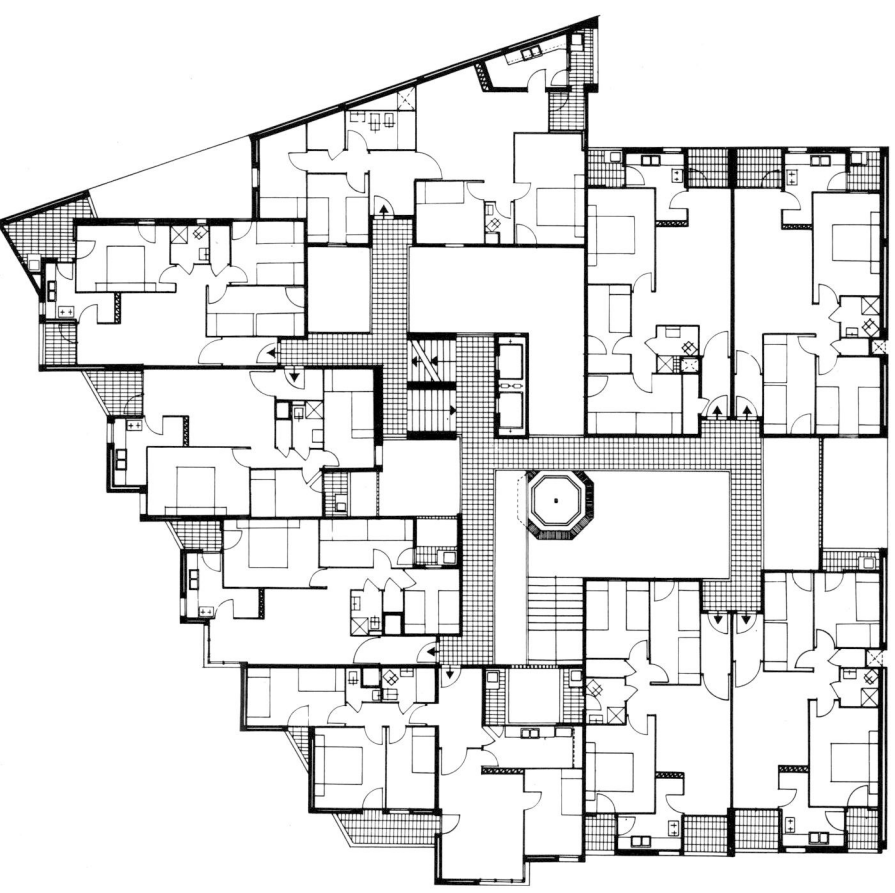

3. View of the courtyard used as an interior public space.
4. The fountain in the courtyard.
5. Gallery access to the dwellings around the court.

Europalma Apartments, Costa de la Calma, Mallorca
1963/64

The stepped housing is situated at the extreme edge of cliffs overhanging the sea. There are magnificent views of the bays of Santa Ponsa and Paguera. It is on the Cornice Road that runs to the north of a tourist development.

It was decided to divide the apartments into a series of small individual buildings to avoid the customary large scale of a single large building which typifies such coastal developments. It was also determined to group the apartments in such a manner as to physically create a village-like form in order to enhance the sense of belonging to a community. The buildings were adapted to the extremely steep slope of the site by staggering each apartment over the other vertically so the entrances are as close as possible to the undisturbed ground level, thereby eliminating all interior access stairs.

The eleven buildings were laid out above and below a pedestrian street that wandered down from a proposed funicular station in a series of eddies formed by small squares until it encountered the sea cliffs and merged with the road where a series of garages were sited. From this central spine, narrow stepped streets lead up or down between the closely packed buildings to give direct access to each apartment much as one finds in actual row houses. Only the first stage consisting of five buildings was realized of the initial programme because of difficulties in the market at that time.

Each unit contains seven apartments with three different plan types. In the central section, there are four semi-detached one-bedroom apartments (60 m^2 including a terrace). In the lower section, there is a shallow duplex apartment (130 m^2) that extends across the entire front of the building with three bedrooms underneath the living room and service rooms. At the back and top end of the building, there are two studios with two bedrooms (80 m^2) that have the additional bedroom in a gallery over the double height living room. Each apartment has a large terrace with views of the sea and garden trough doubling as a balcony and privacy screen to the terrace below.

Stone load-bearing walls were chosen because of their texture and colour to merge the buildings with the rocky landscape. Tiled pitched roofs supplied an appropriate means for stepping the building forms as well as giving a Mediterranean village-like appearance to the housing.

1. Site plan.
2. View of one of the apartment units with flight of steps giving access to the apartments.

3. The stepped walk between the upper and the lower rows of apartment units.
4. Section.
5. Plans (A two-storey apartment with two bedrooms, B one-storey apartment with one bedroom, C one-storey apartment with two bedrooms, D two-storey apartment with four bedrooms).

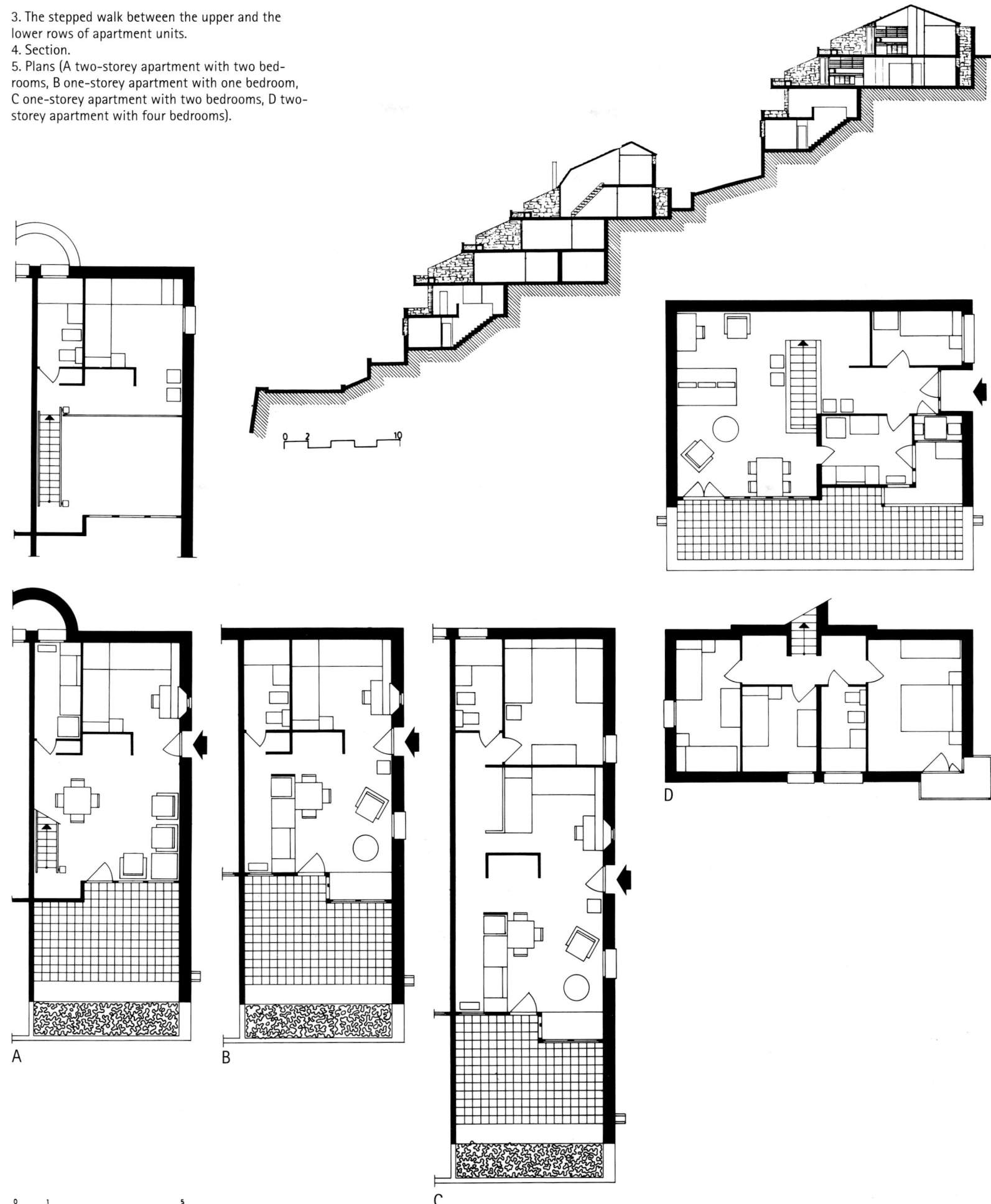

0 2   10

0 1   5

A

B

C

D

Santa Agueda Apartments, Benicassim, Castelló
1966/67

The rape of the Spanish coastline by private developers reached its zenith in the mid-sixties, resulting from the boom in European package tours. In the accompanying commercial frenzy, the tourist was slotted into a high-rise tower, and it was the unrestricted proliferation of these towers that led to the erection of immense hostile walls isolating the shoreline from the traditional settlements set back from the coast.

Included amongst a group of intellectuals and artists from València and Castelló who abhorred such developments was one who had inherited a large field beside the coast on the edge of a traditional summer villa settlement, Las Villas de Benicassim. He asked the architects to provide an alternative model for holiday apartments.

The basic requirements which were agreed to were: to design three to four different sized apartments with large indoor and outdoor living areas subdivided to form physical corners to permit a variety of uses including the possibility of a sleeping area; to manipulate the building section to absorb the car parking beneath; to encourage social interaction along a common access deck leading to the beach; and to group the buildings around a neighbourhood garden to encourage human contact without sacrificing individual privacy and quiet surroundings when desired.

The overall form of the urban design was based upon the preceding criteria, as well as a staggered horseshoe enclosure, adapted to the morphology first introduced by Arne Jacobsen in 1934 for his Bellavista Housing near Copenhagen, and the traditional local image of casually formed village housing with its broken roof lines.

1. Perspective section.
2. Stepped terraced façade.

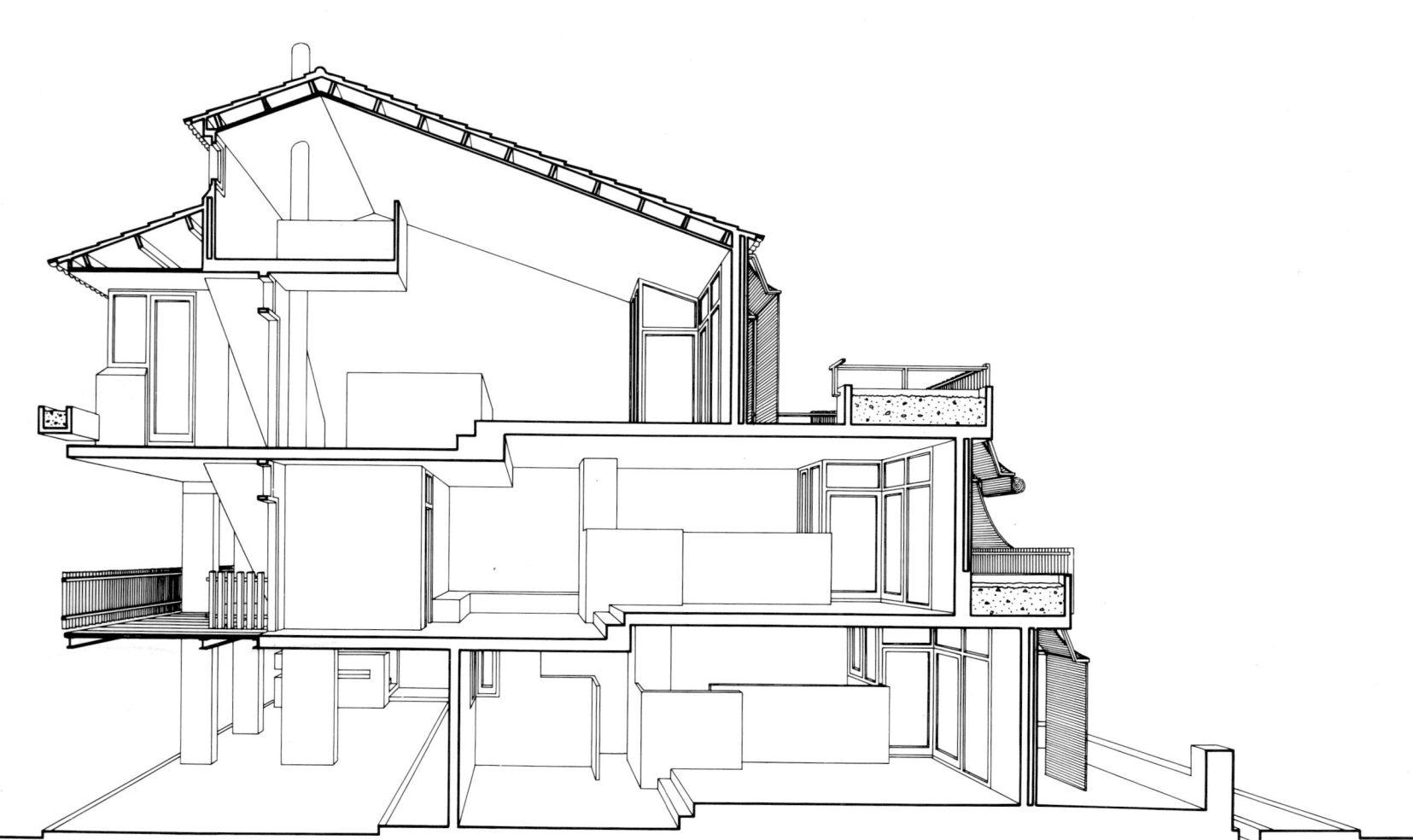

The terraces of each apartment are generously sized to make them really livable. They are protected from the sun and from the gaze of neighbours by a series of green painted wood slatted blinds that drape over cantilevered rods, and a balustrade based on the Renaissance model to give the terraces a solid appearance from the outside, without overdoing it to the extent of depriving them of a certain visual transparency from the inside. The balustrades were made from precast concrete bars fixed to a standard steel section.

Like most enterprises at this time, finance and demand (based on a housing cooperative approach) led to only 118 of the planned 300 apartments being built. Twenty-five years later, the small Santa Agueda community remains as an oasis amongst the massive developments that continue to despoil the Spanish coast, although now, fortunately, the democratic Government has stepped in to restrict this kind of development from happening in the future.

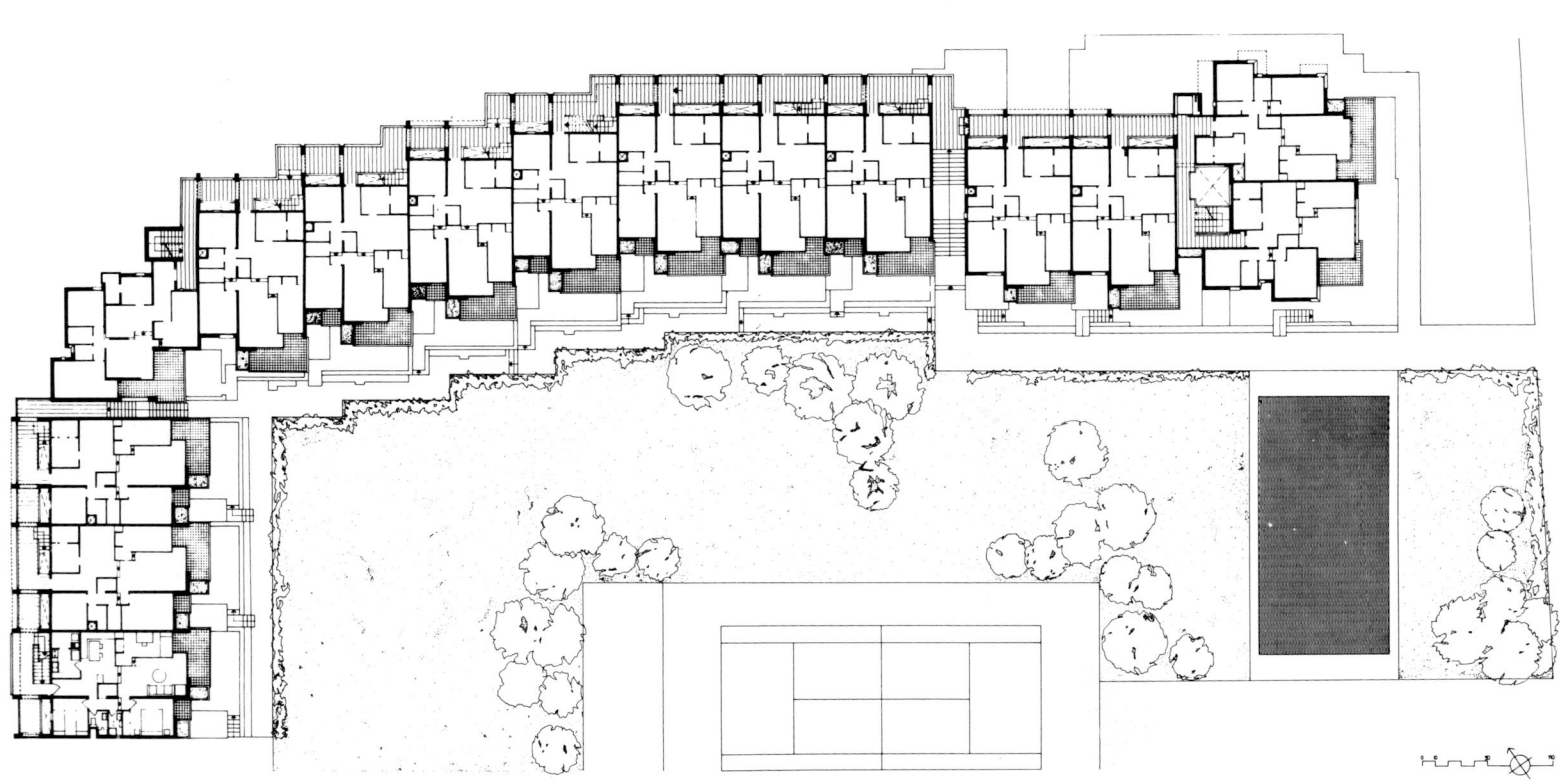

3. Site plan of the first phase.
4. View showing the broken silhouette of the buildings.

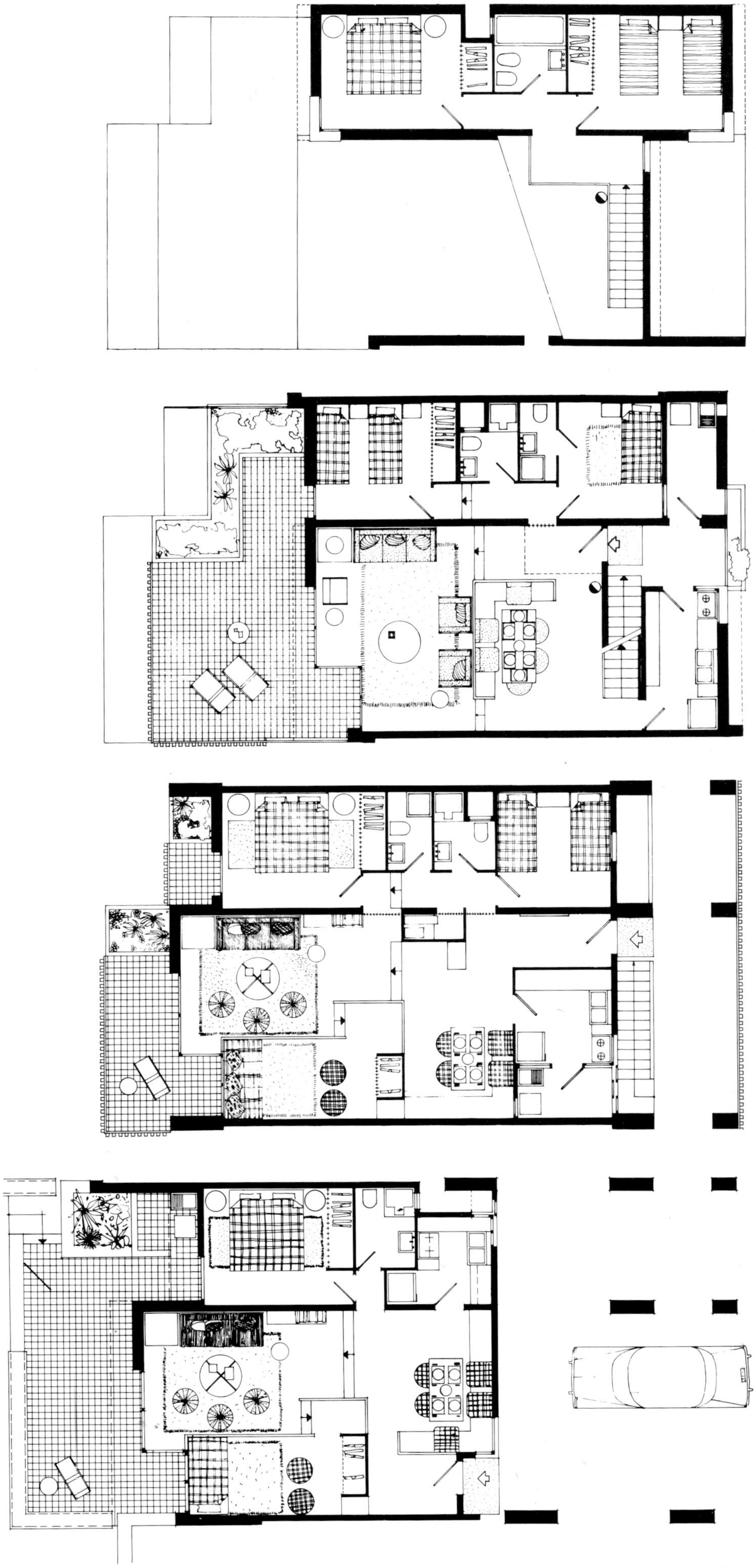

5. View of the corner showing the cascade of draped wooden blinds.
6. The north-east façade showing the gallery access over the sheltered car park.
7. Plans of typical apartments (ground floor, 1st floor, 2nd floor, 3rd floor).

Flats for Teachers, C. Mn. Cinto Verdaguer, Pineda
1967-69

The new Primary School was obliged by the Ministry of Education to provide housing for its teachers near the school. Ideally, an individual house and garden should have been provided for each of the twelve teachers, however, the Pineda village council could only afford a small site for the present block. The village was affected by rising land values and increased tourist activity due to its proximity to the sea and adjacent tourist areas. A compact building was seen as appropriate to likely future building patterns.

The design intention was to give the dwellings the same attributes of an ordinary house set in a street with neighbours. Instead of a stairwell, a stepped street was inserted in a vertical slit in the building that began at the entrance porch and linked the garden to a double height gallery on the third floor. Ten of the twelve dwellings are served by this gallery which doubles as an entrance lobby. It is open, exposed to the weather, and has views like any street or square. The design of the maisonettes, or duplexes side-by-side (the bedrooms are below on the second floor, or on the fifth floor), alone makes this possible. This arrangement maximizes privacy. The fourth floor is reached by two independent cantilevered spiral staircases that have been clipped onto the façade.

The front door of each dwelling is slightly recessed to protect the entrance. Next to the entrance hall is a small study so teachers can receive visitors without disturbing their families.

Times have changed and with it Ministry of Education policy. Teachers are no longer expected to want to live together, which is a reality, and these dwellings are now occupied by teachers and families from the village.

1. North façade showing the double-height gallery with the cantilevered staircases.
2. Section showing the stepped interior street.

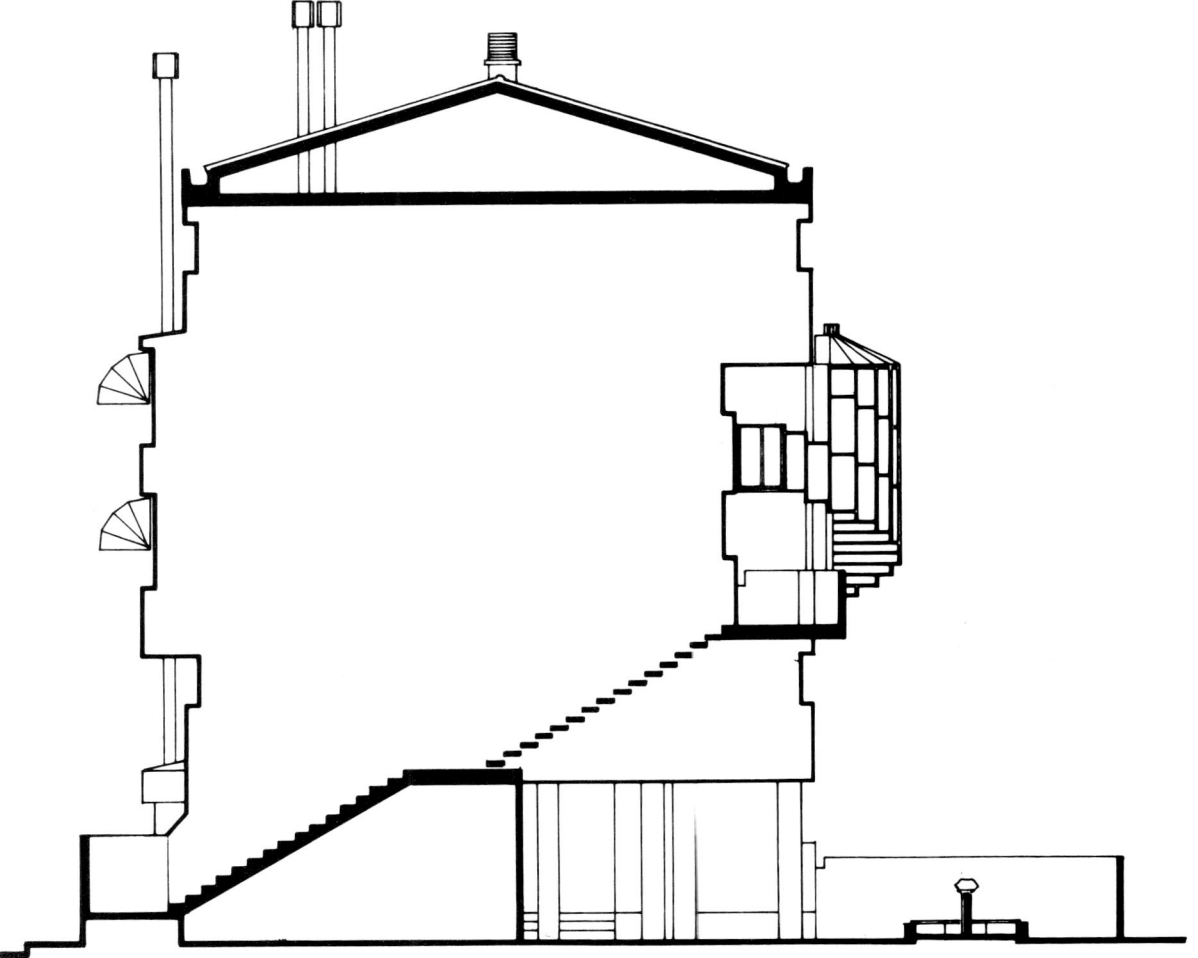

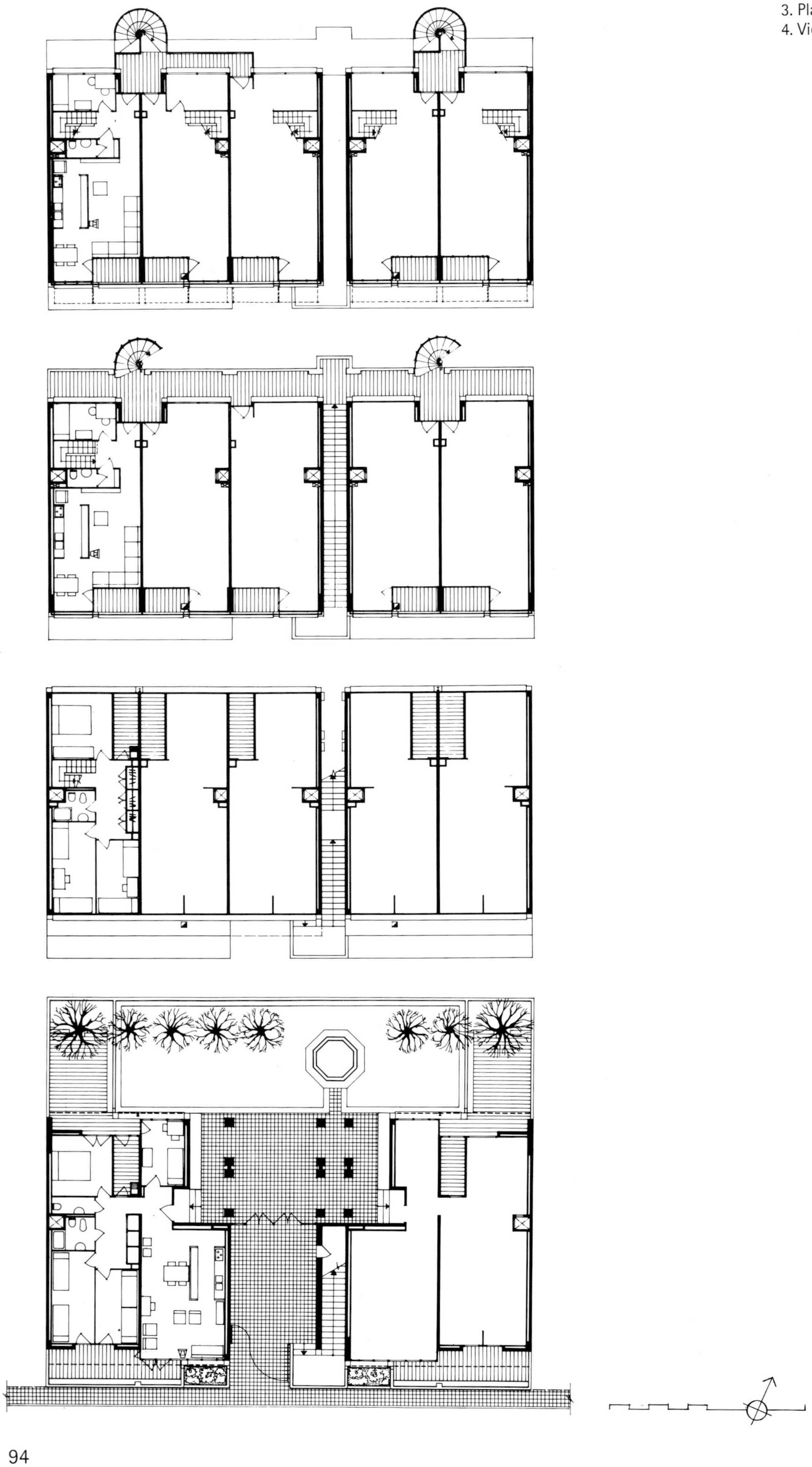

3. Plans (ground floor, 1st floor, 2nd floor, 3rd floor).
4. View from the south.

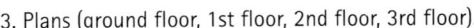

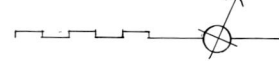

La Salut City Block, Riera de la Salut, Sant Feliu de Llobregat, Barcelona
1969-73

This was begun as a cooperative venture, and later taken over and completed by a private developer. There are 364 dwellings altogether which can be described as offering affordable housing with two basic types of 60 m² and 100 m². Sant Feliu de Llobregat is part of the industrial ring surrounding Barcelona and the site is quite near the centre and market. It occupies an entire city block and is surrounded on all four sides by existing streets.

There were several options given the large size of the site: the housing form could have been designed as a single block much like Le Corbusier's Unité with every dwelling having sun and views; or it could reaffirm the street by throwing up façades around the edges and hollowing out the interior. It was this second option which was chosen. The result is a strongly expressed form comprising an inner ring within an outer ring which follows closely the irregular alignments of the streets. This inner ring encloses an outdoor room in which are found a mixture of private gardens, porches and shops. Here, the residents may sit and talk while the children play in safety. It has a strong urban identity, something assisted by the hard paving and palm trees.

The city block can be traversed diagonally in one direction through gaps left between the buildings at the corners. The interior space is a mixture, it is partially enclosed in one direction and partially open in the other.

The design of the La Salut Block marked an important turning point for MBM in that it represented a return to the values of the corridor street and the urban room similar to the traditional square. This has been a very positive factor in the lives of the new residents integrating them with their neighbours, at the same time helping a strong feeling of community and belonging to grow, with the added social advantages of social cohesion and a safe friendly neighbourhood.

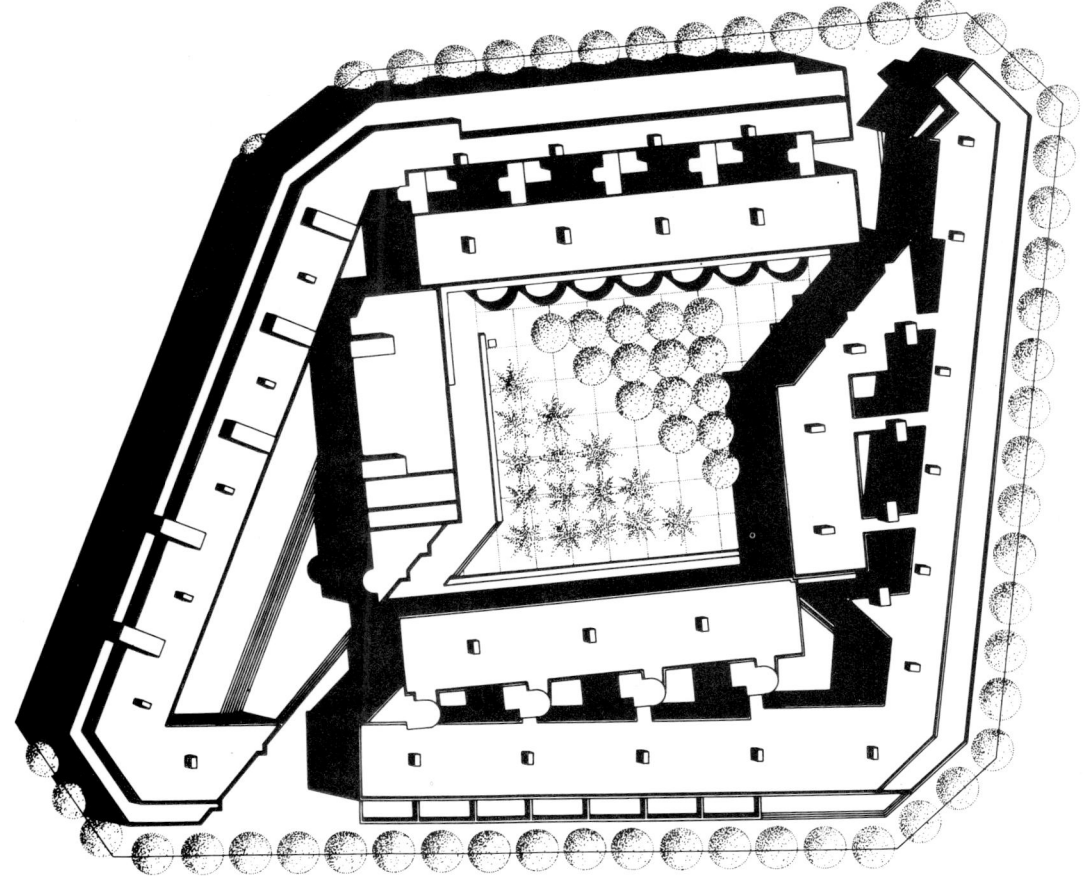

3. The public square formed by the inner ring of
dwellings.
4. Sharp angle of the diagonal cut of the inner ring.
5. Plan of a typical apartment.

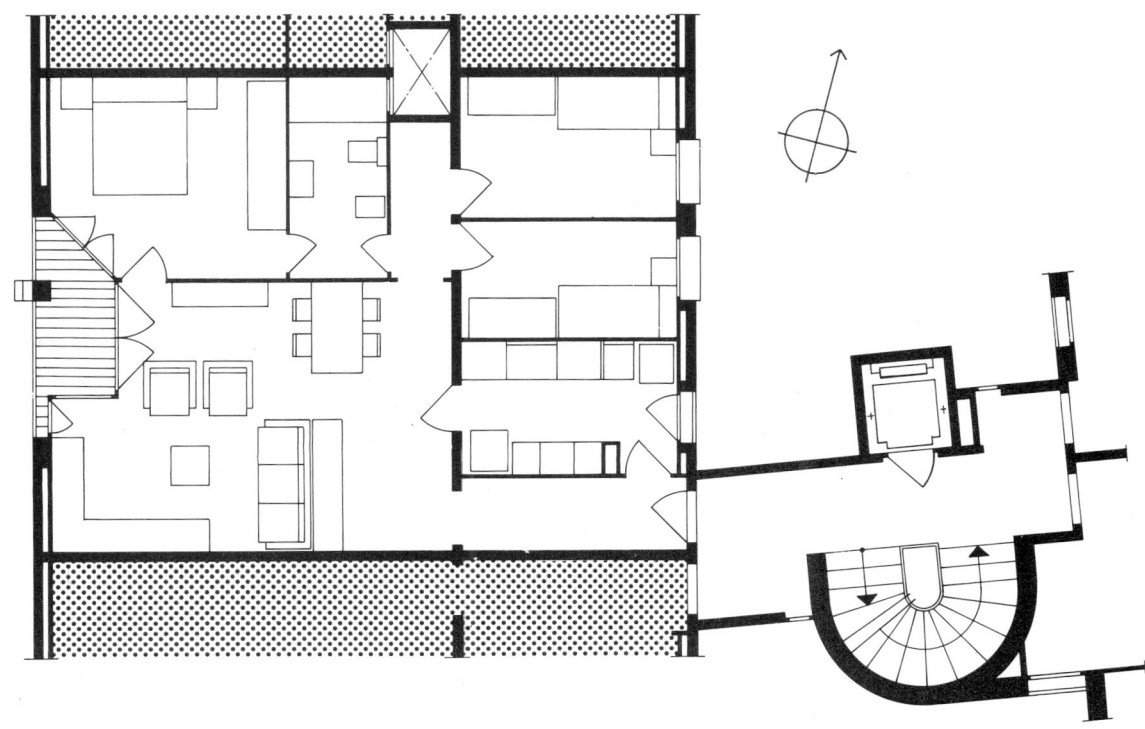

Bonanova Flats, Passeig de La Bonanova 92, Barcelona
1970-73

The Passeig de la Bonanova running east-west between the parish church of Bonanova and the parish church of Sarrià is one of Barcelona's few true avenues. Its wide pavements are a reminder that this promenade once led through fields between the two parishes. It lies upon the lower slopes of the Collcerola hills and until recently contained a string of villas set in their own gardens behind fine railings. They resemble the better residential districts of Cannes or Nice.

Walled-in between the hills and the sea, Barcelona has grown inwards simultaneously increasing its density to extraordinary levels. Now only a handful of the original villas built at the turn of the century are left. They provide ideal garden sites for the new large cooperative dwellings which have replaced them.

The Bonanova Group consists of thirty-two dwellings situated in two L-shaped buildings that face one another across a central garden and square. This diagonal composition creates a south-to-north succession of three garden rooms. The largest and most private is presided over by an enormous linden tree. The central garden is split into two levels, the higher occupied by the original villa garden, the lower forming an alleyway and a hard paved court that runs under the main building. This forms a kind of entry vestibule which neighbours pass in and out of on their way to their apartments; here children play, and cars drive to reach their garages. In summer, neighbours cross this sunken square to reach the third enclosed garden via a flight of stairs which also contains sun terraces and a swimming pool above the garage.

The dwellings have two kinds of fixed core or nuclei. In one, the bathroom is located between the two bedrooms, in the other, the kitchen and breakfast room has an additional annex for service and other uses. Each dwelling has two nuclei of bedrooms which leaves an open plan area between them and the kitchen to meet the communal function of the home. This space has two opposing window-balconies to assure cross-ventilation in summer and to vary the quality of the natural light during the daytime.

Although the pillars and slab floors are reinforced concrete, the outer walls are of brown brick with flush joints with curved corners to emphasize the continuity of surface around the outside. This continuous outer skin is interrupted at five locations by vertical steel-and-glass fins on the living room windows and balconies. These tilt to face south and are painted white for contrast.

1. View from the street.

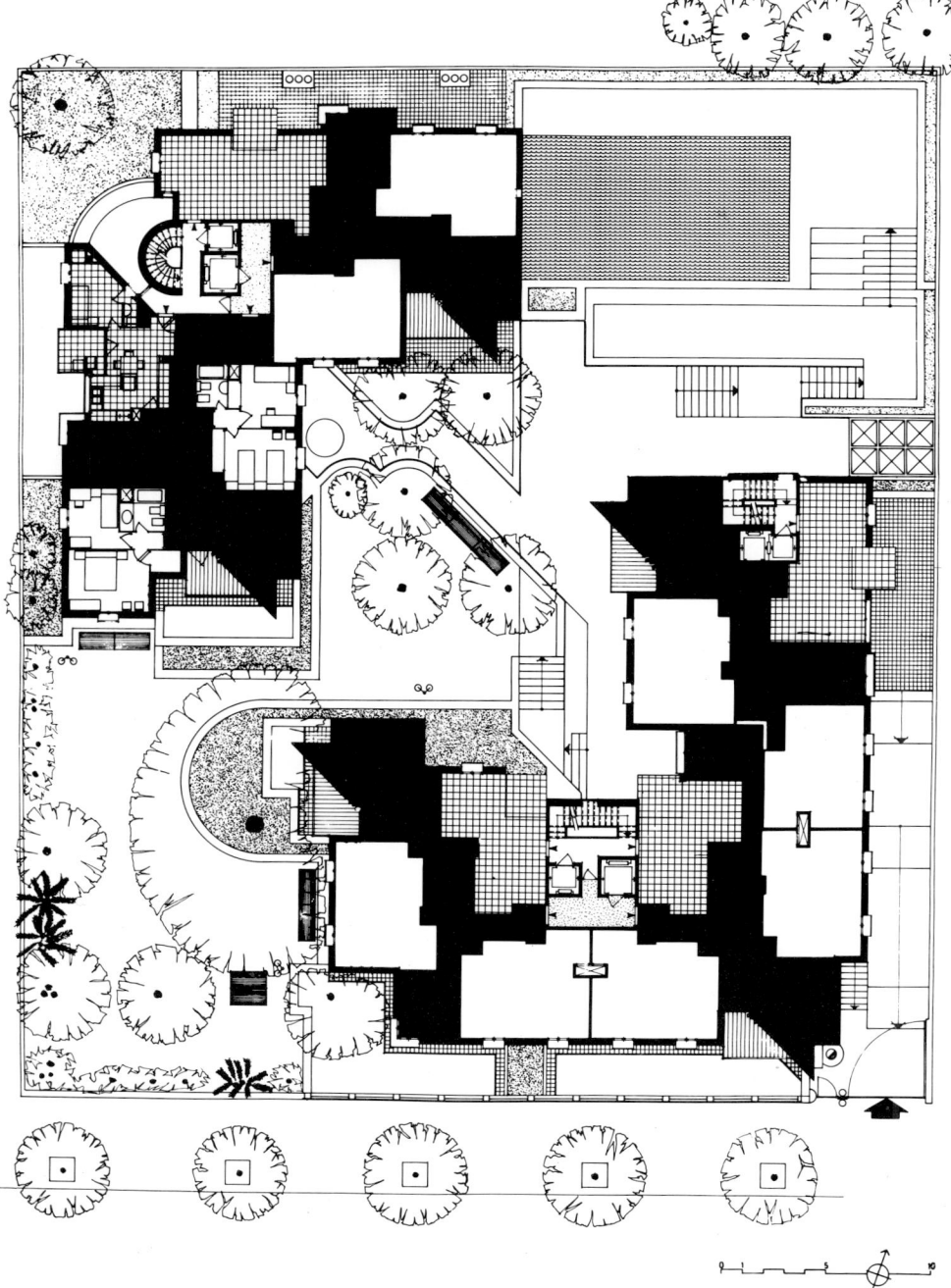

2. Site plan. The black areas show the succession of living spaces of each dwelling.
3. Plan of a typical dwelling.
4. Façade detail with balconies that overlook the gardens.

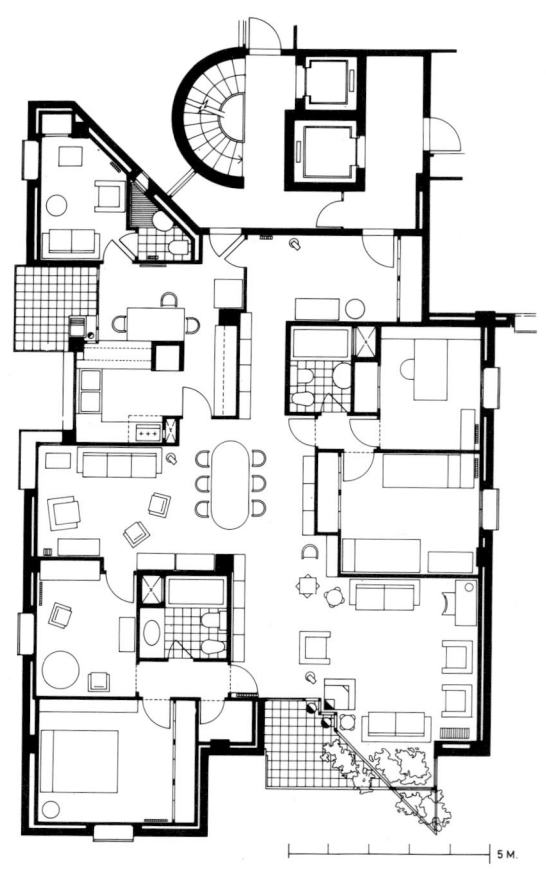

Pals Golf Course Apartments, Platja de Pals, Girona
1971–73

This small group of apartments is situated on a narrow strip of land between the road and the golf course. It was designed especially for golfing enthusiasts coming on weekends, or on holidays, from the areas around Barcelona and Perpignan immediately over the French border.

Not only had all the apartments to face the golf course, but the restricted site imposed a requirement for the car parking to be placed beneath the buildings to maximize the amount of space available for gardens and access paths. The apartments were designed in the form of rows of houses in line with the longitudinal axis, stepping down the slope towards the golf course to produce open terraces for each dwelling.

The row houses were paired to create a narrow interior stepped street that provides access to each apartment, without sacrificing the individual identity of each.

The details and materials echo local tradition in their choice of pinky-brown coloured walls with broad white painted bands framing the aluminium windows, and the blue-green ceramic tiling that caps and marks the stepped wall edges.

As with so many developments for holiday accommodation around this time only one paired housing row, rather than the entire original proposal, was actually built.

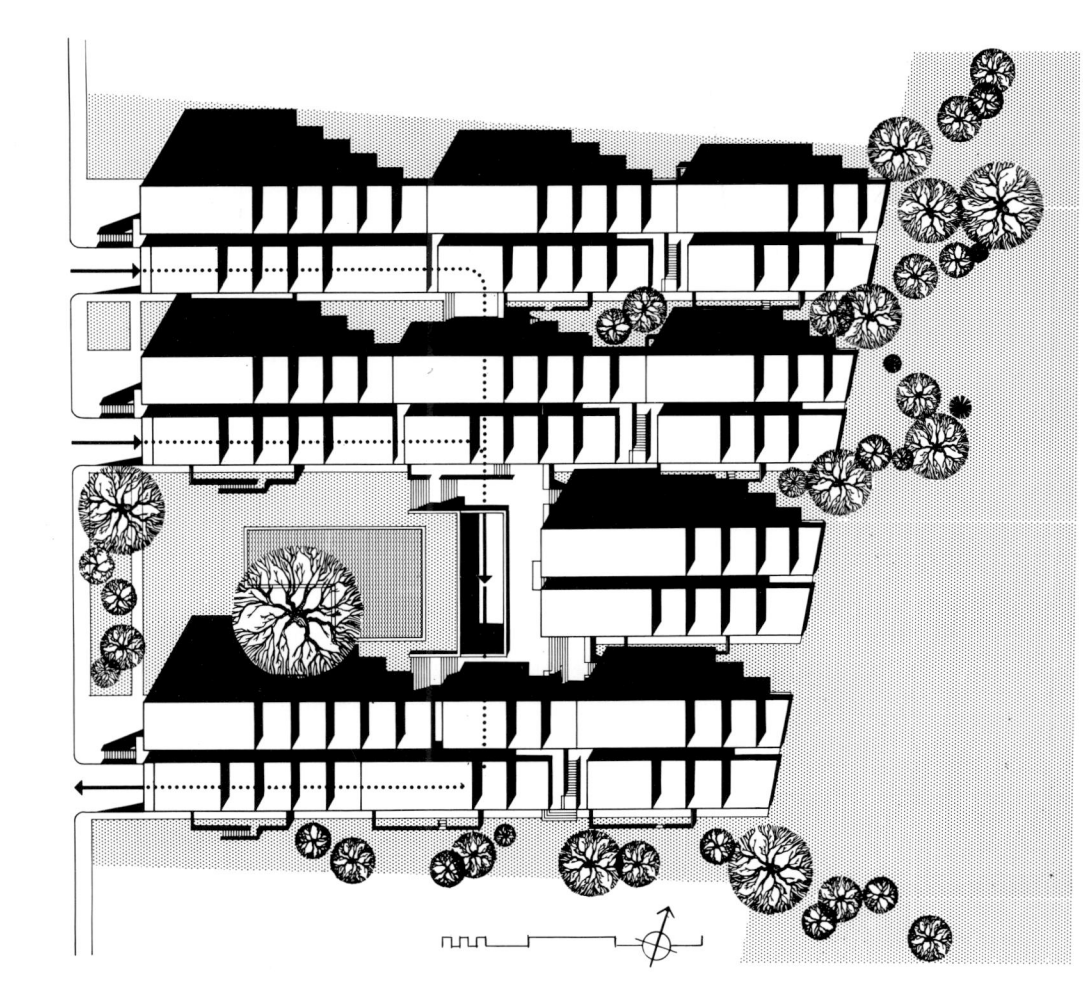

1. Site plan of original project. Only the south building was built.
2. View from the golf course.

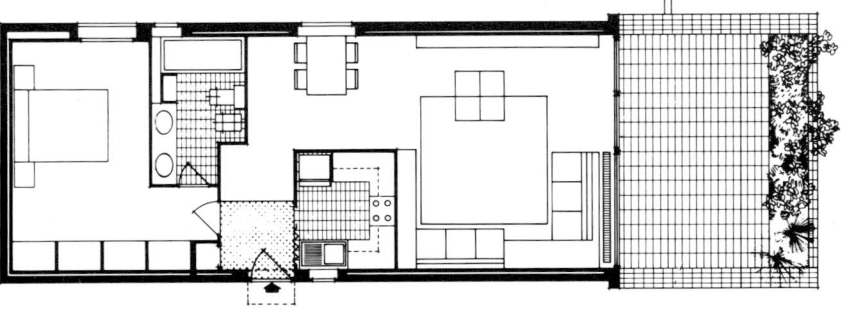

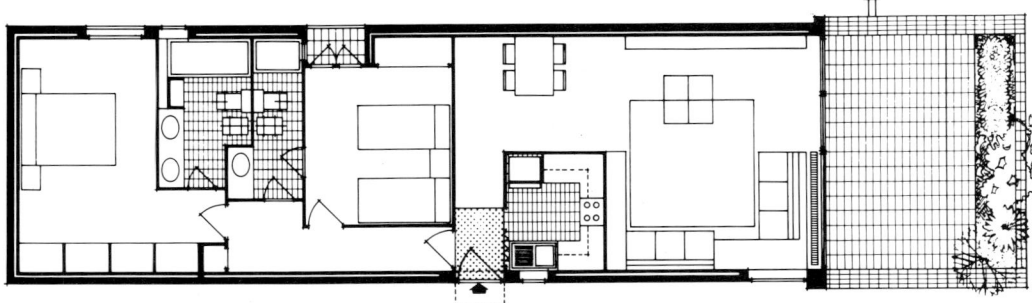

3. Plans of typical apartments.
4. Section.
5. South façade.

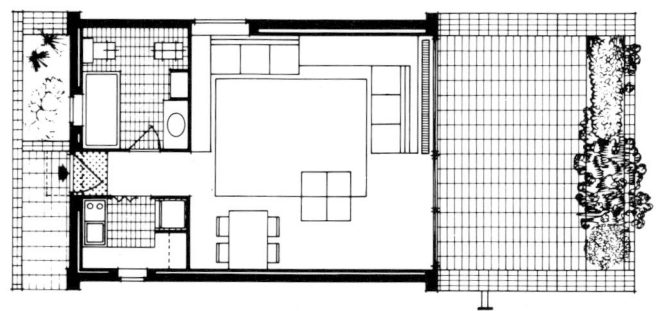

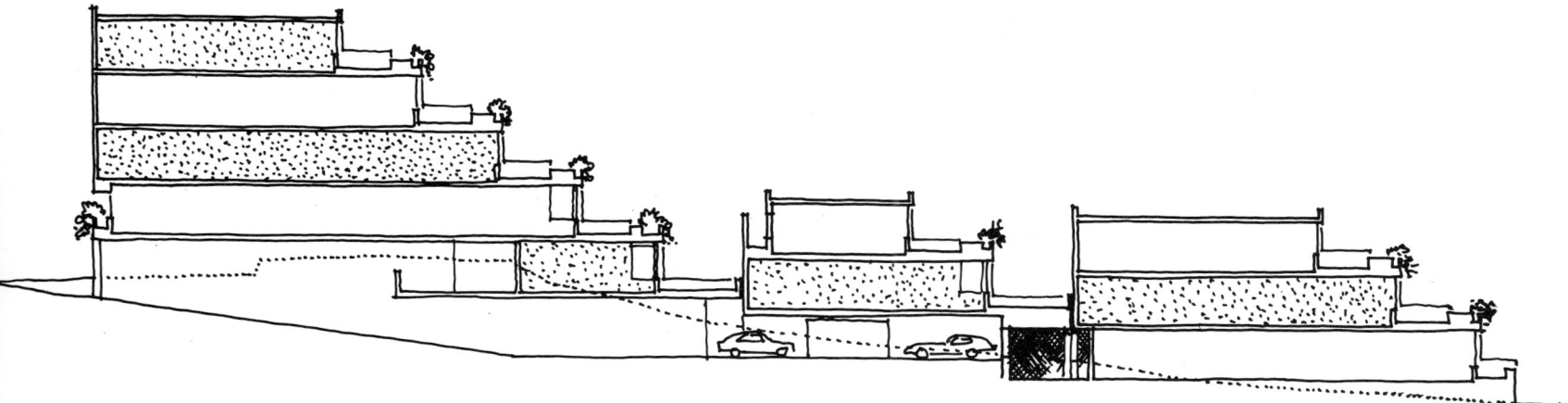

106

Martí l'Humà City Block, C. Martí l'Humà, Sabadell
1974-79

As with many historic industrial cities, Sabadell has grown beyond the first ring of factories, which in their turn have outgrown the old simple sheds and moved on outside the city altogether leaving the sites vacant to be invested with denser buildings for housing, commerce and business.

Some low village dwellings survived on a corner of the block which prevented comprehensive development of the entire site with a perimeter of buildings on all four streets. The buildings were placed along the northeast and northwest edges and wrapped around the north corner in a single continuous form because the available site was concentrated on the north edge about the north-south diagonal of the block. This main outer form is paralleled by a lower four-storey one on the inside, a pedestrian street being produced between the two of them. All the dwellings face south and the majority are duplexes with corridor access between the staircases and lifts. There are private gardens with a swimming pool in front of the lower interior block for use by the residents.

In this instance, for the 145 dwellings (sized between 80 m² and 120 m²) there was no well-defined local character which the architecture could reflect as the partly enclosed new housing block was surrounded by abandoned factories. On the other hand, one of the streets was an important extension of the city's main shopping thoroughfare. The challenge was to establish a strong sense of place and real character in the housing. A more radical approach was deemed inappropriate under the circumstances.

The building regulations which stipulated different height lines for the two streets resulted in a curious geometrical paradox. This was solved eventually by displacing the upper two floors southwards away from the street to keep the same height throughout the building while retaining the visual unity of the building volume.

1. The pedestrian street between the two curved buildings.
2. Section showing the system of access.

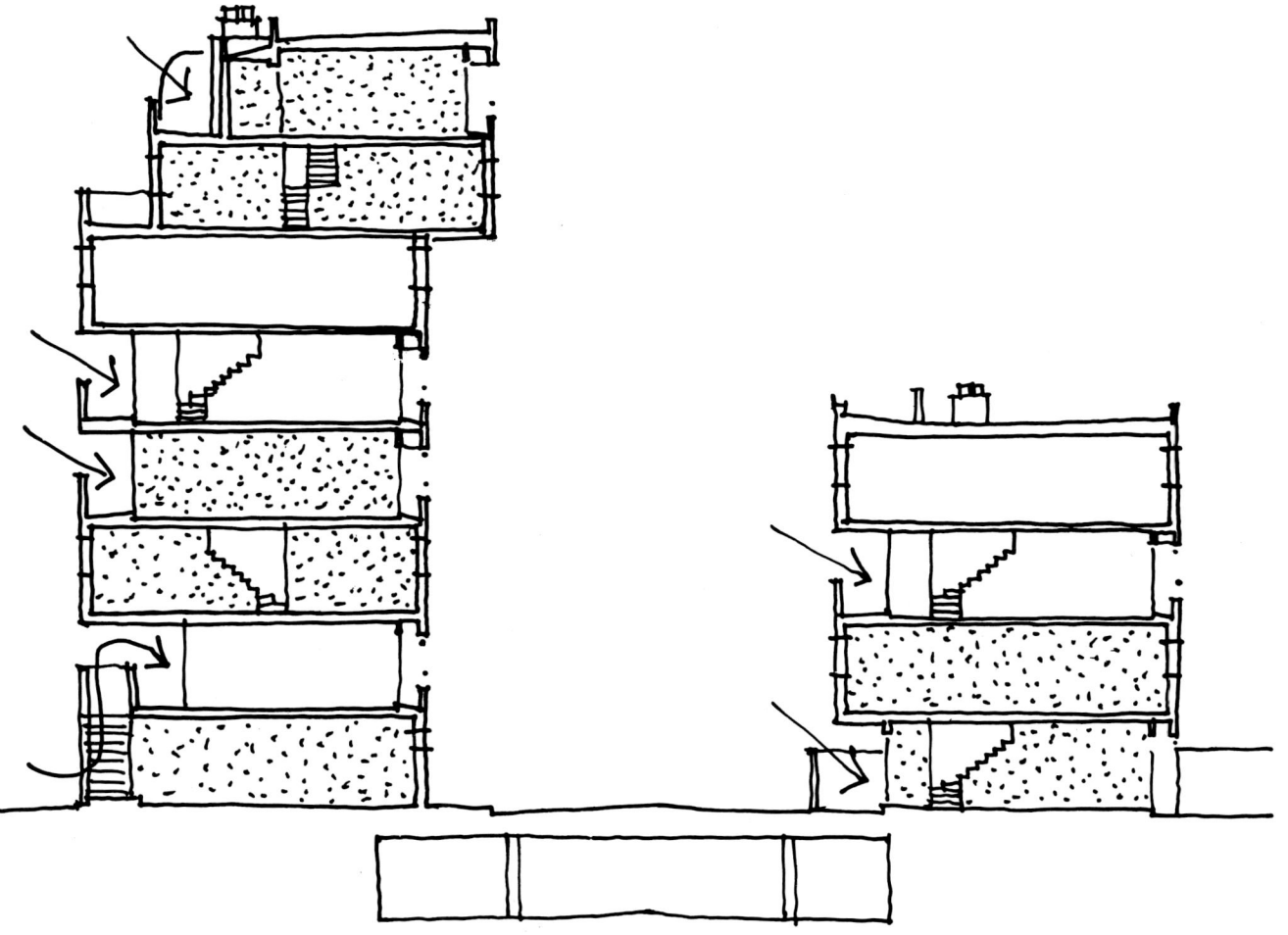

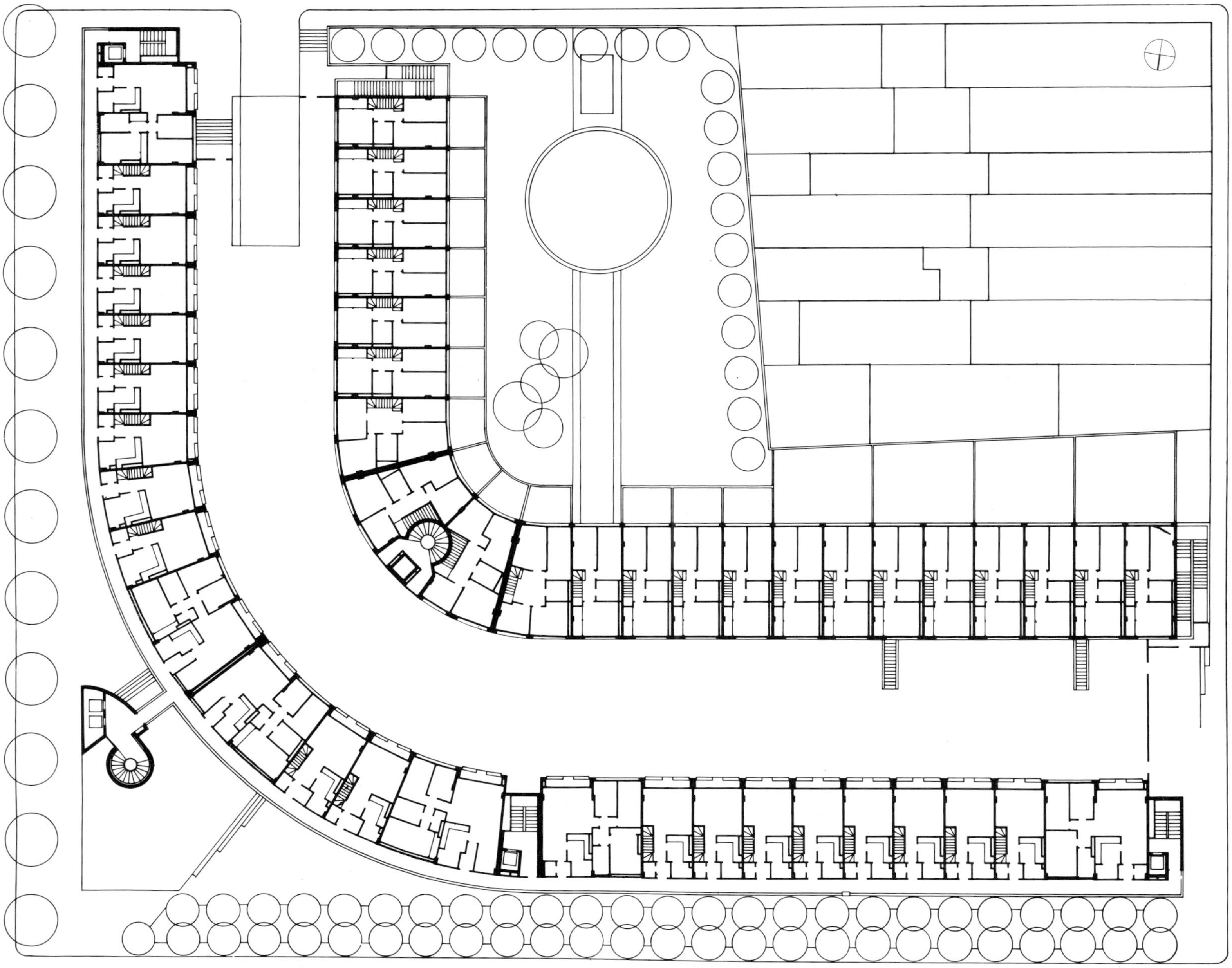

3. Site plan.
4. Aerial view showing how the blocks are adjusted
to the street corner and face south and west.
5. The corner with the separate lift and staircase
tower.

Mollet City Block, Mollet
1983-87

A wide shallow valley called Vallès runs behind the coastal hills at the back of Barcelona. Various industrial cities are situated here at the northern end. Next to the motorway to France lies Mollet. It was here at Mollet that the Autonomous Government, the Generalitat de Catalunya, set about an ambitious new programme for public housing which was to be implemented in stages. A new street grid was laid out with 100 m by 100 m city blocks similar to Barcelona's historic Cerdà grid. Unlike the Cerdà grid, it was orientated to the cardinal points in order that the four outer façades face approximately north, south, east and west.

This particular orientation led to the design of a thin perimeter block to ensure that all the dwellings would receive sunlight at some time during the day. However, the requirement to provide two hundred dwellings meant that the east edge had to be doubled forming a pedestrian walkway between them terminated by lift and staircase towers along the centre with bridges interconnecting the blocks.

The large space at the centre was conceived as a walled city square on two levels to adapt the building form to the topography. All the entrances to the dwellings face the square, although some are duplicated on the street side. The city square acts as a filter for the dwellings, protecting them from the disturbance caused by new and future construction nearby.

The buildings have been given a limited autonomy by the application of well-established typologies detailing access and grouping. The two blocks facing south and west contain maisonettes or duplex dwellings on the upper floors with an access gallery situated on the sunny side running underneath the living room windows. These have a series of protective visual layers. This gallery was seen as an extension of the dwelling, a place where residents could sit and chat, where children could play and where plants and flowers could be placed. It was safe since nearly every living room can be considered a neighbourhood watch for strangers. The form of the building was inflected to break down the monotony of the overlong gallery.

On the lower three floors, the dwellings have direct access to the square. At ground level, above the duplex units, the dwellings have semi-private fronts with stairs rather like a New York street.

The north building has its living rooms facing south into the square with dwellings sharing a staircase, two per floor. The double block on the east side has four dwellings per floor.

There are shops on the lower ground floor facing the street on the south and west.

It is noteworthy that the Mollet City Block was designed after, rather than before, MBM won the IBA Competition for Kochstrasse in Berlin. The Mollet buildings implement many of the features of this original unbuilt proposal.

1. General view of the city block from the south.
2. Axonometric view.

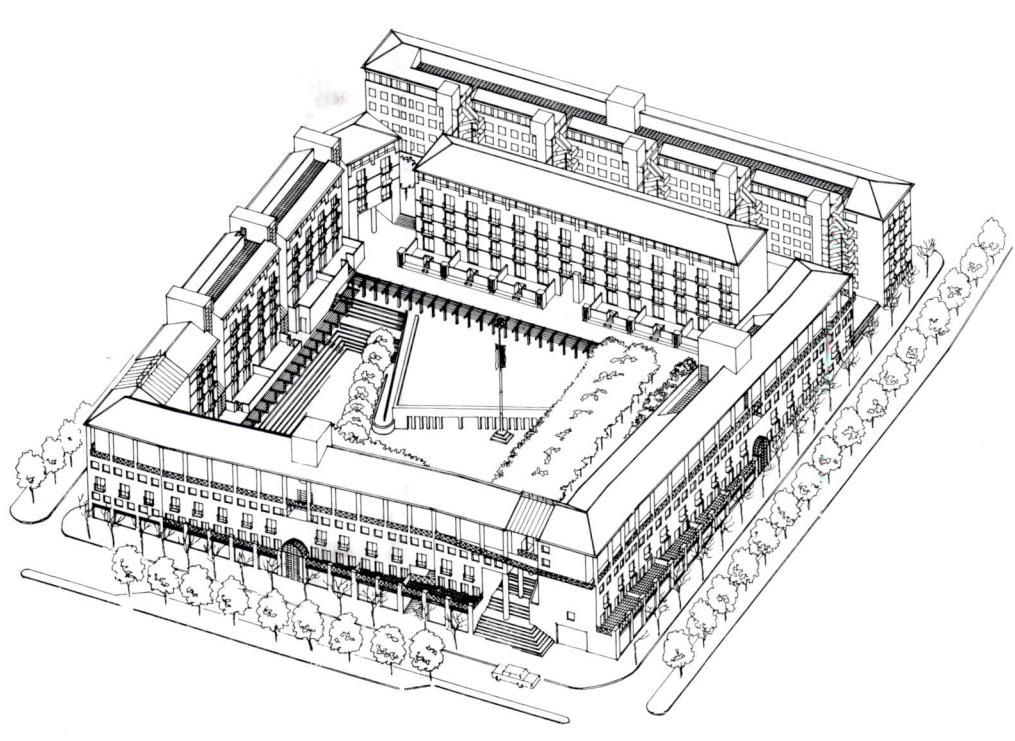

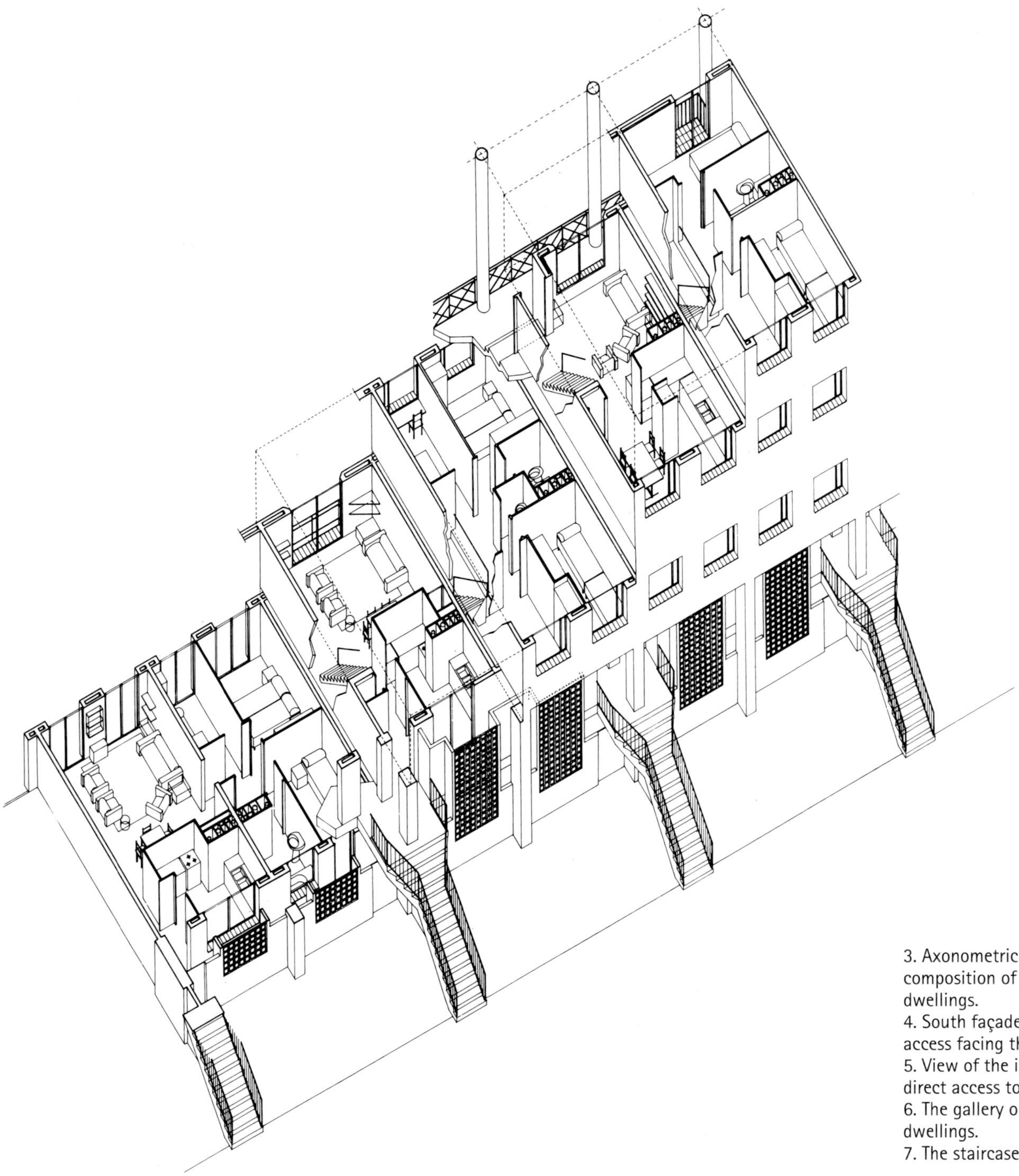

3. Axonometric view showing the internal composition of the gallery block with duplex dwellings.
4. South façade with the double height gallery access facing the sun.
5. View of the interior of the city block with the direct access to the dwellings.
6. The gallery or upper street in front of the dwellings.
7. The staircase and lift towers in the pedestrian

Gateway and Gable Wall Housing, Kochstrasse, Berlin
1985

Each of the three buildings on Kochstrasse contained four entrances: an entrance to the underground car park; an entrance to the new urban area and garden within the city block; an entrance to the Faller/Muschalek/Schröder buildings on either side; and an entrance to the building itself.

Each gateway house was made deeper than the buildings on either side so as to accommodate a higher density of dwellings facing east and west away from the noise of the Kochstrasse on the south. The Kochstrasse façade is in reality the gable end of the building which is repeated to assert the classical entrance typology below the pediment, or »west front« of the basilica church. In this way, the three buildings were given a traditional form of entrance so as to instigate a measured break along the north façade of the Kochstrasse.

The architectural elements used to do this are borrowed from designs of gable wall houses found in buildings near the corner of Friedrichstrasse. These elements are the autonomous brick gable wall set back from the main façade, the glass-brick tower, the hollowed out volume of the porch which visually connects the street with the interior urban space, and the Constructivist styling of the upper street gallery bridge.

The complete north façade of Kochstrasse was designed in association with Faller/Muschalek/Schröder who agreed on the street level porch to absorb the idiosyncrasy of the shops and the continuous gallery on the third floor resulting from the set back of the upper floors to a second plane flush with the gateway buildings. Once this was agreed, the framework was established which allowed each architect freedom to express his own architectural ideas. It was a first important step in advancing the urban design process.

Further up the street, in the same city block, another group of 32 dwellings by MBM present yet another gable end to Kochstrasse, but behind lies a string of Mews-type dwellings with gardens or gallery access which provide an alternative living accommodation to the urban flat of the corridor-street. It picks up a traditional Kreuzberg pattern and at the same time heralds an urban typology that was to be developed more fully in the Olympic Village in Barcelona.

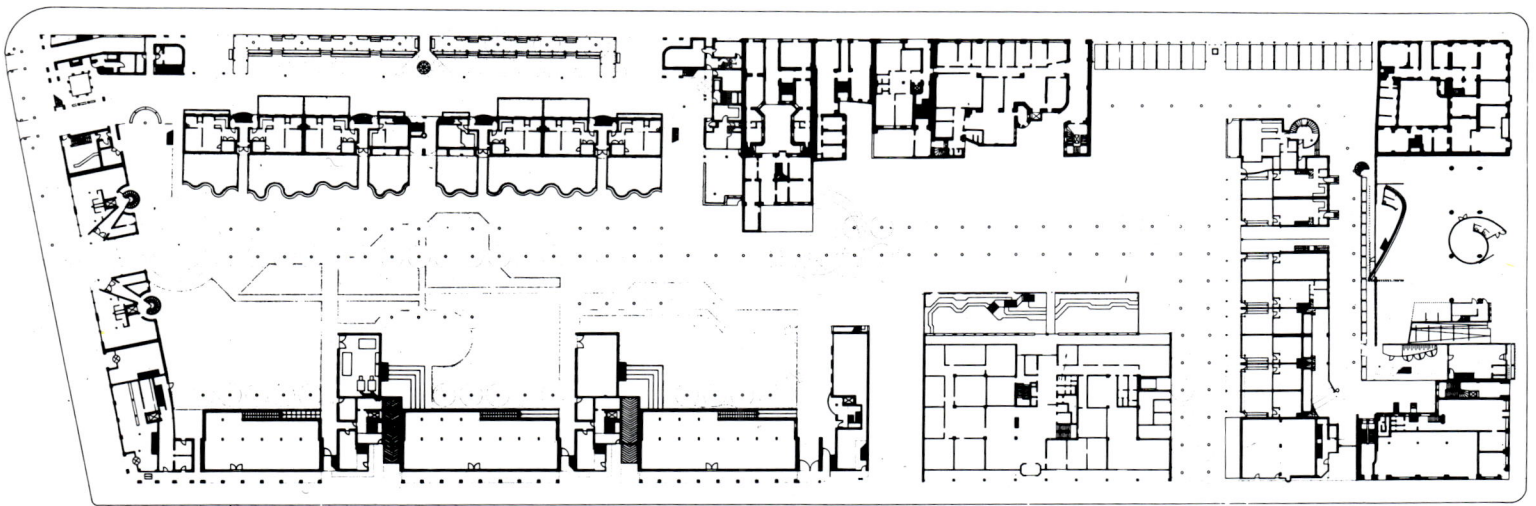

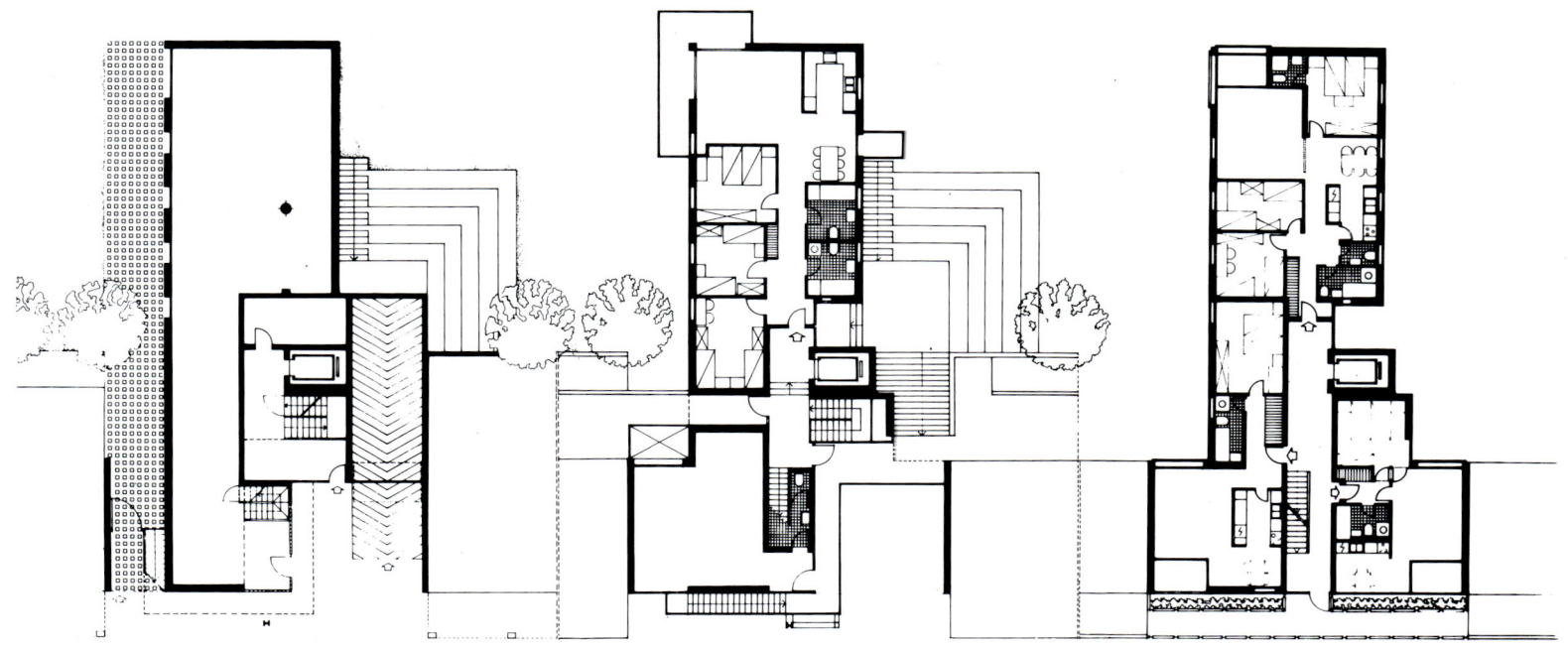

1. Site plan of the city block showing the three gateway buildings and the gable wall building just behind Friedrichstrasse.
2. Plans of the gateway building in Kochstrasse 73, 74, 75.
3. View of the gateway building in Kochstrasse 75.

4. Plans of the gable wall building in Kochstrasse 65.
5. Garden façade of the gable wall building in Kochstrasse 65.
6. View along the entrance alley between Kochstrasse and Zimmerstrasse.

Can Folch Housing, Carrer de la Marina/Salvador Espriu, Olympic Village, Barcelona
1988-92

One of the most important obstacles that blocked the access of the city to the waterfront was the railway line that cut across the streets with a wide sweeping curve that embraced the central Ciutadella park to arrive at the main terminal building. This curve of the railway is just one of half a dozen »accidents« absorbed into the famous Cerdà grid plan of Barcelona that have become part of the city's identity. Following the same curved line a tunnel now carries the trains below the road system allowing free access to the sea and across the city. This curved line has been picked up and re-used as one of the edges of the Olympic Village, 550 m long and six storeys high.

This half-kilometer long building is split in two by the main street carrer de la Marina (formerly Carles I) which runs from Gaudí's Sagrada Familia to the sea. Each half is designed by different architects but with an agreement to use the same grey brick and each to incorporate similar elements when bridging streets and at the ends and edges of the building.

The lower half of the curved building, nearer the sea, contains 150 dwellings between it and the companion building facing Carrer de la Marina. In-between, a triangular space is formed, marked by the old 50 m high brick chimney left as a historical landmark reminding one of the city's former important industrial areas. This triangular space is sunk 2 m below the street surface to create a sheltered shopping precinct.

Since the curved buildings lie on an almost north-south axis both façades have sun either in the morning or afternoon, and each has a view either towards the sea or to the park. Given this unique situation the living and dining areas of each dwelling overlook both sides running across the building but in a zig-zag composition to introduce a diagonal vision and to assist its multiple use. The kitchens all contain a small breakfast area and are located behind the circular bays along the west façade.

There are 27 eight person dwellings, 88 six person dwellings, 31 four person dwellings and 5 two person dwellings as well as shops and underground parking. The total area above ground is around 21.000 m².

1. Plan of one of the city blocks. The curve was generated by the position of the railway now sunk below the street and the park.
2. The sunken court with an old factory chimney.

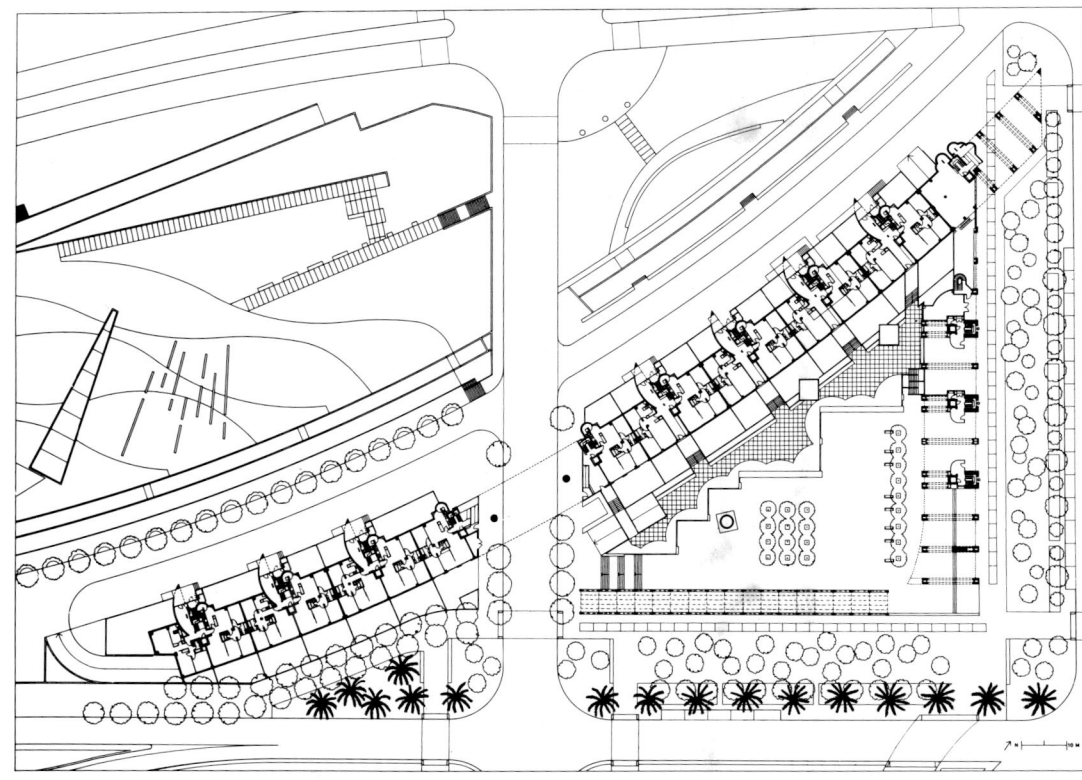

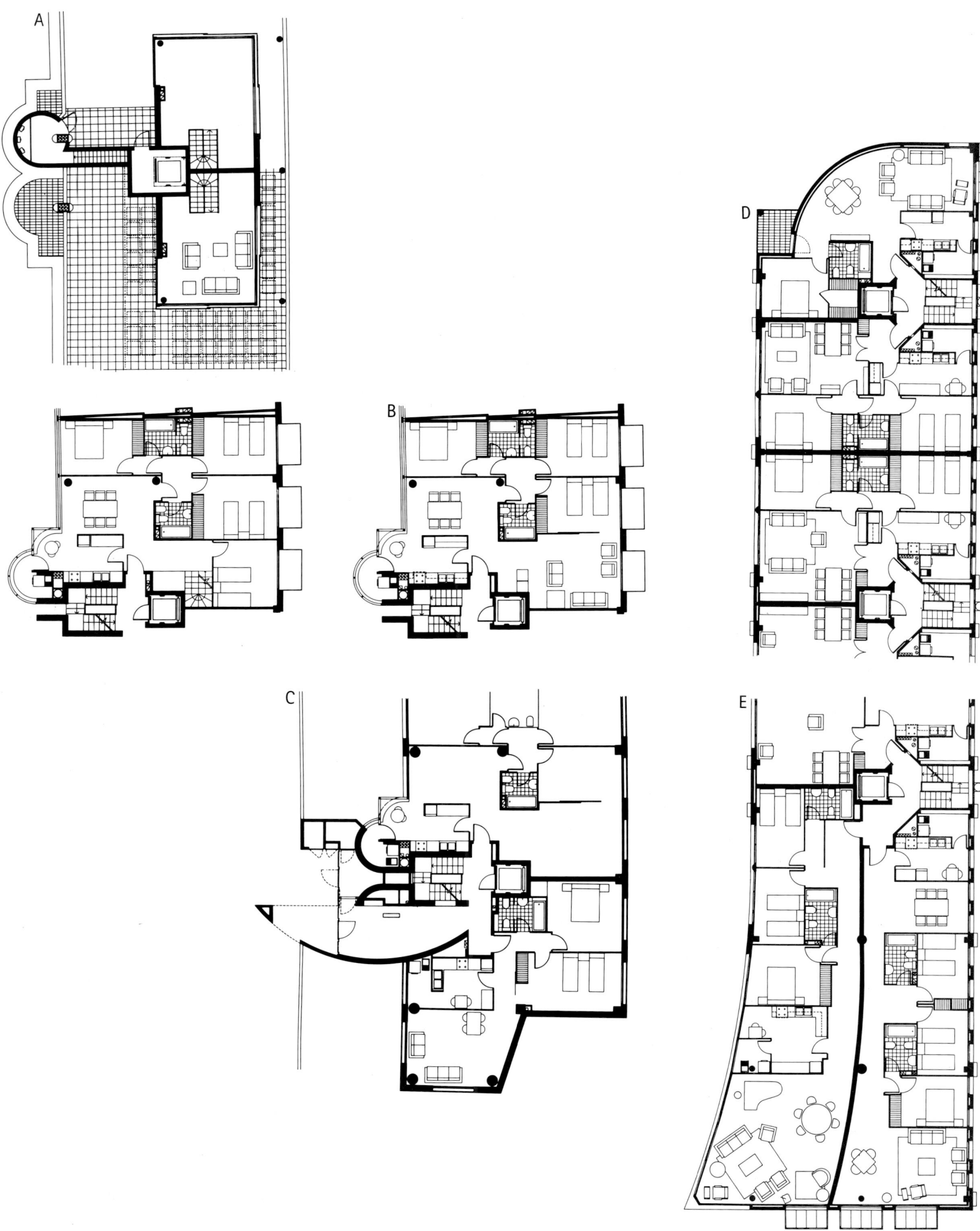

3. Plans (A-C curved building, D/E rectilinear building).
4. View of the buildings from the Avinguda del Litoral.
5. The sunken court with the arched porch on the left and the tower of the hotel beyond.

Schools and Libraries

The post-war baby boom created a demand for new schools everywhere, and this demographic phenomenon, coupled with a new attitude to education which placed increased emphasis on the needs and uniqueness of the individual child, together with the rejection of an authoritarian bias which had long been a part of the educational scene, led to a radical reconsideration of school design practices.

One of the most obvious indicators of this change was the move away from the closed, isolated classroom to open space planning, and experiments with industrialized building systems to rationalize the building process with an eye to taking advantage of potential economies arising from the large-scale and repetition of standard elements that this entailed.

Aspects of these changes, although not all were necessarily involved at any one time, can be observed in the new English school buildings in the late 1950s, notably CLASP, the Consortium of Local Authorities Special Programme started in 1957, the SCSD California experiment, and the SEF programme in Toronto, Canada, in the 1960s.

In Barcelona, Josep Goday designed a series of regular and efficient school buildings for the city council from 1916 onwards, as demonstrated by his 1922 Baixeras School. In 1915, some 15 Montessori schools were constructed. Goday emphasized the quality of the school architecture as a contributing factor in the child's educational development in an official report he prepared in 1917. The 1970s were to witness a renewed period of reform and growth with the firm of MBM very much leading the way.

MBM's schools illustrate many of the new ideas, such things as the building as a city-in-microcosm[69] in the Garbí School, and the application of Rationalism as a method and a language in the Timbaler del Bruc, Thau, and BUP Garbí Schools. Their designs are customarily orientated around a large two-storeyed communal space, which also served as a central meeting place and circulation space, with classrooms, sometimes open, sometimes expressed as cells, grouped around it. The learning areas are either conventional closed spaces, or more often they are opened up and merged with the adjoining hall circulation which is now treated as a learning space or street.

Unlike the USA where there was a wholesale adoption of open planning without any real appreciation of its limitations, the Catalan experiments are more pragmatic and tend to seek a balance between openness and closed spaces that is related to the nature of the instructional task to be accommodated.

Herman Hertzberger's Montessori School at Delft (1966-70) with its intricate interplay of closure and openness, and its merging of the classroom with the central spine of communal space, which was treated as an important educational space, and not merely set aside for circulation like so much plumbing, offered a model for many European schools at that time. The Garbí School (1962-78) is a striking illustration of how advanced progressive Catalan educational planning was in the 1960s. It has a good deal in common with the Delft Montessori School in its informal picturesque planning and focus on a central open communal space, but, as will be readily appreciated, it was designed some years before it. England was the leading country at the time with schools such as Chamberlain, Powell and Bon's 1956 Mies-inspired Bousfield Primary School, London, but by the mid-1960s, Barcelona had caught up.

The Timbaler del Bruc School (1957/58) is an early work indebted to Modernism in its staggered orthogonal planning, and Arne Jacobsen, for its alternation of classrooms and courtyard spaces.[70] From the outset, Rational methods were a leading preoccupation in school design as witnessed by the clarity of the Timbaler del Bruc School plan with its simple disciplined sequence of spaces. Later on, in the Garbí School and the Sant Jordi School (1967-69), there is a conscious effort to introduce an element of playful arbitrariness into the planning by avoiding, wherever possible, straight rows of classrooms along corridors so the spaces are more relaxed and open, more unpredictable, less authoritarian and rigid. This is the case with the Garbí and Sant Jordi examples, but the Thau School (1972-74) marks a retreat from the earlier picturesque forms to a regular orthogonal organization of the space without sacrificing the ideas of the dual use of circulation spaces, or the emphasis on communal foci.

The Garbí BUP School (1975-78) is an exceptional instance of the formal quadratic *parti*. It has four learning areas each square in the four corners of a large square floor tray, so placed that they leave a cruciform corridor into which has been poured the principal staircase, two sets of toilets, and seminar rooms. Externally, the school resembles a large house with its cleanly etched windows arrayed in three regular rows across the four elevations.

The industrialized expression of Thau, which is apparent from the details and materials, glass block screens, coffered concrete floors, metal adjustable sun screens and overall white appearance contrasts with the interest in texture of the earlier work with its brick, timber, and canvas, lending a softness to the school environment and a conspicuously domestic atmosphere. In the case of the Catalunya School (1981-83), located in a tough industrial wasteland surrounded by factories, the school took on some of the same qualities as its surroundings. It looks like a factory, but on this occasion, it is very much an Italian factory with its assertive concrete frame expressed at the ends and brutal unpainted concrete blockwork. Inside, hard materials, steel mesh balcony balustrades, glass block screens, exposed painted I-beams reinforce the industrial character encountered outside. There is no attempt to deny the factory paradigm, with the classrooms arranged in a linear manner along the central interior street. Thus, MBM's schools provide a condensed survey of the larger stylistic shifts in their work.

Looking back, the Thau School remains the outstanding work which is just as impressive in its achievement now as when it was finished. It retained elements of the earlier intimacy and individuality of the spatial repertoire experienced in Garbí and Sant Jordi, but in addition, there is a much greater control over, and confidence in, the deployment of the architectonic materials.

The vacation village for children at Canyamars (1961-65) with its explicitly Corbusian vocabulary, red walls and tiled roofs borrowed elements of the Mediterranean vernacular to relate it more to its hillside location and produce a scale in keeping with the children. It is a delight to visit, even if some of the details such as the thick cork ceilings have not stood up to the test of time. The building forms follow the ridge line in a slow snaking curve, stepping back and forth as they do so.

The heavy wooden trusses supported on thick brick piers, concrete beam seats, and rain water spouts, are all convincing reminders that this was the heyday of Brutalism. But it is a Brutalism tempered by MBM's special brand of Realism, an idea that has a moral dimension, as well as an aesthetic one. This involved taking responsibility for designing the buildings so they meet the needs of city children who have come to the country to learn about nature, and to experience something of the freedom that country children take for granted, together with an aesthetic which draws its inspiration from the ordinary. The red walls, juxtaposed against the piercing blue of the sky, simple traditional shapes, and sculptural manipulation of the masses, all assist in evoking a feeling of being on holiday.

The Library at Can Sumarro, L'Hospitalet de Llobregat (1982-84), which was developed around the sensitive rehabilitation of an existing set of farm buildings is one of MBM's most seductive works, partly because it is small and easy to relate to, partly because the juxtaposition of the old and the new amplifies those traditional resonances in the MBM vocabulary. The architect's task was less one of designing a new building, than one of touching up, and inserting new elements into the existing, to adapt the spaces to the new library functions. The result is in many ways much more pleasant, and much more sympathetic to the reading of books than would have been the case with an entirely new building.

The entry through a narrow gate under a classically simple porch with its Neo-Rationalist concrete columns is reassuring in its understated simplicity. The gentle entry ramp allows the visitor to look back at the courtyard and reappraise its qualities a second time. The children's reading room in the barn with its solid brick arches is secure and protective, but it could equally have been claustrophobic but for the ingenious, and equally simple design of a double line of roof lights on either side of the ridge, made possible by crossing the rafters. The principal reading room looks out on an enclosed courtyard landscape with palms which heighten the serenity of the architectural space itself.

Holiday Centre for Young Children, Canyamars
1961–65

The centre is located a distance from the Catalan coast and is set amongst woodland and abandoned vineyards. The complex provides accommodation for 72 children in two groups with monitors.

The buildings, divided into three sections, have been fitted to the hillside location. Two have been provided to serve as dormitories, while one is used for communal activities. The ground plan was conceived to permit a flexible use of the facilities to meet possible future uses while at the same time merging with the natural setting. The three buildings are linked by covered walkways around a spacious courtyard which, however, has not been enclosed on its northern side where it opens onto woodland. This courtyard provides a focus for social activities that is strongly identified and acts as a cushion between the individual and group and the larger spaces of the countryside beyond the holiday centre.

The entrance is from the south and leads directly to the Director's flat and administrative offices and reception. Each part of this building has a covered outdoor space designed for craft activities.

The construction is very simple incorporating painted brick walls inside and outside, exposed reinforced concrete, and timber trussed roofs clad in clay tiles.

1. A corner of the large court formed by the buildings and adjoining wood.

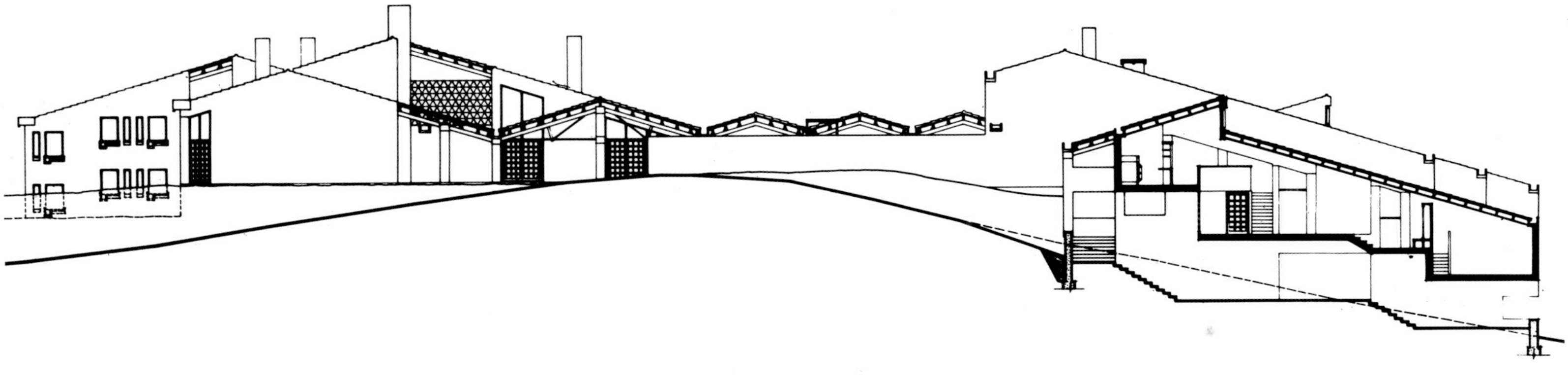

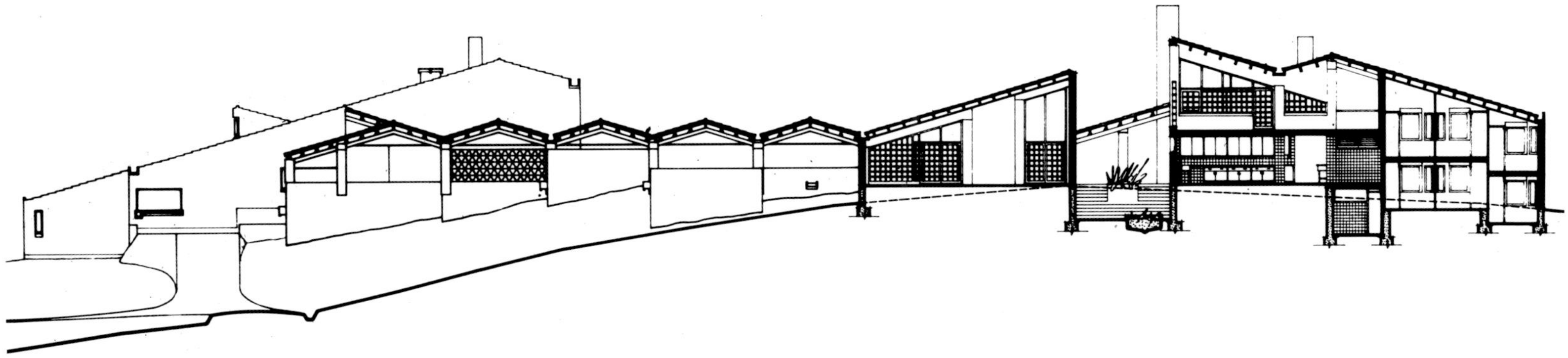

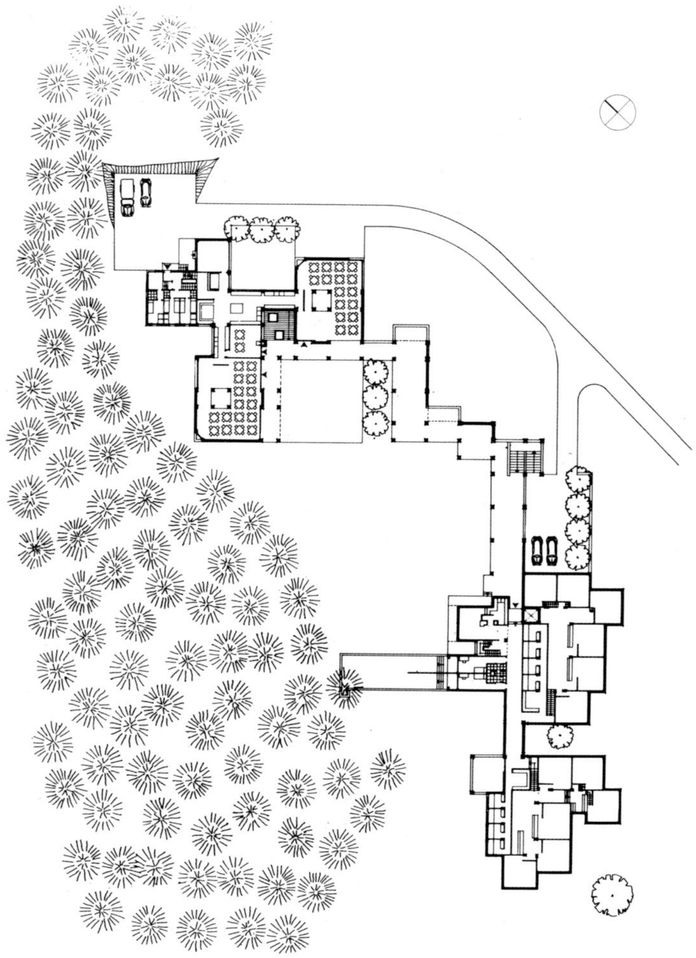

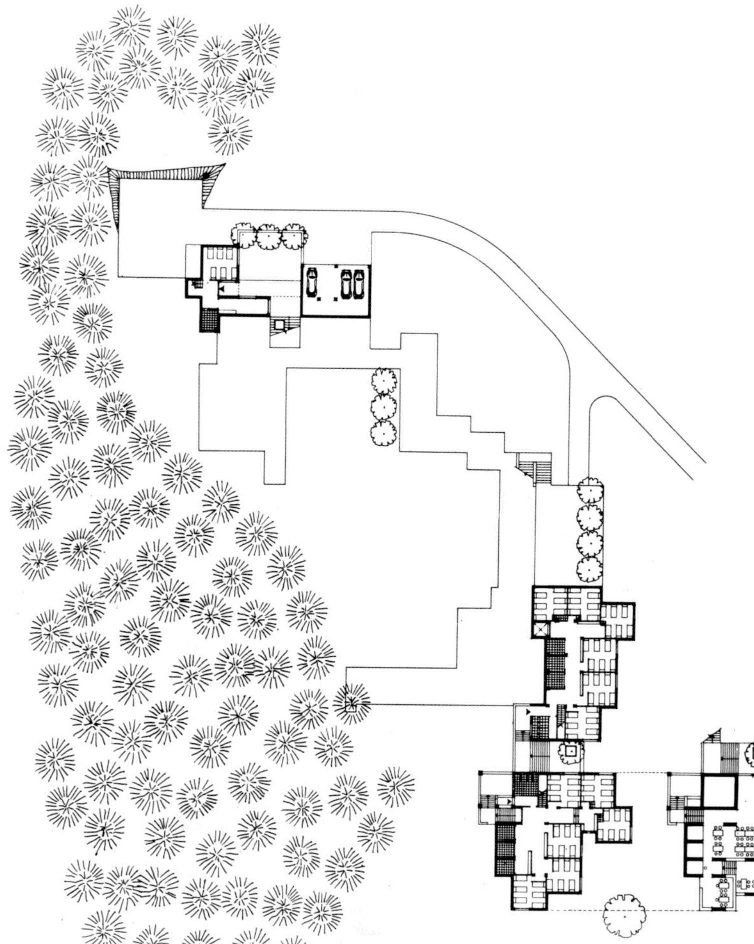

2. Sections.
3. Plans (lower ground floor and upper ground floor).
4. The gallery over one of the dormitory units.
5. View from the south showing the open-air class-rooms in the porches under the dormitories.

Garbí School, Esplugues de Llobregat, Barcelona
1962-78

Located at the western end of the Via Diagonal that cuts across the Cerdà street grid, the school lies just outside the Barcelona municipal boundary. The school, which was founded prior to the Civil War, continues to implement progressive educational ideas and practices dating back to the 1920s. It began at a site on the beach in Barceloneta before moving to its present location.

The present school has of a nursery, primary and secondary departments. At first these facilities served 400 pupils but later they were extended to accommodate 840. The construction of the first phase (1962-65) of the building programme was carried out in collaboration with a team of educators who were keen to break away from the traditional classroom. This resulted in an arrangement of teaching spaces around an open central area, much in the manner of a town square, with this space being used as a dining area.

Shortly after the school was opened work began on extensions (1967/68). The original concept was retained, based once again on the central public area, around which an open-air stepped street was added leading from the new entry on the opposite side of the school which had to be shifted to accommodate the construction of a nearby motorway.

The support of a strong parents' association which was instrumental in funding the new building during Franco's dictatorship also ensured the continuation of the tradition of liberal and lay education. Architecturally, the entire space within the school was used for teaching and learning (including the washing facilities), in order to destroy the isolation of the classroom and create a sense of the school as a social community. Because of the confined area of the site, the roof was designed for teaching and play activities.

Reinforced concrete column and slab construction was adopted to permit future change. Timber joinery finished with a natural varnish complements the fair-faced brick and glazed tiles which have been used throughout.

Adjoining the primary school an independent building was later designed for the senior students. It is a simple cubic classroom block with a cross-axis structure that suspends the classrooms above the lower column-free ground floor multi-purpose hall.

1. Partial view of the primary school from one of the roof terraces.
2. South façade showing the use of domestic elements: brick, coloured tile, varnished wood and awnings.
3. Site plan of the nursery and primary school with the secondary school in the east corner.

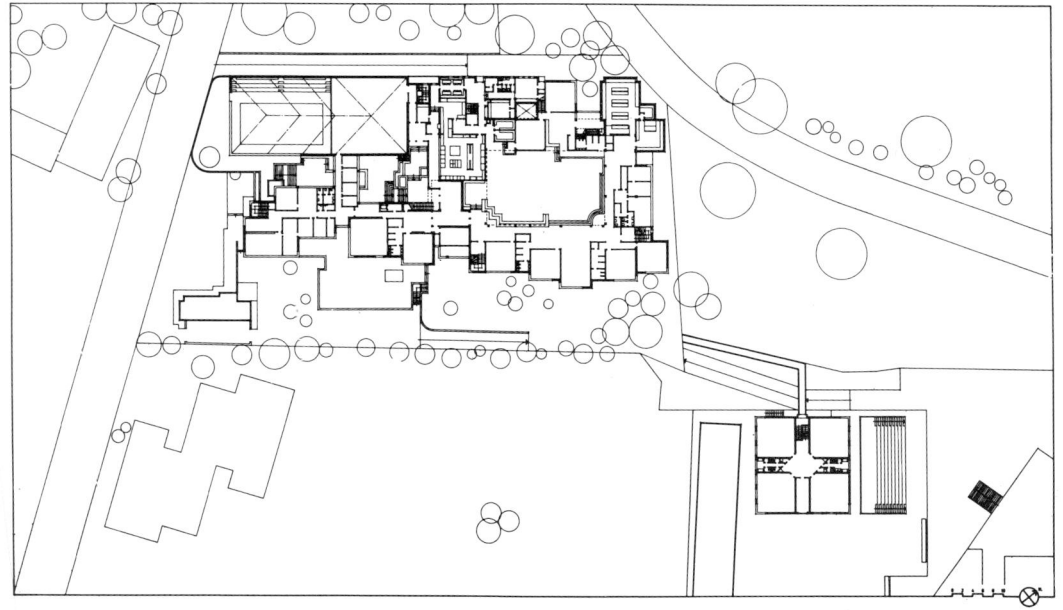

4. The »village square« or community space also
used for midday meals.
5. The intermediate space on the first floor between
the »houses« (classrooms) and the »village square«.
6. The swimming pool with its stepped roof.

7. One of the classrooms with its adjoining open space for additional activities.
8. The secondary school from the sports ground.
9. Façade detail of the secondary school.

Sant Jordi School, C. Mn. Cinto Verdaguer, Pineda
1967–69

This nursery and primary school for 250 students is located in the small coastal town of Pineda north of Barcelona. The arrangement is similar to the first phase of the Garbí School, however, in this instance, the common central area is divided into two sections, one of which serves as a gymnasium.

To overcome the restrictions of the small site which was inadequate for normal outdoor play activities, the roof was designed as an extension to the playground with a court for sports on top of the gymnasium and hall.

The library and hall have been designed so that they can be used at weekends and during the school holidays by children and family members from the neighbourhood. An important modification was made to the nursery school which forms an integral part of the main building by raising the floor to reduce the scale of the rooms. The play area of each nursery classroom is protected by a low wall to prevent the smaller children from coming in contact with the more boisterous older children.

1. The roof-top terrace is used as an additional playground.
2. Plans (ground floor, 1st floor, roof-top terrace).

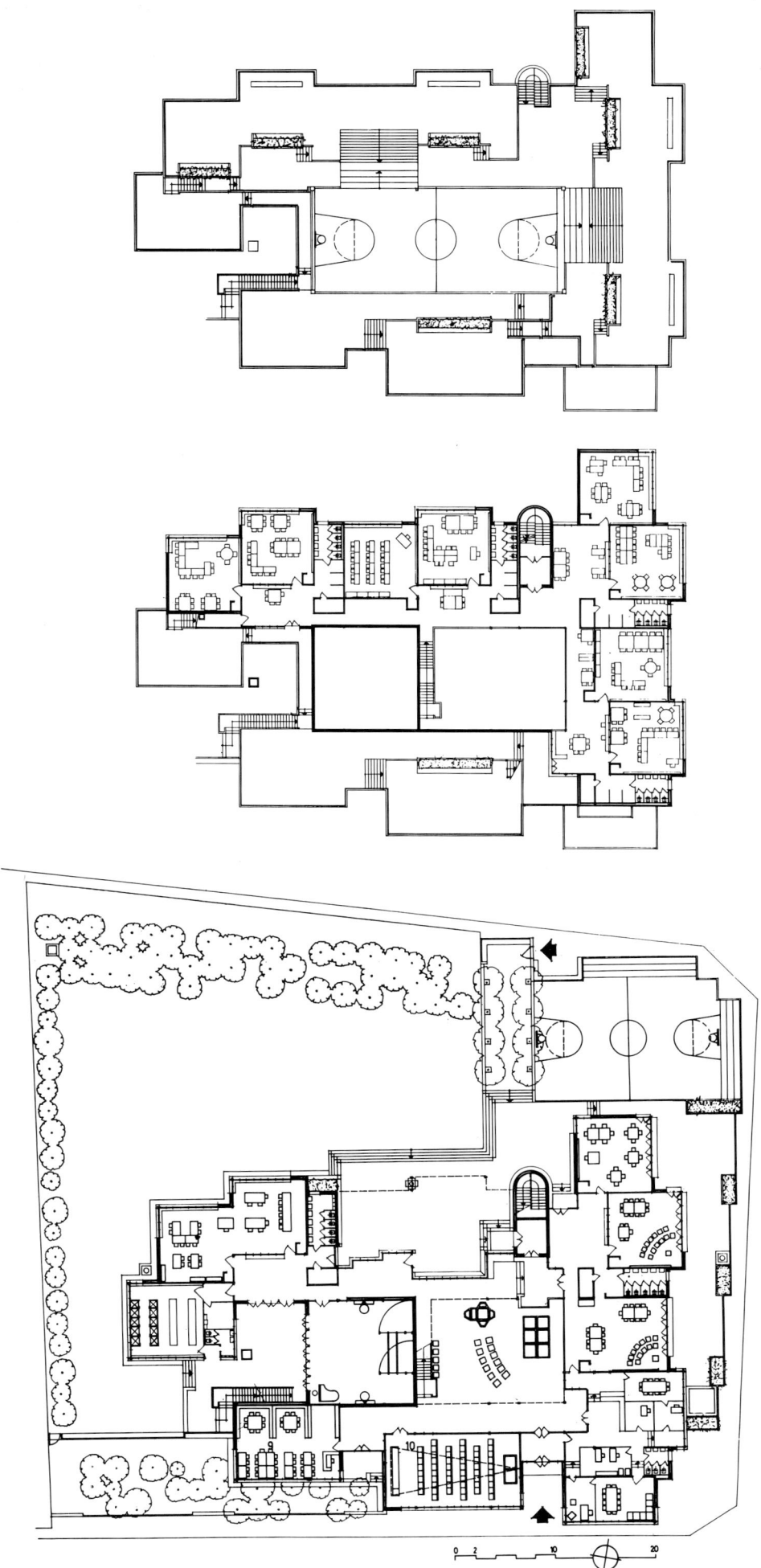

3. View from the south.
4. Entrance to the school with the cylinder containing the staircase link to the roof.
5. The multi-purpose hall with the surrounding galleries.

Thau School, Ctra. d'Esplugues 49–53, Barcelona
1972–74

The Thau School is a mixed all-age school for 1440 pupils included in which are nursery, primary and secondary departments. It resulted from a restricted architectural competition but, because the building had to satisfy the criteria of the Ministry of Education to qualify for a public subsidy, it is more compact than it might have been considering the radical form of the competition design.

It is customary for all pupils to remain in the school for the midday meal. The school is organized around this requirement with the result that it is both a school in the customary sense as well as a restaurant and kitchen. For this reason the nursery school had to be placed close to the kitchen, but with its very own specially scaled space to allow young children to eat at a slower pace and to learn to feed themselves.

For pedagogical and psychological reasons it was decided to isolate the secondary school in another smaller building farther up the hillside from the all-age school. An amphitheatre has been inserted between them which serves both as a boundary and a common meeting area.

Each building has an open multi-purpose area surrounded by classrooms arranged along the southwest and southeast façades facing the sun. This assists in reducing the heating requirements in winter but it has the disadvantage that the summer heat must somehow be controlled. This is accomplished with adjustable louvred blinds fixed with a 500 mm gap in front of the glass to allow the hot air to rise and be dissipated.

Suspended from the roof slab along the fully glazed northwest and northeast façades the staircases, which resemble stepped streets, connect the floors with the entry visually as well as physically. Internally, exposed concrete block is used for its acoustic quality and for low maintenance.

1. North-east façade of the larger building.
2. The open-air theatre from the north-west stair-case in the larger building.

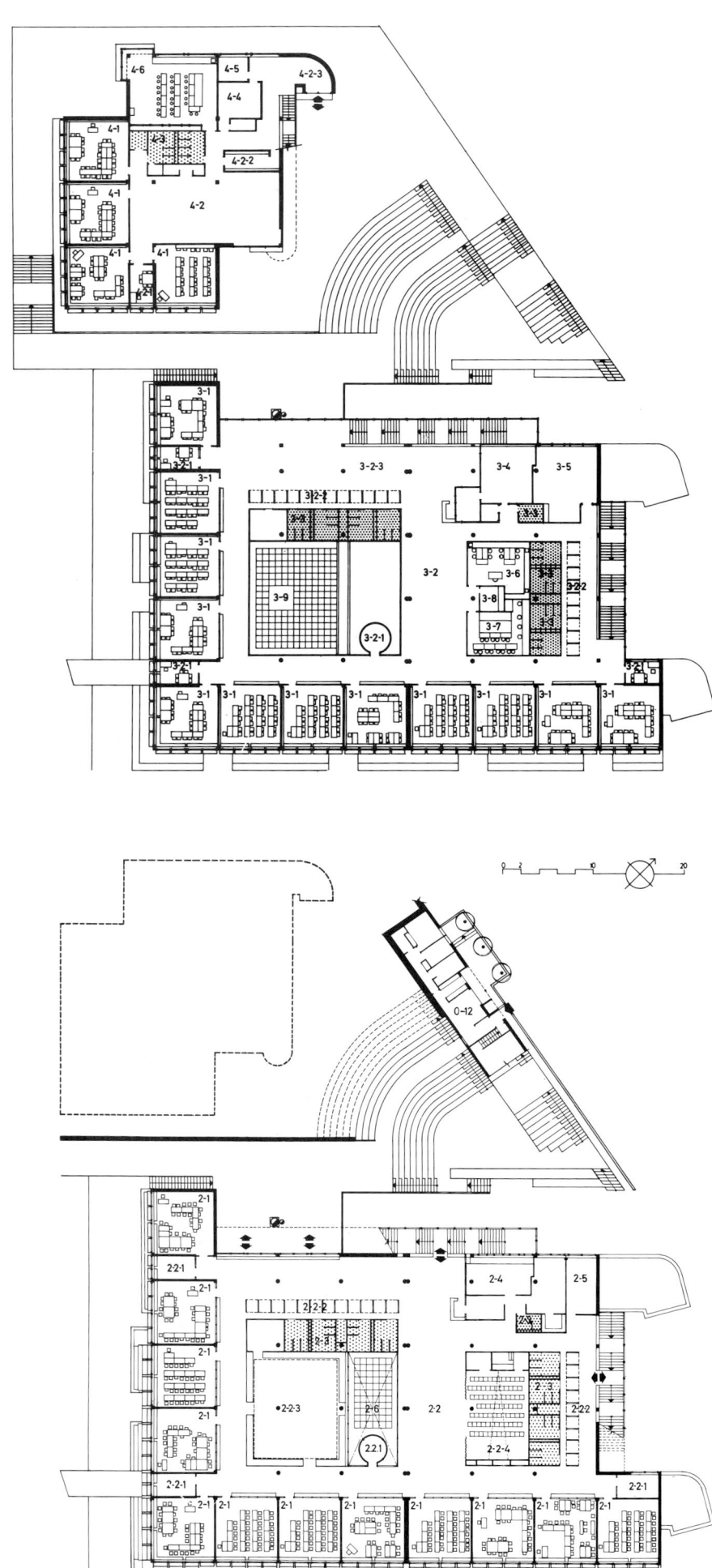

3. Plans (1st and 2nd floor).
4. The north-west staircase looking north-east.

Catalunya School and Institute, Sant Adrià del Besòs, Barcelona
1981-88

The building can be viewed as an interplay between a standard nave envelope and a series of autonomous spaces within it considered as a sequence. The prefabricated nave structure is basic and ordinary with regularly spaced frames that establish a simple repetitive rhythm. Within this, the school programme has been inserted. Mostly the spaces are contained within the linear envelope, but some extend outwards beyond this boundary.

There were two options which determined the internal location of the teaching-learning spaces. One was the desire to ensure maximum contact with the ground to encourage outdoor learning. This led to the administration and laboratories being located on the upper floor level. The other was to widen the circulation corridor to convert it into an internal street housing resource facilities and accommodating other common activities that heighten the school community's identity.

The Catalunya School was designed as the first of three schools, but ultimately only two were built. The second is an Institute, or senior school, designed on the same principles but with a more complex programme and an additional floor of classrooms.

1. Aerial view of the two schools. In the foreground is the primary school.
2. South-east façade of the secondary school.
3. South-west façade of the primary school.

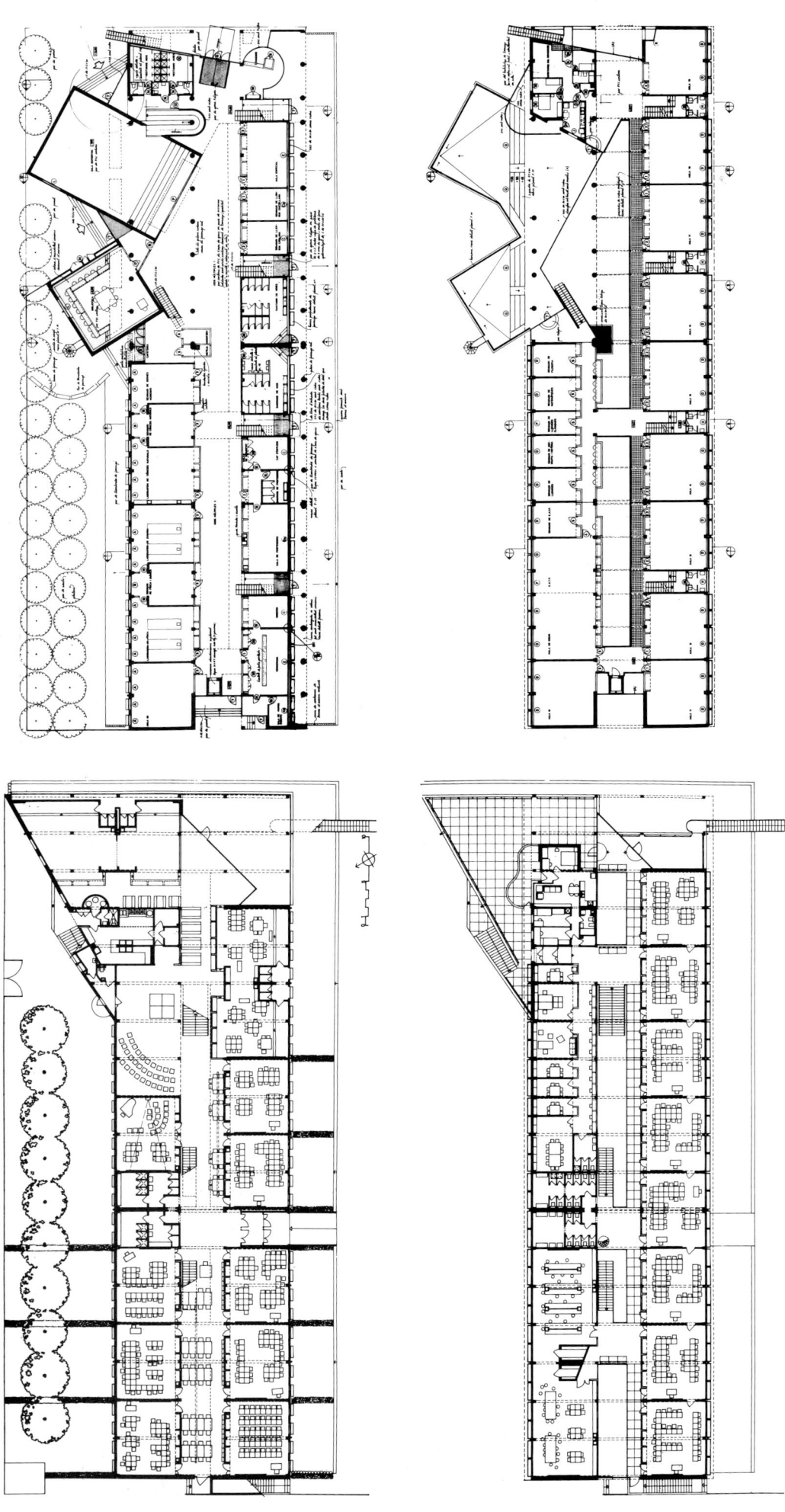

4. Plans of the secondary school (ground floor and 1st floor).
5. Plans of the primary school (ground floor and 1st floor).
6, 7. The central spine of the primary school.

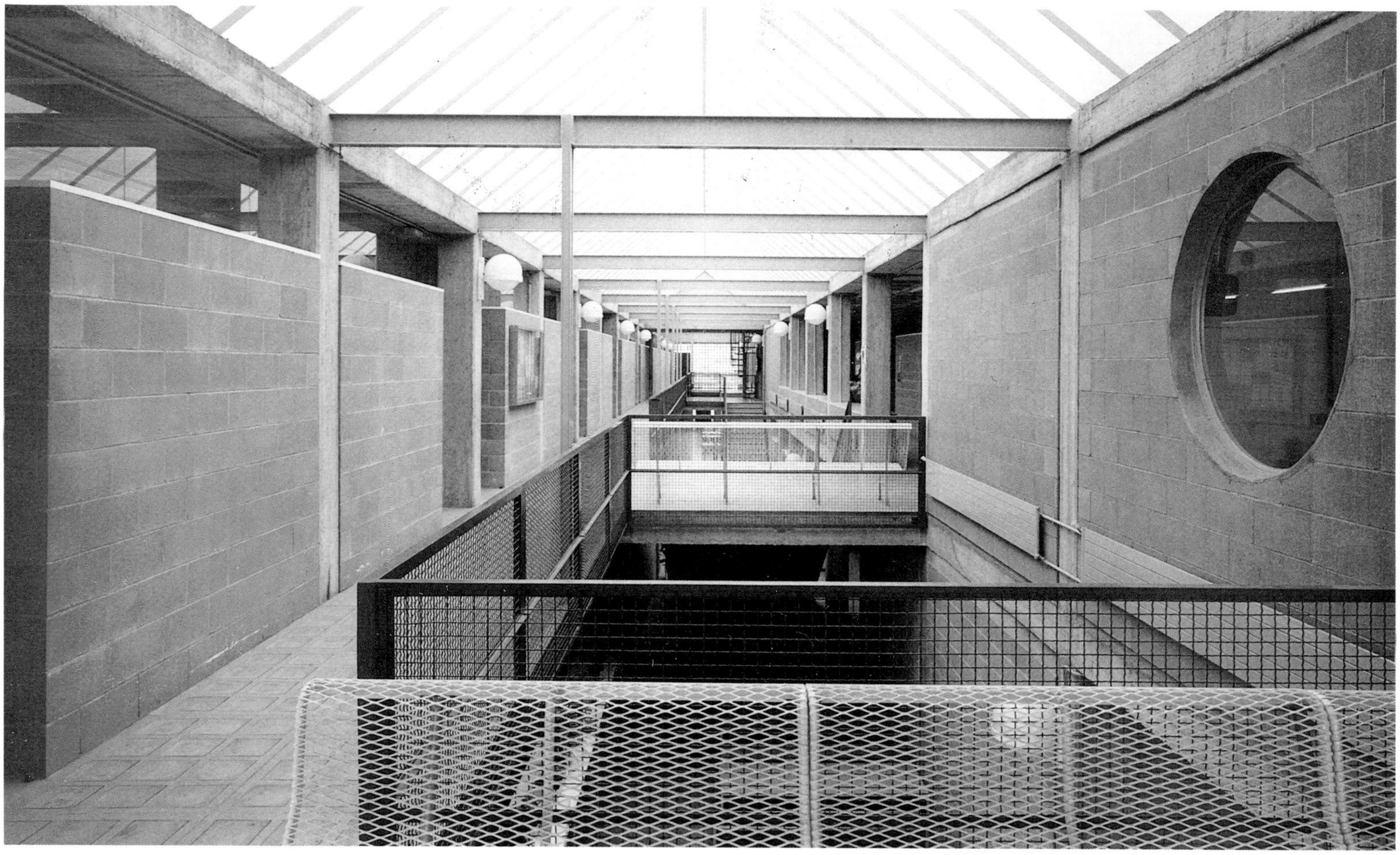

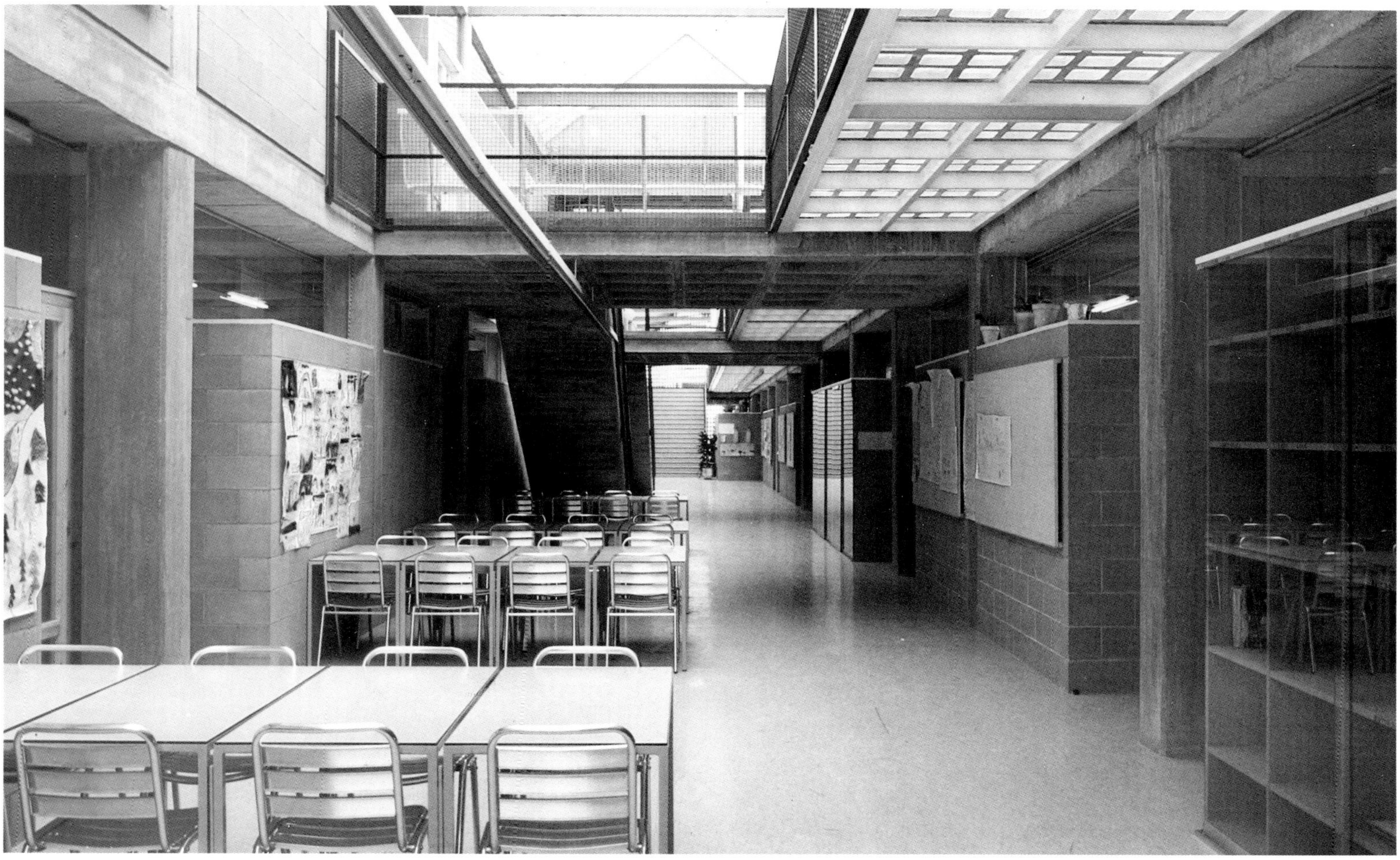

Refurbishment of the Can Sumarro Farm House as a Library, C. Barcelona 138, L'Hospitalet de Llobregat, Barcelona
1982-84
Interior design: I.D.P.

The farm buildings consisted of two separate structures which shared an enclosed courtyard: the larger of the two faced south onto a separate courtyard which had originally been the means of access to the farmhouse and the cow shed. To the north of this, an old barn and straw loft framed the first courtyard. The farmhouse, dating from the 16th century, was restored as a model example belonging to the area. It houses the administration and a collection of rare books and documents.

The criteria adopted for restoring and adapting the farm group was to preserve the form and scale of the existing buildings, repairing or replacing damaged elements where necessary with traditional materials. However, when a new window was required this was made using contemporary industrial products and construction techniques to emphasize the difference between the old and the new work.

The two-storeyed attached out-building overlooking the southern court is now the library, while the room which formerly contained wine vats on the north has become the periodical room. A ramp was added beside this to provide access to the upper floor. This addition, glazed on one side, is repeated in the form of a sun porch along the south wall of the barn, which has been converted into a children's library.

1. Plans (ground floor and 1st floor).
2. The children's library.

3. The ramp that was added to the farm-house on the north side.
4. View from the east towards the courtyard and the converted barn that is now the children's library.
5. View from the main library room into the south garden court.
6. The garden court and the farm house with the new windows of the main library.

Industrial and Commercial Buildings

While the bulk of the MBM practice has been housing and apartments supplemented by schools, a sizable portion of the work consisted of factories, retail, offices, and more recently hotels. This spread of work is typical of the larger architectural office. The 1960s and early 1970s were a period of vigorous expansion of the Barcelona economy and this led to repeated factory commissions in the years from 1964 to 1971.

The first stage of the Piher-Badalona Factory in 1959 represented the beginning. Piher proved a consistent client whose success as an industrial entrepreneur was mirrored in a number of factory buildings. These were specialized plants. In 1964, a second stage was added to the Badalona Plant, followed by the first stage of the Piher-Navarra Factory in 1966, a factory at Granollers in 1971, and the second Badalona Plant in 1971. Besides Piher, MBM designed factories for Giró and Haïssa at Badalona.

In the early factories each bay was emphasized so the form reads as an accretion of individual bays. The individuality of the bays was stressed by continuing the V-roof profile over onto the ends at Tudela in 1965. This solution made its first appearance in the Piher-Badalona Factory in 1959. James Stirling and James Gowan's Leicester Engineering Laboratories had a similar lozenge motif applied diagonally, but its date 1959-63 falls mid-way between the Badalona and Tudela factories.

The second stage of the Piher-Badalona Factory had a clean prismatic form with a continuous stair suspended down one side in a long chute-like sequence of ramps. This marked the beginning of a new approach and move away from additive forms based on the single bay, to the neat container, the factory as a »can«. The Piher-Granollers Factory in 1971, designed three years earlier, is the outstanding example with its uncomplicated metal external envelope, with air-conditioning machine rooms and ducting exposed on the roof. The ducts were carried across the roof and down the sides to connect with internal ducts in a deep services sandwich beneath the first floor.

There is a notional conflict between the neat container and services expressionism, one hides the industrial processes it houses, whilst the other treats the exposed ductwork as a kind of industrial sculpture. The Haïssa Factory (1969-72) came a little later. The roof has been turned over to cars and offices, the latter are arranged slightly skewed to the rectangular base of the main factory floor. A long screened vehicular ramp admits cars to the roof.

Services expressionism reached its climax in the Iluro Building at Mataró in 1974. Here, four ducts were bent to form separate lines so they snake their way down from the roof and plug into the successive floor levels of the spiral interior. This mechanical operation has been strikingly expressed on the street.

The new Nestlé Office Building at Esplugues de Llobregat (1983-87) is sited behind the first eight-storey Head Office built in the 1970s which has an inoffensive curtain-wall façade. The two buildings are connected by an enclosed walkway which crosses a landscaped garden with lawns and water ponds on the lower side.

A sizeable part of the facility, including a conference centre, storage and translation facilities, is buried under the park. This is connected to the upper ground level and the enclosed walkway by a brilliantly detailed and gem-like stair in steel painted blue capped by a sinuous bright yellow hand rail. The stair is pure sculpture. The conference auditorium is dominated by a diamond grid of fluorescent tubes reminiscent of Arata Isozaki's 1978 Kamioka Town Hall.

The eight-storey office tower, identical in height to the old Head Office, is another exercise in the »container« aesthetic, but on this occasion it is a sheer immaculate glass container from which large chunks have been extracted from the precise wedge-shaped ends. These triangular incisions, one at ground level marking the juncture with the covered walkway connection, the other six storeys up on the opposite side facing the expressway, are a kind of literal cross-section through the building rather like an illuminated anatomical manikin. The brilliant red columns immediately attract attention, whether the building is first seen from the expressway at speed, or at a more leisurely pace on foot through the glass roof of the connecting walk. The brilliant red columns are a distinctive sign for the new Nestlé Building.

One detail is indicative: this is the clear glass strip at the edge of each floor. Instead of hiding the office floors, as was customary in curtain-wall detailing, MBM chose to expose not merely the floor edge, but have taken it a stage farther in their see-through detail, by displaying the steel bracket supports of the curtain-wall. This is a polished demonstration of Realism, updated to the 1980s, because we not only see and admire the finished wall in all its taut elegance, but we are invited back-stage and shown how this has been accomplished. There is a certain bleak honesty about the performance, but this is not the complete story. Details such as this add greatly to the impact of the forms.

Light is very important. It was the Mexican architect Luis Barragán who pointed out that human beings need half-light, the sort of light that imposes tranquillity. In a large hotel today they also need to have their privacy protected, to be part of a large vital community, but at the same time, to feel they are able to withdraw into absolute privacy when they feel the need to do so.

MBM's hotel in Puerto Vallarta, Mexico, completed in 1990, beside and facing the sea, is an exercise in filtering and reflecting light, shutting out its excesses in the tall chimney-shaped light catchers over the extensive lobby areas which make such a distinctive and arresting introduction to the hotel. Projecting concrete window hoods are painted green, blue, and terra-cotta inside to soften the reflected light to the hotel rooms.

Tourism is changing. No longer does the tourist demand the identical and predictable in his accommodation. The universal hotel room, so long the bane of the creative architect, is giving way to an architecture whose forms are imbued with the texture of its surroundings. More and more, people travel to learn about other cultures, to experience something new, to immerse themselves in an altogether different human universe. Hotel architecture is beginning to reflect this in buildings which are much more regional in inspiration, which take their ideas from their immediate surroundings, rather than being designed from a remote office in New York.

MBM were ideally suited to the task because of their sensitivity to the region and their hotel at Puerto Vallarta shows this. It is a large affair comprising low five-storey blocks arranged around a central garden crossed by shaded pergolas. Red tiles on the roofs lend a welcome domestic feel. The central lobby and dining areas, bars, etc. are dominated by two ten-storey towers that overlook the garden and beach areas. Behind is the forest of light catchers arranged in a uniform grid. This is what the hotel guest sees on his arrival, the low distinctive silhouette of identical light catchers, red walls, and a forest of columns leading into the building interior.

The hotel accommodation is simply expressed with precise rectangular openings puncturing the solid white of the walls. Along the upper levels, red *gelosia* lattice screens break down the light to the hallways and terraces. The forms have a simple monumentality. The public spaces are generous and serene. Rather as occurred in the Villa Escarrer, the character of each of the major spaces takes on its own peculiar ambience, but it is an ambience inseparable from Mexico itself, inseparable from the vitality and richness of that country and its people.

Piher–Badalona Factory, Riera Cañadó s/n, Badalona, Barcelona
1959–64

For the manufacture of electronic parts, this industrial factory group is comprised of a large workshop area and a complementary service building. The workshop was characterized by a series of steeply sloping metal roofs to provide evenly distributed north light and ample room for the equipment and manufacturing activities. The saw tooth shape of the roof was extended to the end walls with the openings in this instance facing the south.

Offices are included within the main volume of the workshop building, along the nave on the north. A canteen and changing rooms are provided for the staff in the smaller service building.

Some years later, this building was dismantled and moved to the city of Tudela where it was re-erected for use by the same company.

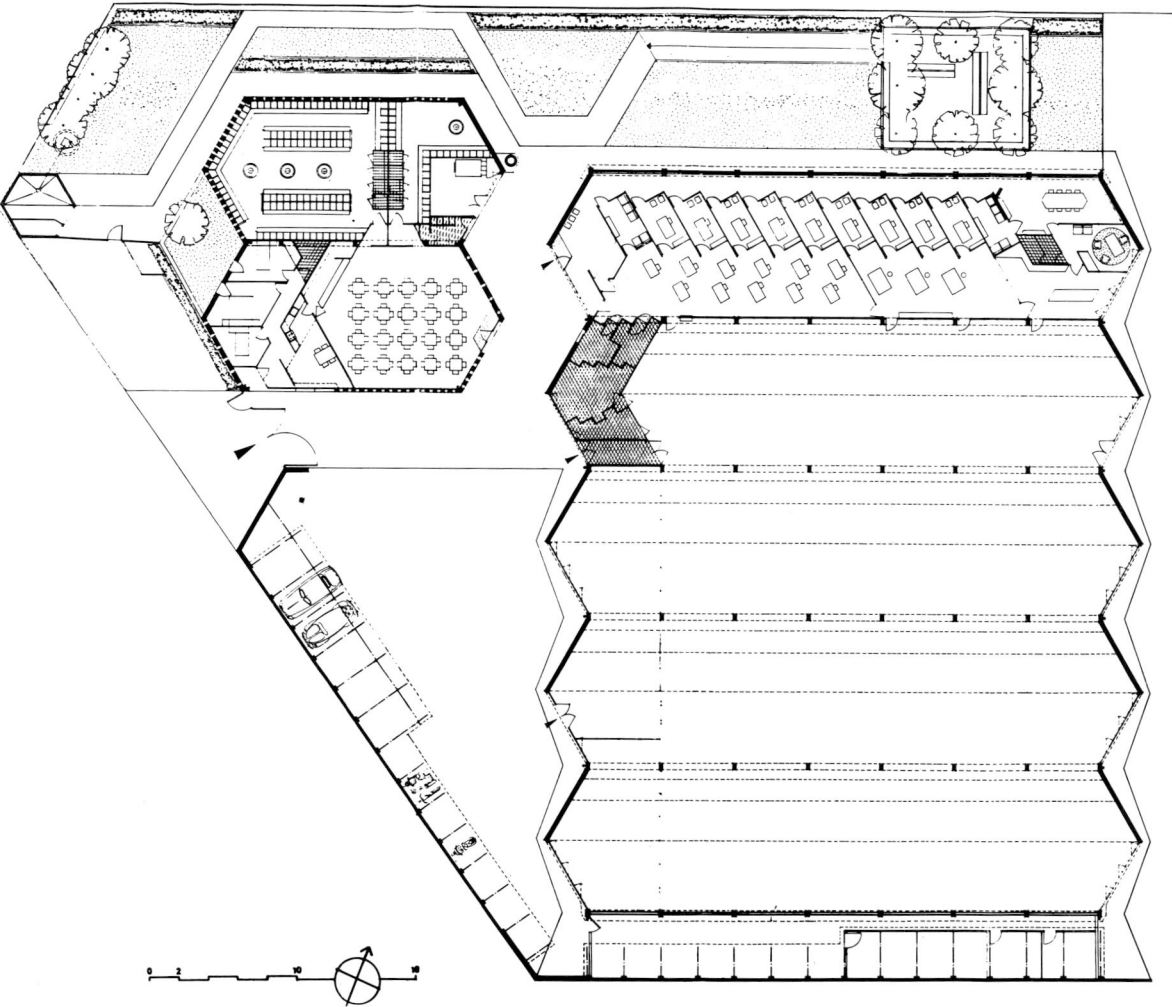

1. Plan.

2. The industrial bays from the east.
3. Section.
4. Interior of the industrial bays.

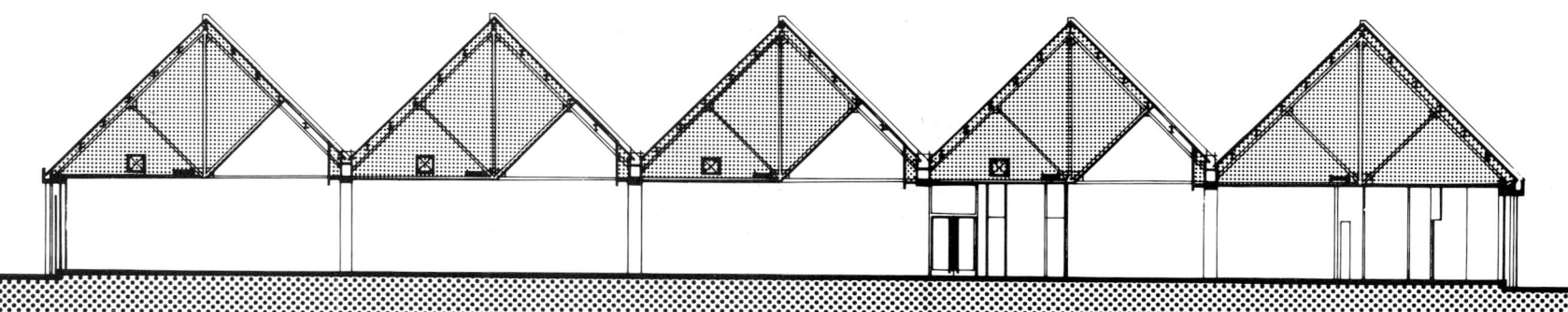

Piher-Granollers Factory, Av. San Julián s/n, Granollers
1968-71

The workshop, housed in a parallelepiped of 46 m x 46 m x 3 m raised 5 m above the ground level, required the most exacting conditions of controlled light and air conditioning for the production of semiconductor micro-chips. The service area with facilities for access, changing rooms, canteen, offices, stores, workshops and loading bays is positioned below this main production floor. Above it is a service area for all the mechanical and technical installations. The sandwich section was chosen to ensure maximum flexibility for the workshop production floor.
The air-conditioning duct work and other mechanical installations were exposed on the outside of the façade and roof to provide an almost decorative contrast to the hermetic severity of the electronic workshop shed.

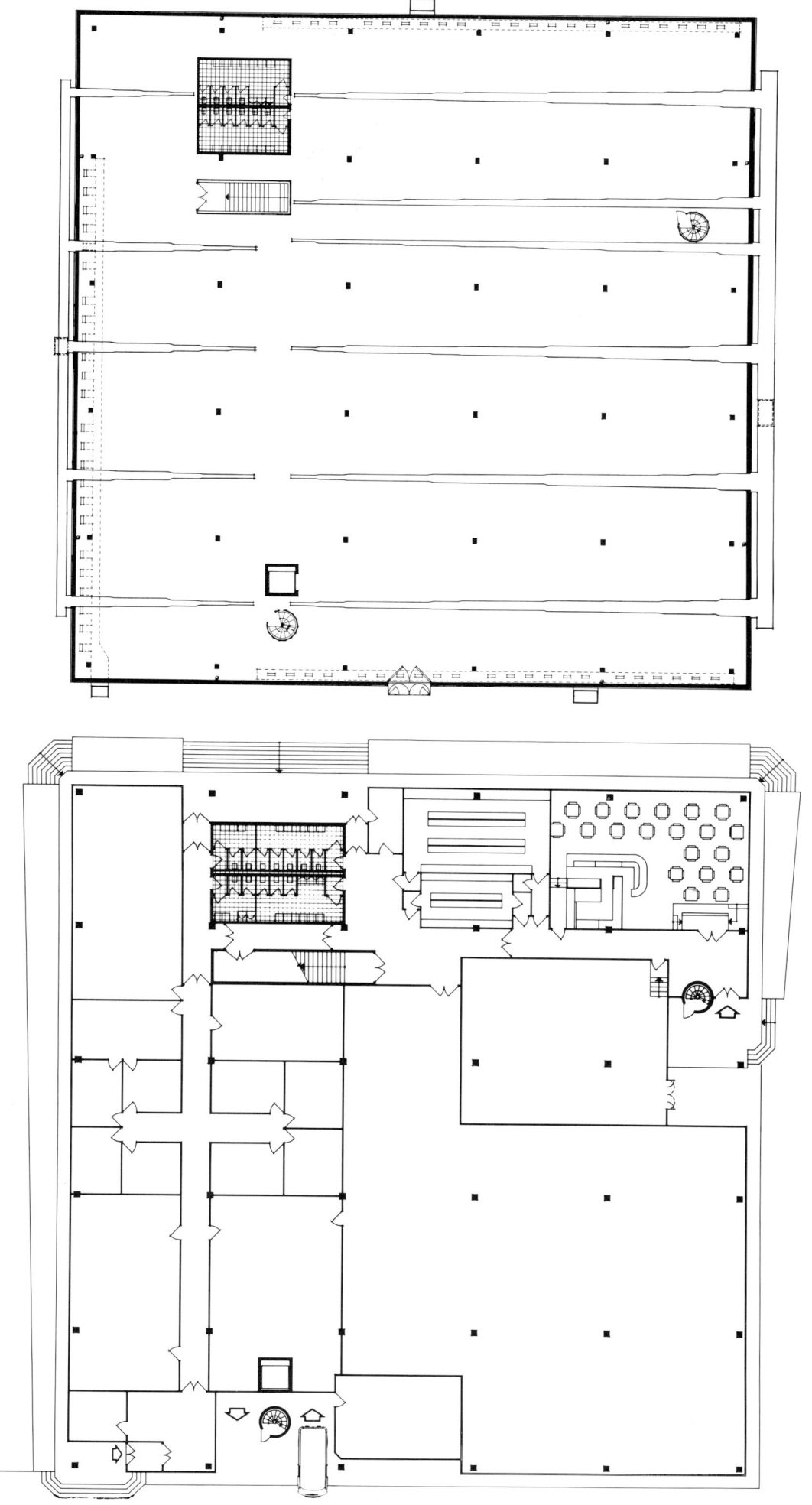

1. View from the north-west.
2. View from the north-east.
3. Plans (ground floor and 1st floor).

Nestlé Office Building, Av. Països Catalans 33–49, Esplugues de Llobregat, Barcelona
1983-87
Interior Design: I.D.P.

This new office building for the Nestlé company at Esplugues, Barcelona, is an extension to a comparatively recent building completed in the 1970s. The design requirements were established following lengthy consultations between the architects and the client concerning the space, image, maintenance, as well as envelope restrictions imposed by local building ordinances caused by the presence of surrounding roads and a nearby motorway. These factors, plus visual and solar conditions applying to the site, determined the exact location and form of the new building.

A paramount concern of the client was to ensure almost identical working conditions to those provided in the existing 1970s offices in order to avoid conflict amongst staff and to permit the free movement of personnel and office furniture between the two buildings. This factor established a basic module of 1.2 m for internal divisions outside the structural grid to avoid conflict with the columns. The total area of the new building above ground is just over 7,000 m².

There are six basement levels under the intervening garden, five for parking for 380 cars serving the two office blocks, and one level of basement, 900 m² in extent, containing a public conference hall and an experimental teaching kitchen and dining complex.

The design of the glass curtain-wall was taken to extreme lengths in both its technological as well as visual refinement. Its prismatic form is emphasized by the absolute reduction of the supporting mullions to a flat neoprene gasket; the »goldfish bowl« effect of tinted glass upon the interior offices was minimized by the introduction of clear glass

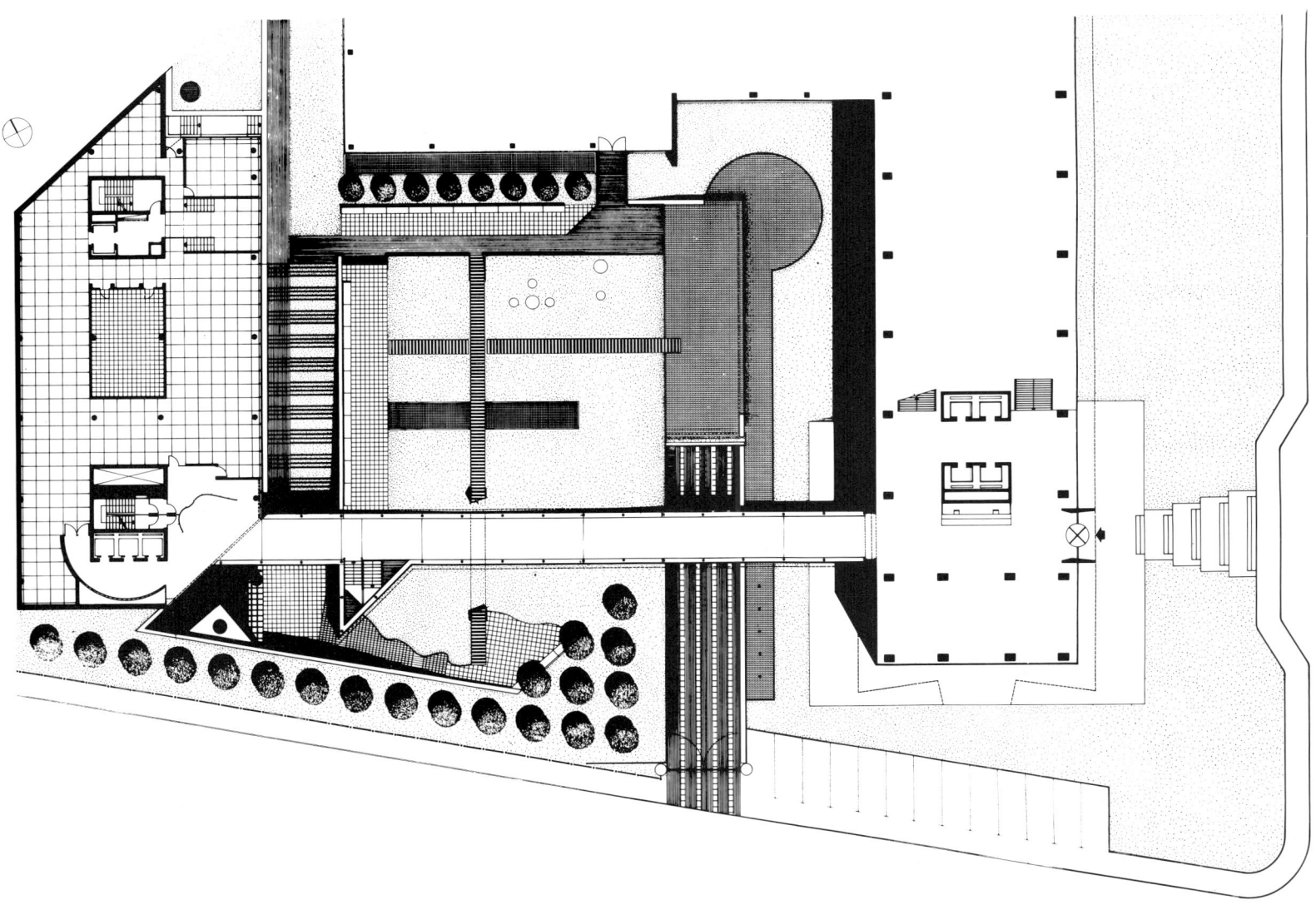

1. Site plan showing the new and old buildings.
2. The cut in the lower corner of the prism indicates
the location of the entrance.

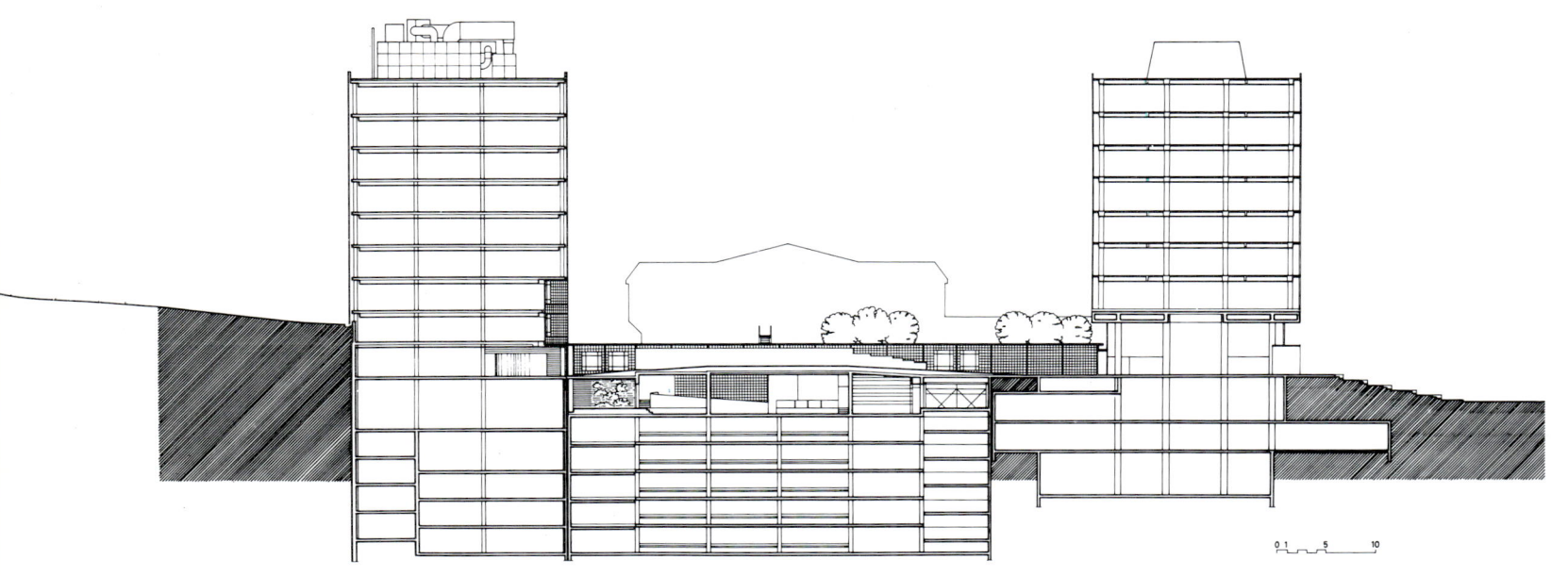

3. Section.
4. South-east façade. The clear glass strips allow the users to have a reference to the natural light.
5. Plans (basement and typical floor).

corresponding to the depth of the false ceiling, thus allowing office workers the chance to see the outside naturally; clear glass was also used in front of the floor slabs, where tinted glass was obviously unnecessary, and the steel supports to the curtain-wall were exposed and painted a bright yellow to add a certain decorative functional expression to the façade; a darker grey coloured glass is used to face the blank end walls, base, and roof thicknesses to convey their different functions.

The two office buildings are connected by an enclosed pedestrian passageway that is partly buried and partly exposed, and so is a mixture of tunnel and bridge. It is a bridge where it flies over the garage ramp and the sunken garden to access the conference centre, but a tunnel where it runs through the garden. The connecting passageway is constructed of steel, clear glass, glass bricks and white tiles to merge it completely with the garden. To avoid monotony that is a by-product of uniformity, the height of the tunnel has been deliberately varied by grading the floor level upwards towards the centre.

The conference centre has been rotated 45 degrees to enable a better ratio between the conference table area and the public area and to blur the boundaries of the hall to allow a more flexible use for receptions and different sized groups of the public.

The principal concern of the architects was to avoid the anonymous »international curtain-wall office block« stereotype and to create a sense of place that related both to the existing buildings and their immediate surroundings and also to its commanding position at the motorway entrance to Barcelona.

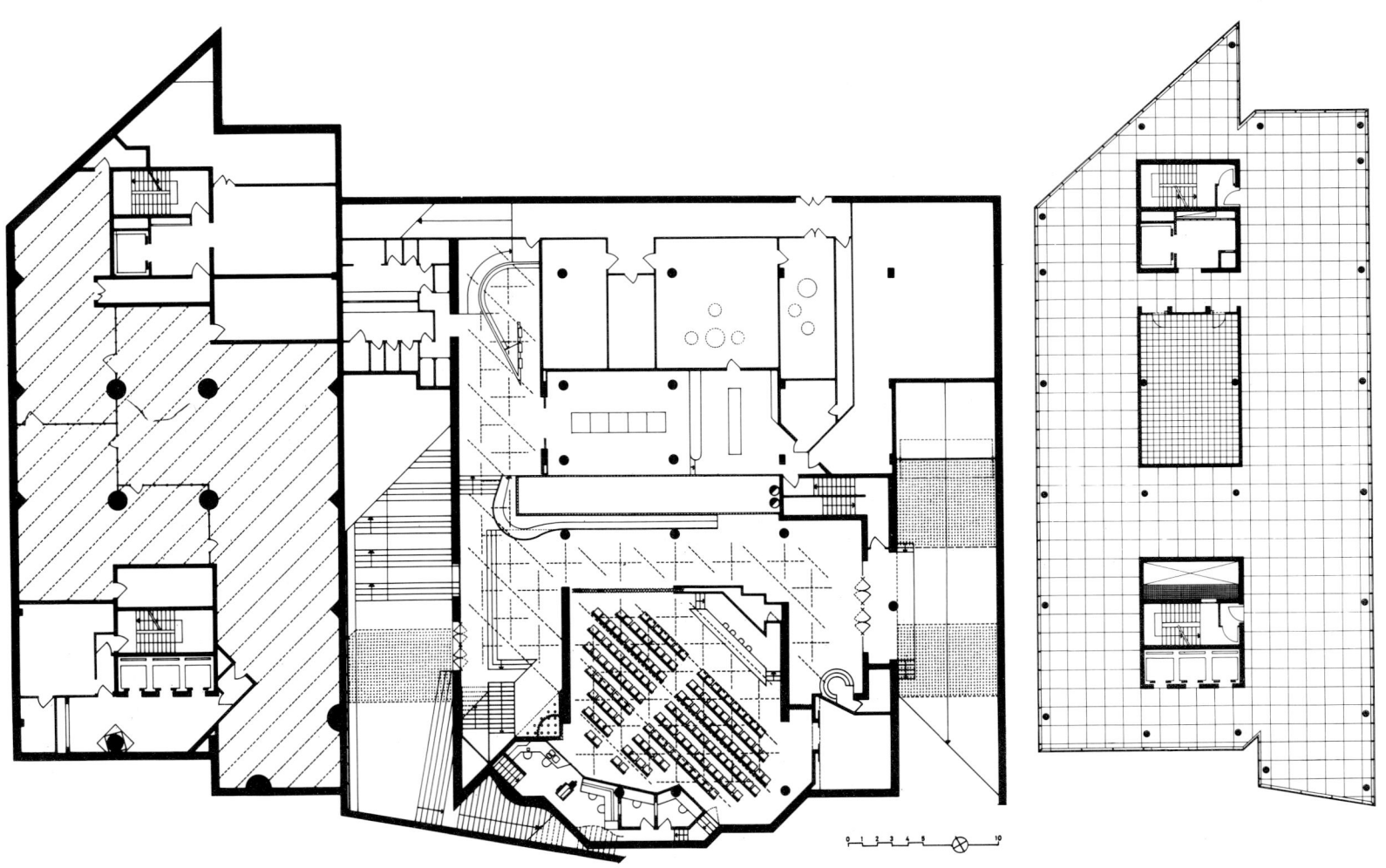

6. Detail of the conference hall.
7. Vestibule to the conference hall.
8. Passage that cuts through the garden to connect the two buildings.

Hotel Melià, Puerto Vallarta, Mexico

1987-90
Site Architects: Miguel Murguía and Raimundo Castillo del Angel
Interior Design: I.D.P.

At Puerto Vallarta on the Pacific coast of Mexico, the onshore sea breeze moderates the tropical heat. Formerly a small out-of-the-way fishing village, the settlement gained world attention with the filming of John Huston's *The Night of the Iguana* there in 1964 with Richard Burton and Ava Gardner. An international airport financed by the Mexican Government facilitates tourist access from the U.S. which is at its height between Christmas and Easter. Every conceivable variation of what is considered to be Mexican architecture has been tried by the international hotel chains which have entered the market. Pseudo-Mexican architectural concoctions, either built or proposed, compete for attention.

The hotel occupies a 215 m wide by 275 m deep plot of land connecting the main avenue that runs along the northeast boundary, with the beach and a lagoon-like marina.

The clients asked for 400 double bedrooms together with a considerable amount of free leisure space, both within and outside the hotel to encourage hotel guests to spend much of their time in the hotel until the next Boeing 747 arrival at the weekend. A spectacular entrance was demanded to make a powerful first impression; all rooms had to have a view of the Pacific Ocean, and the swimming pool and gardens along with their bars and restaurants were there to complete the attractions.

Because of difficult financial factors in Mexico, the entire project had to be completed in 18 months. This difficult target was achieved.

The idea was to produce an autonomous landscape, one that was open to the sea, and to use the hotel building to prevent the gardens from being overlooked by neighbouring buildings. The building was designed so its form and scale approximates that of a large Spanish colonial monastery, five floors high and with 40,000 m^2 of built floor area. The entrance lobby, continuing the analogy, replaces the church in this composition, and consists of a hall of 4,000 m^2 divided into 49 modules of 8.25 m x 8.25 m x 8.25 m, each capped by a pyramid-shaped breeze catcher of concrete. The hall is inspired by the Mosque of Córdoba (785). The proportions are similar. The lobby is open except on the north and east where the space is shielded from its neighbours and the street by a separate low wall. This enhances the sense of removal from the street at night.

The corridor-access to the bedrooms responds to the gardens outside. On the lower floors it merges with the garden, while immediately above this, there is a double storeyed concrete grille for privacy. On the upper floors, the corridors are exposed under the sheltering eaves of the tile roof. This was done to avoid any suggestion of cheapness usually associated with exposed corridor-access in hotels. Simple construction methods were adopted with reinforced concrete, load-bearing walls, coloured rendered surfaces and minimal details used throughout. The hotel architecture relies on the interplay of the spaces and effects of sunlight to impress the visitor.

1. The great lobby looking towards the Pacific.

2. View showing how the hotel forms the wall of the garden.
3. Edge of the south-east wing of the hotel showing one of the open staircases.
4. Plans (typical floor and roof).

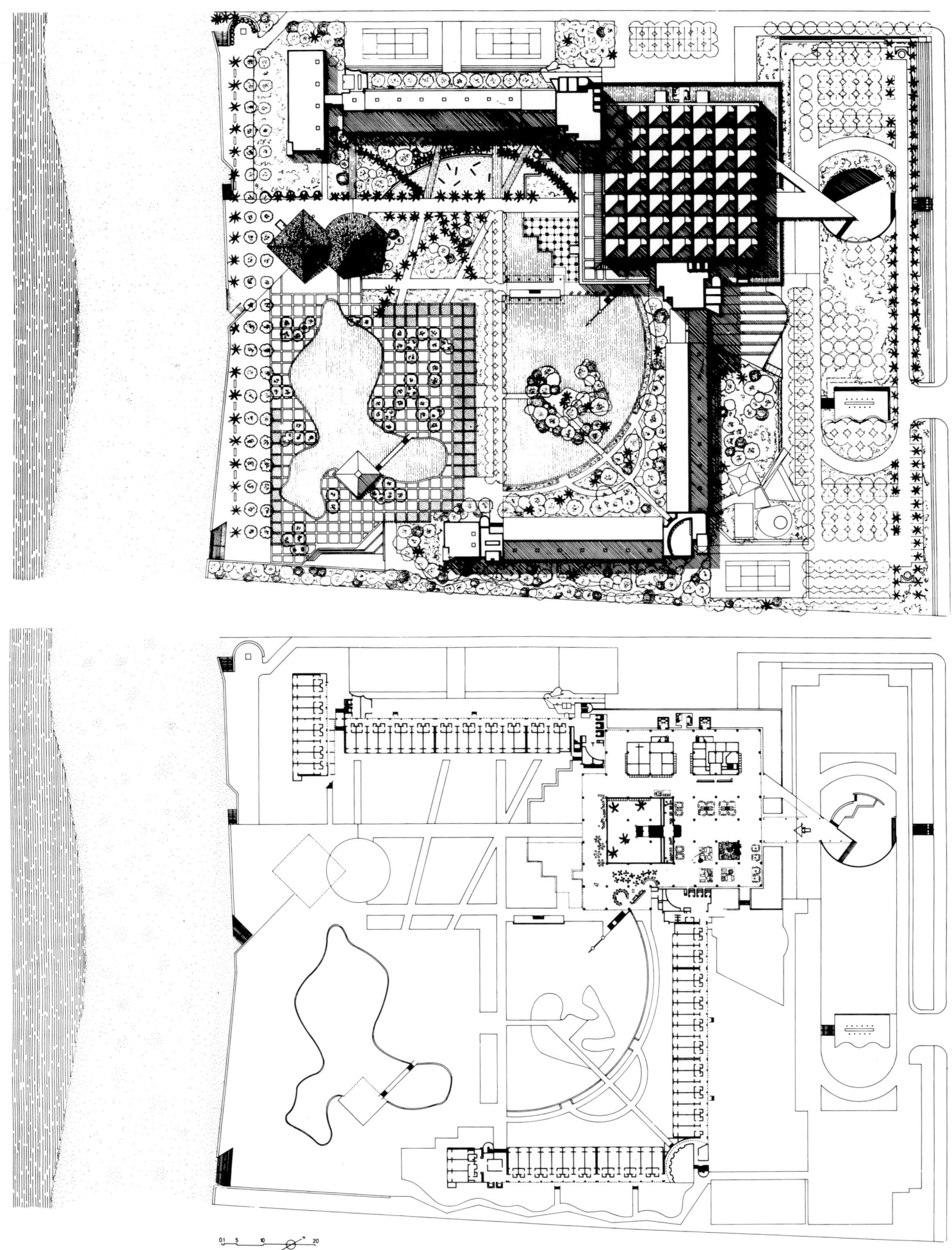

5, 6. The lobby is covered with prismatic light catchers and natural-ventilation chimneys.
7. The open-air corridor along the outer façade of a bedroom wing.
8. Timber pergola in the garden.

Pavilion of the Future, Expo '92, Sevilla
1988-92
In collaboration with Peter Rice
Collaborating Architect: Jaume Freixa

International exhibitions provide an opportunity to experiment, to stretch architecture beyond its accustomed limits. In the instance of the Pavilion of the Future, the conditions of the commission were quite specific and unusually emphatic. These stated that:
1. The pavilion was to house an exhibition of advanced technology indicative of the future in various fields, although the precise programme of the exhibition was not known at the time the building was designed. The pavilion is one of the few permanent constructions, but, once again, its function after the conclusion of the Expo was uncertain. Most probably, it would be connected with the university and research.
2. The location of the 400 m x 60 m site results in the east façade, which faces towards the city, being the representative façade of Expo itself.
3. The architectural character of the building was to be an expression of new technology, or at the very least, the result of an investigation in this area, forming an integral part of and indicator for the exhibits on display inside.
   These specific requests were answered in the following manner:
1. A long hangar-type building 21 m high surrounds a second interior container building along the east façade which holds all the service installations, vertical and horizontal circulations. This made for greater flexibility and freed up what was left over. A removable intermediate floor enables extra floor space to be added within the main exhibition space should this become necessary.
2. The 36 m high east façade is a long highly transparent membrane, rather like an enormous garden pavilion, from which the metal roof has been slung. The façade is al-most independent of the rest of the building. Its independence further advertises its role of introducing Expo '92 to the public, a kind of symbolic bill-board for the exhibition itself. It is the only true façade the pavilion possesses since the roof tilts down to the ground on the west side to shade the building from the hot sun.
3. The exploration of technology is demonstrated in the structure of the transparent eastern façade which was designed in collaboration with the engineer Peter Rice of Ove Arup. It comprises a succession of arches built with Porino granite in extremely small elements, strung together and stiffened by steel tubes anchored to the stone joints. The arches are brought into a state of compression to support the roof which is hung below them, its weight being distributed through a bicycle-wheel-like framework. The aim was to use a traditional material such as stone in a manner that made use of high technology. This was considered appropriate in the context of Seville's traditional architecture. It suggests a link between the progressive image of Expo '92 and the historical European city.

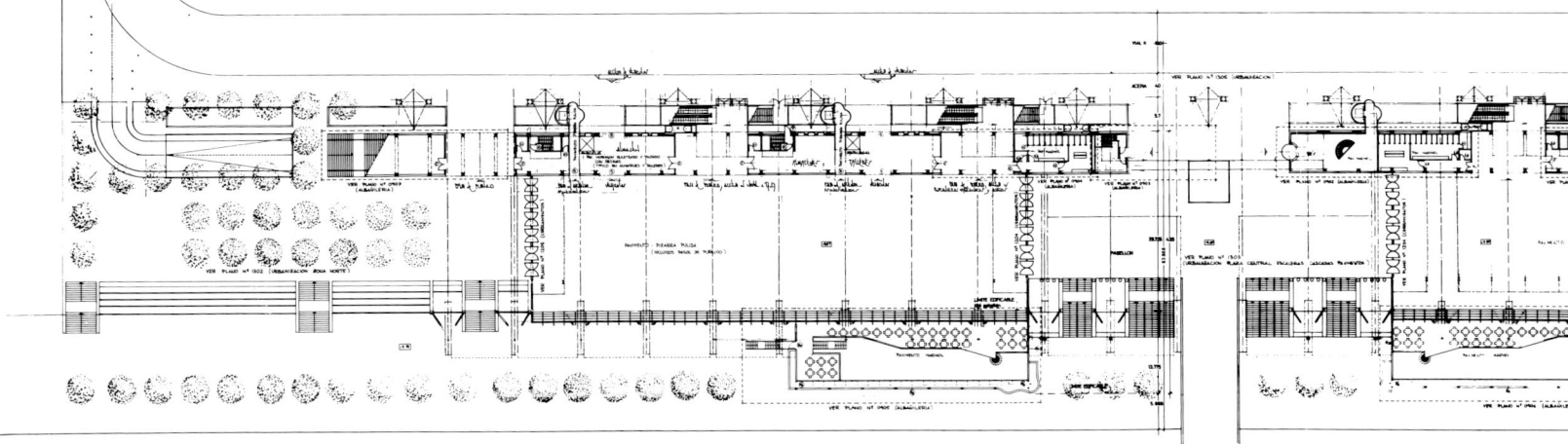

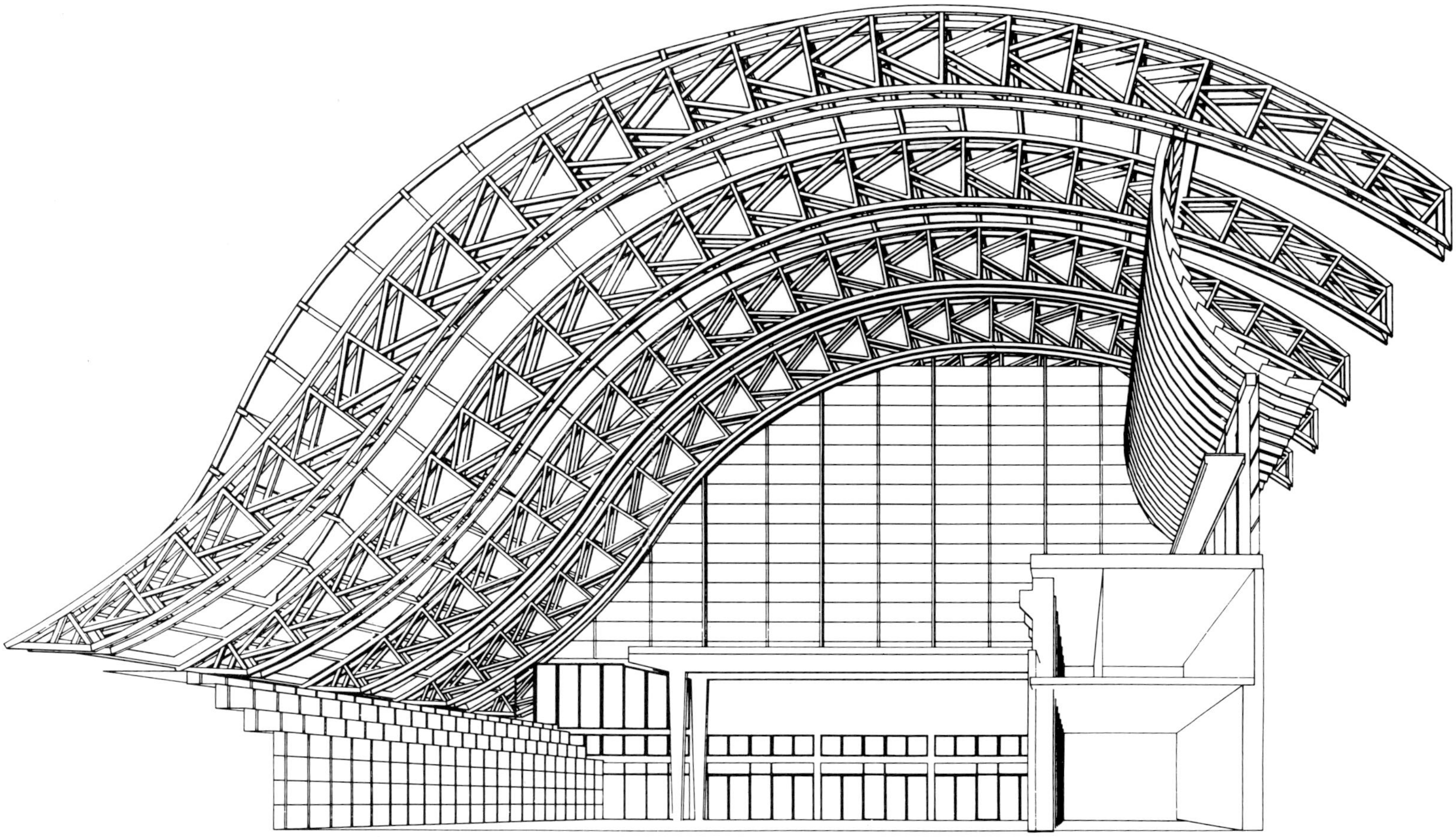

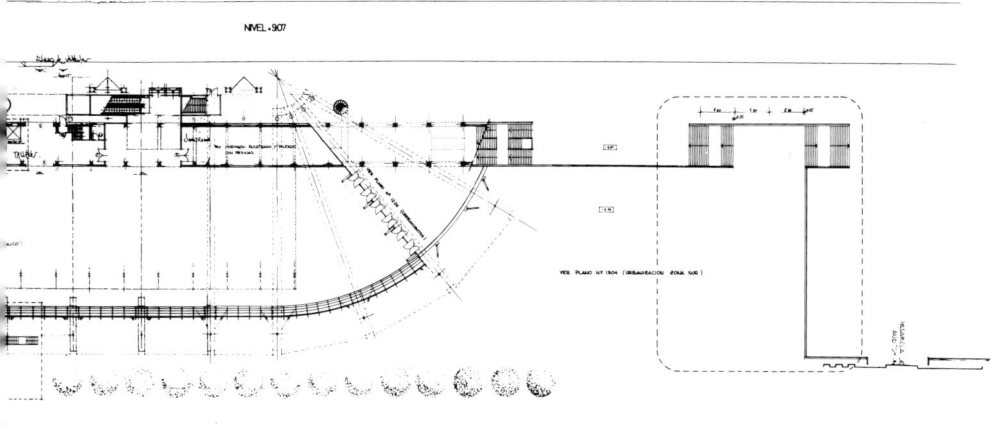

1. Preliminary section.
2. Plan.
3. Perspective section of the roof without the stone
arches.

4. View of the pavilion from the city of Sevilla.
5. The main façade from the gardens.
6. The tilted undulating roof that protects the pavilion from the hot afternoon sun.
7. Detail of the structural arches from which the roof is hung.

Harbourmaster's House, Olympic Port, Barcelona
1989-91

The port provides a visual link between the city of Barcelona and the Mediterranean. One of the principal objectives in the design of the new Olympic Port was to maintain an unimpeded view of the sea horizon from the promenade. In the past, port structures, industry and railways were placed in-between cutting people off from the sea.

Ports have their own buildings and these can intrude unless properly considered beforehand. To control this, and to adjust the aesthetic to meet future functional needs a standard 12 m x 12 m x 12 m cube was chosen as the basic spatial building block for at least three different buildings, only one of which, the Harbourmaster's House, was built. It has an area of 320 m².

The Harbourmaster's House is based on the same internal spiral composition of four quarter levels per floor as the earlier series of buildings represented by the Casa Almirall. In addition to accommodating the Harbourmaster, it. has offices for the Port Management, the Generalitat de Catalunya, the Coastguard or »Guardia Civil« and the Navy. The spatial arrangement proved ideal for this multi-tenantable use. An independent outside staircase was added for their use.

In addition to protecting the building from the intense heat in summer and hiding the unsightly air-conditioning machinery, a wood umbrella mounted on the roof also provides a picturesque conclusion to the cube while serving as a sheltered platform for viewing the entire port area. The external walls are sheathed in white marble fixed proud of the main wall structure on stainless steel clips in order to leave a ventilation gap as a further cooling measure. Internally, the public spaces are finished in light grey concrete blocks with floors of beige coloured linoleum.

1. Plans.
2. Aerial view.

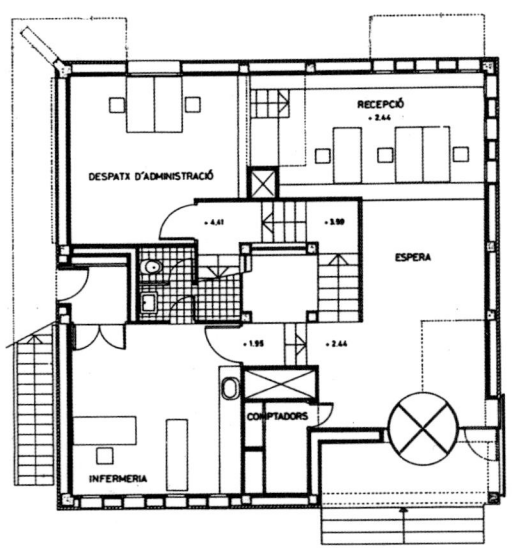
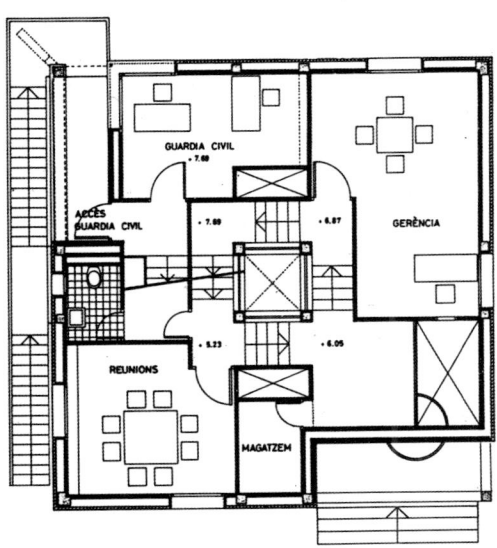
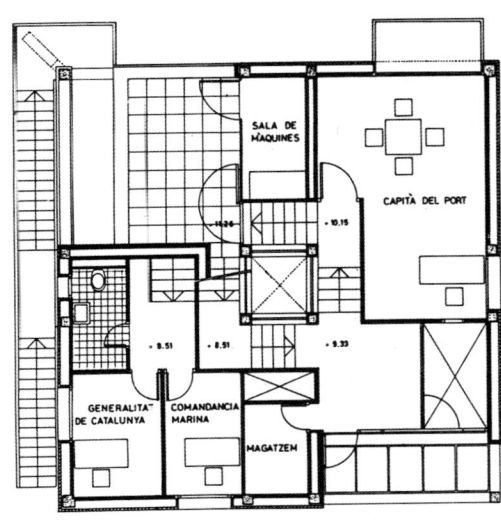

Ecclesiastical Interventions

One of the most beautiful examples of spatial orchestral compositions is the egress canopy from the sanctuary of the Black Virgin of Montserrat. Montserrat, or the sawn mountain, resembles the monoliths of Central Australia, the Olgas, and it seems strangely out of place so close to Barcelona, a serrated, jagged silhouette seen in the distance which looms ever larger as the pilgrim approaches the mountain.

Montserrat is one of those sites, like Delphi or Thingvellir in Iceland, where people feel centred in the universe. It is a natural *axis mundi*. As such, it is a rallying centre with special powers of attraction, a protective mountain in times of trouble where people can gather together and forget their differences in a common cause. The Virgin of Montserrat is the patron saint of Catalonia and an encouraging symbol for all Catalans.

It was Schiller who said that »Montserrat sucks a man in from the outer to the inner world«[71]. The egress canopy beside the sanctuary is a gentle intervention, an architectural umbrella held over the pilgrim as he or she emerges from Schiller's inner world, on their slow return to their own outer world.

Pressed between the rough conglomerate rock face and the west wall of the sanctuary, the egress is a narrow channel of space which is deflected two thirds along its length by a protruding chapel. The experience of emerging from the dimly lit sanctuary into the daylight and surrounded all around by the mountain is not unlike leaving the underworld. Candles flicker in their red glass holders. Overhead, a light barrel vault of perspex steps down the gentle incline, levitating on green painted steel I-beams built into the rock.

The perspex semi-cylinders break into separate vaults in individual steps, narrow vaults over the steeply inclined sections, longer horizontal sections where it is flatter, so we see through between each perspex vault to the trees and buildings beyond. Tactfully, the designers recognized any intrusion as a distraction, and so have provided this wonderfully sculptured permanent umbrella to shelter the pilgrim from the rain. What they have done is very simple. The problem of connecting the vaults on an inclined base has been avoided by dividing them into short lengths, a procedure which immeasurably enhances the richness and interest of the space.

Richness, too, is the hallmark of the renovated Romanesque remains of the Encamp Church, Andorra. MBM have re-roofed the ancient ruins with a protective slate roof which extends the interior forward of the dominating solid stone tower. This has been a job of working with the Romanesque fabric on equal terms. The new work is not subservient; it belongs to this century in its simple carefully calculated recall of Modernisme which is most apparent in the timber detailing and geometrical forms of the seating with their striking use of blue. The brilliant red ceiling washes away the coldness of the stone and responds to the sumptuousness and glitter of the gold altarpiece. Romanesque and Modern have been harmonized in this beautifully restrained interior. This is typical of MBM; the ability to deal with the past without belittling or betraying the present.

Egress Canopy of the Sanctuary of the Virgin of Montserrat, Monastery of Montserrat
1980–83

The Benedictine monastery at Montserrat is an important centre of learning and music besides its being the popular sanctuary of the image of the Black Virgin. Both the mountain and its monastery are focal spiritual symbols of the Catalan people. The religious devotion accorded to this strange abrupt rock formation is inexplicable simply in terms of its history – something more is involved. The identity of the Catalan people is indelibly tied to this particular site. Not surprisingly, it is now a popular pilgrimage and tourist attraction.

The massive queues of people lining up in preparation to filing past the image of the Black Virgin which stands behind the main altar conflict with the dignity of the Benedictine liturgy. The two needed to be isolated by the construction of an alternate route to and from the image behind the altar. This was achieved by cutting an entry through the south chapel on one side. This established a route through a narrow pass between the church and the nearby rock face over which towers the mountain. The architects covered this passage with a lightly framed steel vault structure covered by clear plastic. The vaults overlap and step down the slope. Instead of resting the canopy legs on the ground, the steel supports are fixed in the rock face to allow pilgrims to move unhindered and in direct contact with the mountain itself – an essential complement to the image of the Virgin of Montserrat.

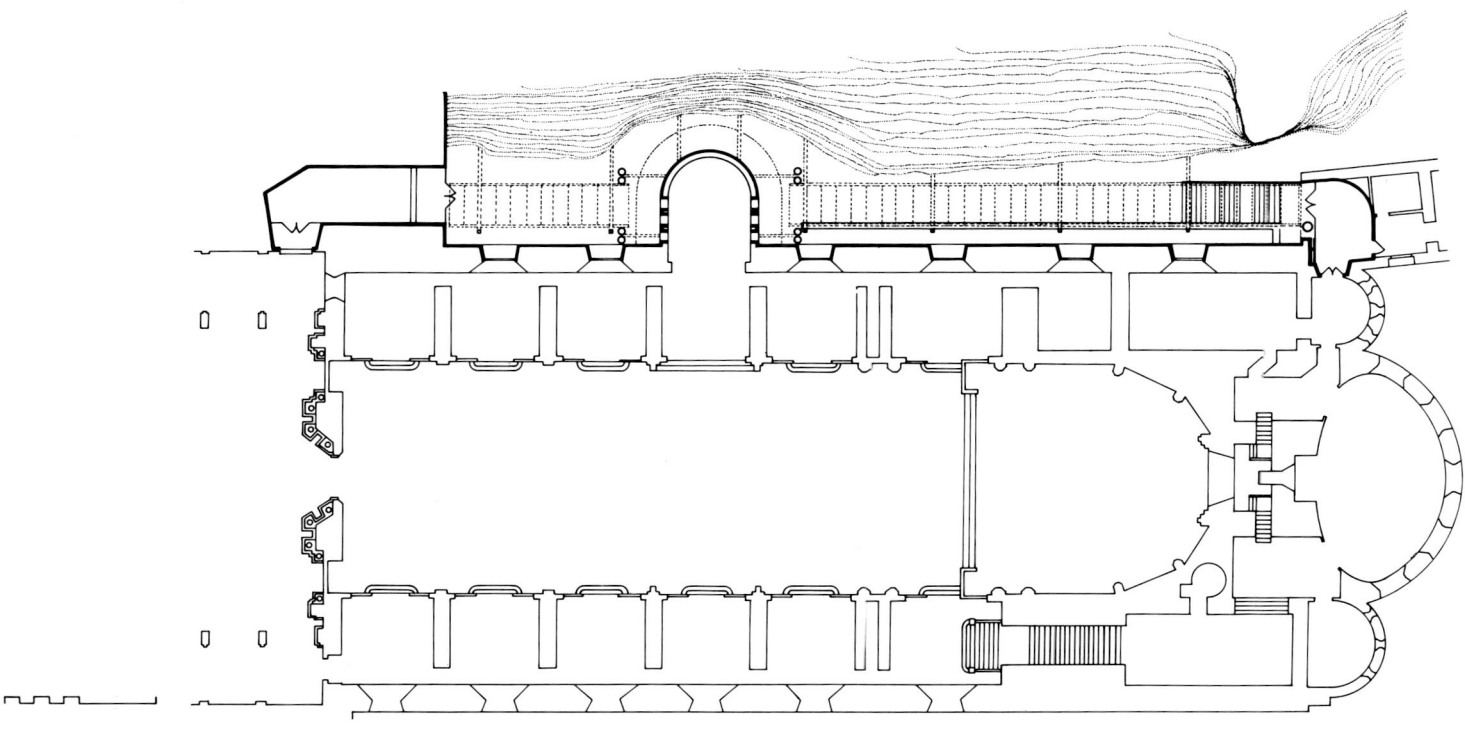

1. Plan showing the covered way between the
monastery church and the mountain.
2. The light transparent roof that provides a fragile
cover to the pilgrims.

Restoration and Refurbishment of the Parish Church of Santa Eulàlia d'Encamp, Encamp, Andorra
1987–89

The Pyrenees are richly endowed with Romanesque churches. They were mostly sited at the edge or just beyond the village because they served the parish scattered along the valleys or on the mountain sides in addition to the villagers. Half urban and half rural, they were a mixture, neither one thing nor the other. In this regard, Santa Eulàlia is quite typical.

With the passing of time the church had become something of an »ugly duckling« in Andorran architectural heritage. A hole was left by the removal of the cemetery to the north of the church and this was being used as a car park. The apse had been torn down in the 1930s and replaced by a nondescript wall, and the inside gained an ugly suspended asbestos ceiling and a crude cement tiled floor. The original beauty of this eleventh-century building was hidden behind the recently added finishes and ornaments which, no matter how worthy as objects of devotion, contributed little to the enhancement of the original.

The aim of the work was twofold: one, to restore the historical monument itself and above all its setting, and two, to increase the capacity of the church which proved inadequate on such occasions as weddings, funerals, and the principal religious celebrations. Additional accommodation was needed so it could properly fulfil its function as a parish centre.

The parish rooms, one of which acted as an annex to the church, were located in the hole on the north. The roof at this place formed a new public space. Since the existing somewhat ugly concrete retaining wall was still exposed, a long porch was provided running parallel alongside the church nave to cover it. The parish office is at one end of this. Curved suncatchers admit light to the rooms below.

The nave was extended eastward, the popular Baroque reredos relocated on the new east wall, in-between, the nave is flooded with light and views to the outside shut-out. The new and the old are clearly distinguished to avoid confusion. The aim here was to respect the traditions of church architecture going back 1000 years into the past without compromising the expression of the present day.

During construction the base of the original walls of the eleventh-century apse were discovered and this necessitated a change in the design to accommodate the different floor levels and the interruption due to the unusual placement of the baptismal font.

The acoustics of the church were carefully considered to ensure that in its role as a parish centre it would perform well on such varied occasions as concerts, and mixed social, civic and religious gatherings.

1. View from the south showing the new extension to the right of the twelfth-century bell tower.
2. The public court on the north side of the church.

3. View towards the new east extension.
4. View from the community hall towards the altar.
5. Plans (main floor and roof).

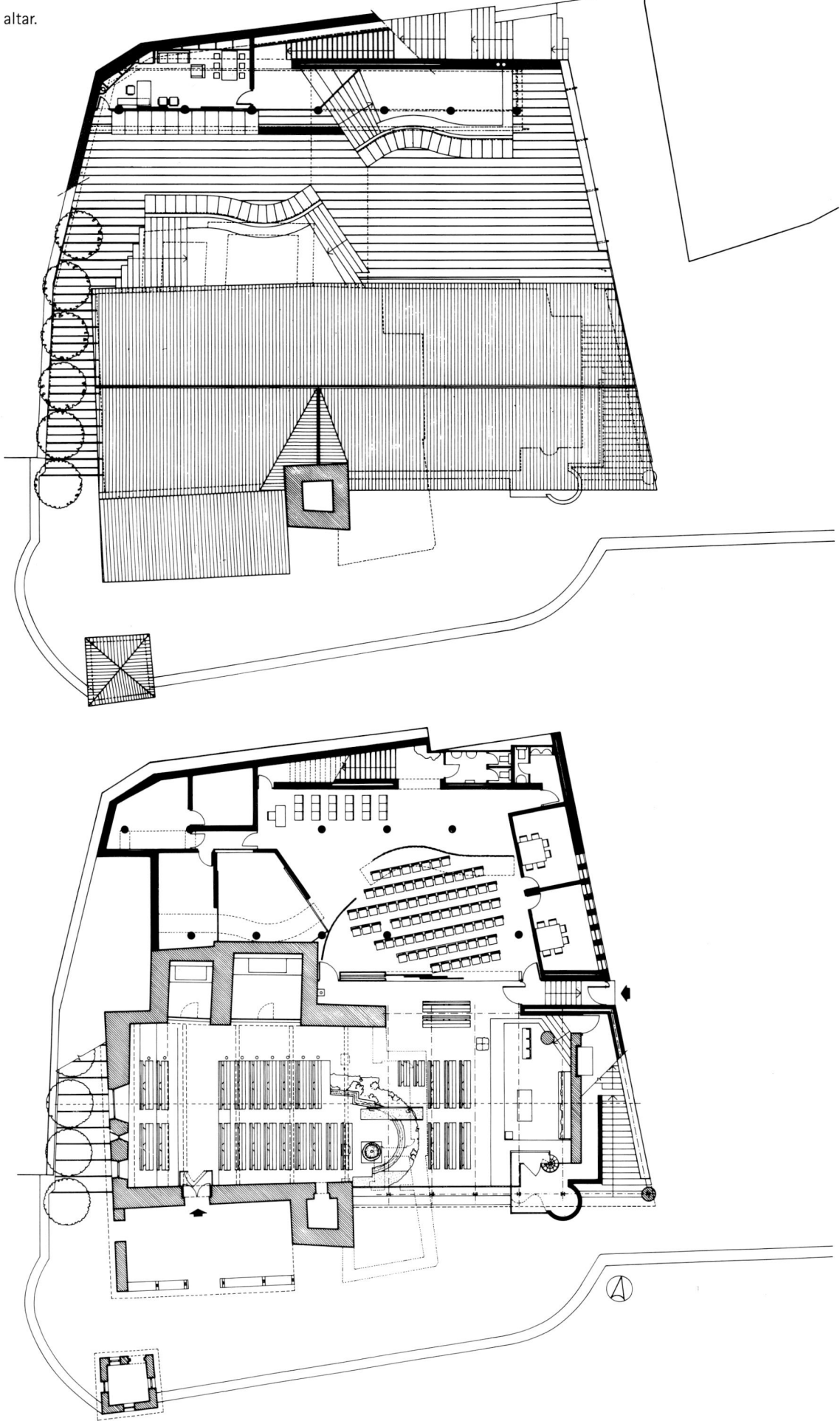

Urban Design and Parks

In the city, buildings are less volumes in space, less sculptural objects lacking physical boundaries, than the urban equivalent of walls and piers which subdivide and channel urban space into its constituent rooms and hallways. Buildings frame the spaces; they define and organize space by the creation of screens, gateways, and foci within the city.

MBM's designs for their Berlin housing should be seen in the showcase context of an international collection of leading architecture in the tradition established at the Weissenhof settlement at Stuttgart back in 1927, and the approach owes something to the Expressionism of Hans Scharoun's house, though there is a suggestion of Constructivism in the Kochstrasse entry porches.

In the competition scheme, the Friedrichstadt architecture is two things: a civic scenery meant to monumentalize the street so it becomes an important and dignified focus for everyday life, but behind the sober façades and rhythmic colonnades, it is all quite different. The internal edges, the second layer, are far more sculptural, shaped according to internal necessities, but masked so they do not disturb the equanimity of the street.

Two brooding towers with steep hipped roofs guard the entry from Wilhelmstrasse, from here, the space spreads out with avenues of trees on either side. On one side, abounding Zimmerstrasse, set back behind an impressive crescent-shaped colonnade, the block has a curiously serrated inside edge interrupted by openings every so often in an unpredictable manner. Mannerism and Classicism appear to have discovered a common principle. The upper two storeys of the Zimmerstrasse block have an open colonnade such as one met with in the Mollet Mansana.

The Friedrichstadt Residential Unit demonstrates the extent of MBM's facility, the firm's ability to translate its ideas on housing to a quite different cultural and urban milieu without any apparent hesitation or tension. The forms have a confident German feel to them, as much as the Barcelona housing is Catalan.

In the later project, built or under construction, the Kochstrasse apartment buildings are designed as three identical units linked in series, each with its formally assertive porch, indicating its function as the main entrance or »gateway«, over which a gallery provides a unifying horizontal element between all three. The built residential wings thrust out into the interior of the block, reinterpreting a traditional Berlin urban form.

The Villa Olímpica (1985-92) is the most ambitious housing project to date, both in terms of the complex requirements for the Games and afterwards, and in terms of its large size. The challenge is to avoid monotony and undue repetition without arbitrariness.

The project fell into two parts: the great curved eastern wall of housing that intersects with the Passeig de Carles I and looks back across to the extended Ciutadella Park, and the three superblocks along and behind the Avinguda del Litoral. One is an edge, the others are islands surrounded by streets with a protected nucleus of open space.

The Mendebaldea square and enclosure in Pamplona (1986-92) was devised with the intention of imposing some degree of order on a disorganized part of Pamplona. It is a fairly typical type form with the important difference that one side has been left open to allow the outside landscape to invade the central space. The strategy adopted in this instance was to construct the square with a dual alignment, the first to indicate the scale of the porticoed square itself, and the second to adjust the new intervention to the heights of the other highrise blocks and towers in the vicinity and so create a gradual transition between the new and the existing. This was accomplished by two U-shaped walls, the outer higher than the inner one, a paved square, avenues of trees and a diagonal V-*pèrgola* which links the inside with the outside. A pedestrian walkway between the two blocks at first floor level provides access to apartments and shops. There are a series of stairs connecting it to the principal points of entry to the square.

The square has been reserved for pedestrians and is entered through two impressive gateways. Some traffic is allowed into the square.

The other important element was the provision of a generous park nearby on the south as a retreat from the oppressive traffic on the north. This was achieved by forming a semi-enclosed block which abutted the traffic on one side while it opened onto the park on the other.

In 1989, MBM were engaged on a series of successful urban design projects in Siena, Birmingham, Hamburg, followed by Aix-en-Provence and Clichy, Paris, a year later. In two (Siena and Aix-en-Provence), they were awarded first prizes from among a selection of international entries. These schemes all have a great deal in common in that they seek to preserve the existing urban morphology and stress the role of the street as an urban artifact and scenic backdrop to everyday city life. The street is deployed to lend a quality of nobility to public life, a dimension of grandeur (almost of monumentality) to the special rituals of city living. But the street has an even more formidable contribution to make as the chief organizing element, in partnership with the public square and block, in the city composition.

These recent urban experiments since Nova Icària apply the previous ideas and can be classified into two categories: those which emphasize the city network of pathways generated by a grid of semi-closed cells; and the ribbon or linear pattern expressing movement. In one, the street and square are related in the traditional manner of Renaissance urbanism, in the other, an assembly of parallel zones steps back from some physical or topographical edge.

The Birmingham Business Exchange, Open-enclosure of Grasbrook, Hamburg, and Aix-en-Provence proposals illustrate the former model with varying degrees of complexity and statements of closure, but in each, the city fabric has been expressed in terms of a basic cell structure. This becomes the building block of the city.

The second ribbon or strip pattern which responds more to the needs of traffic than the city, is illustrated by the scheme for the bus-pedestrian interchange for Siena and the ambitious new development proposal for Clichy by the Seine. The Clichy proposal is reminiscent of the Barcelona waterfront scheme with its combination of roadway, park and water edge with long curvilinear building façades providing the man-made counterpart to the natural edge of the river bank and some measure of continuous closure.

The Siena project is one of MBM's most interesting to date. It is located in the Piazza Gramsci next to the Viale Federico Tozzi and incorporates the historic Palazzo Ciacci. The bus interchange has been placed under the ground level parallel to the Viale Federico Tozzi and this function is allowed to dictate the west façade treatment in stepped layers. The main form curves around into the square against the irregular shapes of the surrounding buildings and then tilts itself returning behind the cylindrical drum of the theatre next to the Palazzo Ciacci. MBM have not been able to resist the temptation to express the ideal city as it was depicted by Piero della Francesca, but they have transformed his serene circular temple in the centre of the square into a Constructivist theatre in the round with its ligaments and musculature exhibited in an arresting and thoroughly twentieth-century way. The form of the building has been determined by the requirements of the motor vehicle, it is linear and irregular and designed to fit neatly into the available space of the city. The façades respond to the space and forms nearby, on the east, the façade is a gentle concave transparent curtain which wraps around behind the assertive cylinder of the theatre. A pedestrian bridge and ramps connect the two entities.

Aix-en-Provence is a far more developed proposal. Two precincts one along the Rue Tardieu, the other focusing on the Place de la Rotonde have been linked to construct a rough »Z« by diagonals welding the top and bottom bars of the urban figure. The diagonal slash is occupied by a conference facility, casino, and a Salle de Spectacle. These are served by a bus and rail interchange. Once again the city block with its empty centre has been reapplied in a widely varied range of shapes which are ruptured at selected locations to plug them into the city's lines of movement.

Following their reconstruction of the Barcelona waterfront, MBM have applied similar notions of edge to the south bank of the Seine at Clichy, Paris. This is an extensive proposal for three sectors: the Cables de Lyon, Porte de Seine and GDF/Dupont, affecting an area of some 400,000 m². In essence, the architects have stationed nine towers along the river bank with their feet in the water. Behind them is a deep park combining water and land forms in a recreational landscape. This is bordered by a serpentine roadway with regular avenue planting whose alignment is reinforced along much of its length by curvilinear building forms which curl around at the ends to form stops. This formal punctuation in the city forms ties into the existing avenues and bridge crossings of the Seine.

MBM designed many parks, seeing the park as a special kind of urban architecture, employing different materials, but engaging similar principles of order, arrangement, movement, perspective, and placing of art. In Spain, there is a lack of differentiation between the landscape architect and the architect. Besides their La Creueta del Coll Park, Barcelona (1981-87), and Sant Oleguer Sports and Leisure Park, Sabadell (1983-86), MBM prepared schemes for parks at Rosario (1980) and Córdoba, Argentina (1981), the La Città Rifugio della Natura for the Triennale di Milano, Turin (1987), and the Urban Park at Gerona (1988).

The Sports and Leisure Park at Sabadell and the Park de la Creueta del Coll were conceived as urban spaces. They are extremely architectural and geometric in their layout, much more open and hard than is normal in northern Europe. The landscape, even in the cooler winter months, is dusty. Dust is everywhere. Hence the park is less of a metaphor for paradise, than urban spaces, which have been designed to provide relief from the congestion of the housing block, somewhere for children to play in safety away from motor cars, for old people to rest, and for families to stroll in.

The swimming pool, designed for masses of people in summer, is the focus of the park. It is here that there is a concentration of planting and activity. MBM's most important achievement, the large park set on the hill at Creueta del Coll in the centre of a neighbourhood, is sited in a large abandoned quarry. Water is an organizing medium, from the ornamental pool above the main swimming basin, water serves to unite the various outdoor spaces and becomes the central focus of the park. Things go on around it, the circular edge of the water is continued on to complete the circle as a shaded esplanade, irregular terraces, carved out of the hillside and raised on rock embankments, stare down at the lake. A palm-covered rectangular stage juts into the water at the centre.

Above the water basin, Eduardo Chillida's massive horned concrete block dangles from four steel cables anchored in the old quarry rock face, its inverted reflection reaching upwards to the pronged arms of the suspended sculpture. The entrance to the park is announced by a tall corten steel totem from Ellsworth Kelly.

The clear order at the centre evaporates towards the edges as it spreads outwards into nature, becomes less regular and more assimilated with the geology and terrain of its rugged surroundings. It is a mixture of geometry and geometry-in-decay, order giving way to disorder, to more complex forms. The details, as exemplified by the large pipe handrails on the upper terraces, are bold and in keeping with the scale of the park. The esplanade has a light expanded metal mesh shade *pèrgola* linking the entrance to the farther end of the water basin by way of a circular route circumnavigating the square.

The Sant Oleguer Sports and Leisure Park at Sabadell (1986) contains running tracks and athletics facilities besides the large 100 metre diameter swimming basin, changing rooms, and adjoining parkland. The pool is intersected by a serpentine promenade which has a stepped landing for access to the water at two points, and an island with a small harbour on one side for boats. Quite a bit larger and much more open than the park at Creueta del Coll, the planning is more formal and simpler. Linear and serpentine motifs intertwine. This combination was repeated for the nature refuge at Turin where angled buildings are placed along axes and treated as sculptures mounted in a landscape dominated by a serpentine canal and linear avenues.

The park is a special type of urban space, one in which there is a reference to the natural, however casual or brief, and acknowledgement of the wider biological connections to growing things left behind outside the city, of a paradise at the beginning of historic time from which man was expelled when he commenced his journey to self-consciousness. It is typical of MBM as members of the »third generation« of Modern architects[72] that they should view architecture as subservient to space, to its room-making function in the city.

Friedrichstadt City Block, Kochstrasse/Friedrichstrasse, Südliche Friedrichstadt, Berlin
IBA competition, 1st prize
1981

The proposal for »City Block 4« was made in the wider context of laying out four blocks which together constitute the sector adjoining the Berlin Wall dividing West and East Berlin. There were a number of fundamental criteria: these were the maintenance of the street as a primary urban generator and the creation within each block of public space with an independent structure of its very own so as to give each block a unique character. In the case of the street, this meant building up to the street alignment and stressing its form.

These two criteria were answered by the use of a single architectural device; that of linear blocks which simultaneously defined the street on one side, while they contained and isolated the interior space within each block on the other. The ends of these long blocks have been emphasized by the addition of towers which also strengthen the containment of the inside space. As emphatic gestures, the towers emphasize the identity of the enclosed space at the same time relating it to the prevailing urban grid outside it.

A three-storey car park was designed in the gap left between the north building and the Zimmerstrasse. This car park, placed between the residential block and the Berlin Wall, was used to hide the Wall so it could not be seen. It also made it possible to convert the entire ground floor into commercial premises when the Wall was taken down, thus presenting a lively façade to the Zimmerstrasse. With the removal of the Wall, the car park enabled the Zimmerstrasse to take on the appearance of a street.

1. Perspective of the interior of the city block looking towards Friedrichstrasse.
2. Perspective along Kochstrasse looking towards Wilhelmstrasse. Note the introduction of the curve to recover the former character of a street saloon.

3. Site plan of the four city blocks around the
Friedrichstrasse-Kochstrasse crossing.
4. Axonometric view.
5. Elevations.

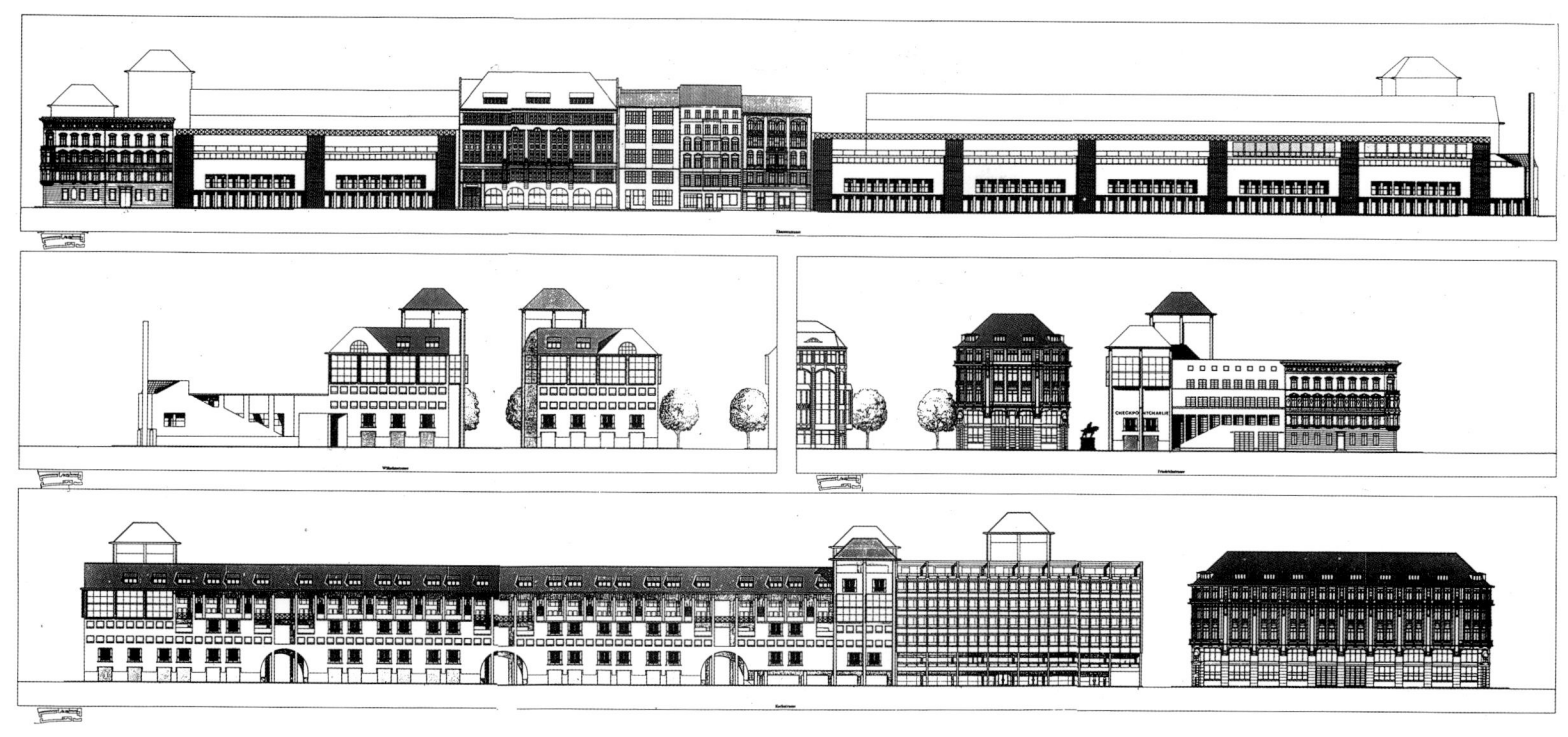

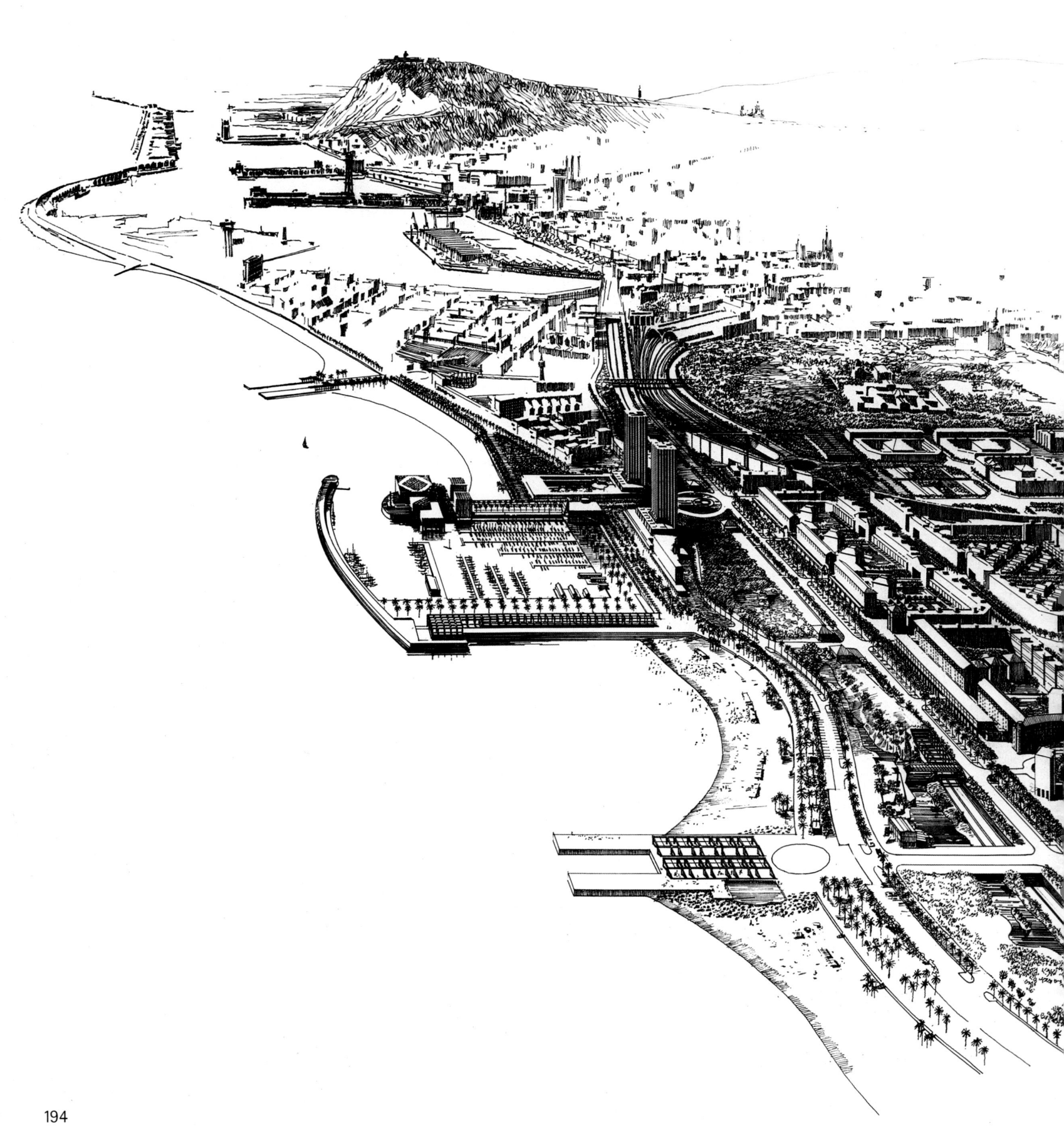

1. Perspective view looking towards Montjuïc and the old city.

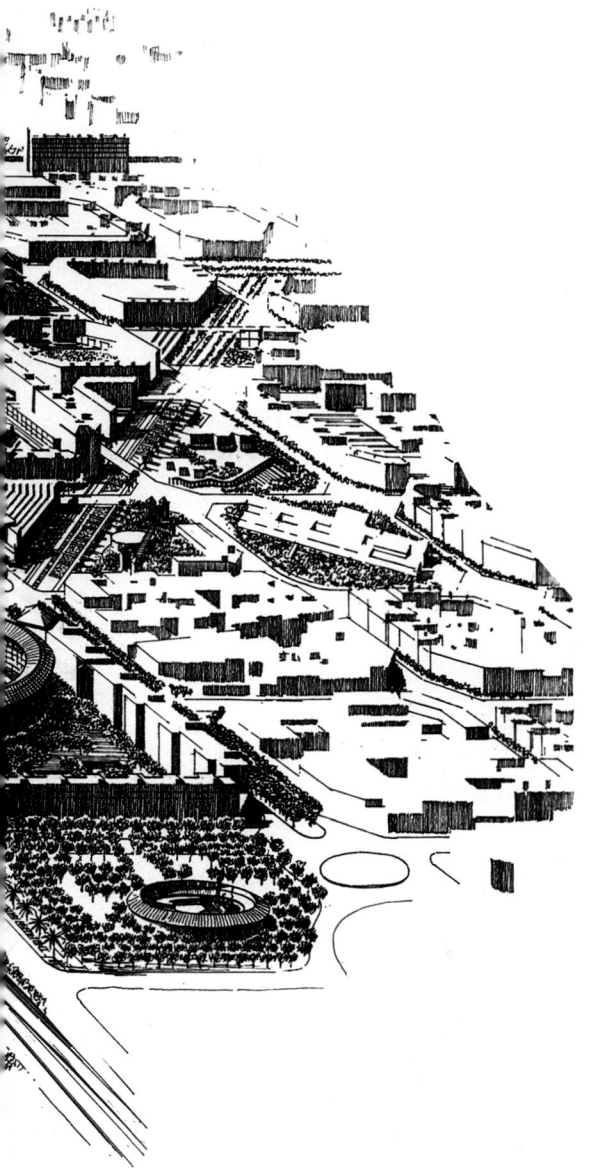

Nova Icària, Olympic Village, Barcelona
1985-92

Commencing in 1980, the City of Barcelona determined that it would set about reconstructing the city by means of specially targeted projects applied to key nodes in the urban fabric. Later, the plan was enlarged to tackle problems that were metropolitan in scope. This ambitious plan included four areas which lay between the nineteenth-century grid and the 1960s suburban sprawl. One of these was a disused triangular shaped area jammed between the Old City and the neighbourhood of Poblenou. The redevelopment of this sector would realize the historic ambition of Barcelona for contact with the shoreline of the Mediterranean which, until recent times, had been blocked by the presence of the port and industry. The 1992 Olympics provided the requisite impetus to implement the proposal.

The project affected a site of 79 hectares separated from the city by railway lines. It contained disused factories and warehouses mostly from the nineteenth century and a handful of houses. Thirty-five families were displaced and relocated in new homes nearby. The bulk of the area was to form the basis of the new neighbourhood. Now called Nova Icària, the design is based on three premises:

1. reconstitution of all infrastructures, i.e. beaches, railways, coastal ring-road, and the metropolitan network of storm-drainage and sewage that runs through the site,

2. continuation of the traditional Barcelona morphology of the corridor street, but in such a manner as to adapt it to new building typologies developed as a result of the impact of the Modern Movement in the twentieth century, together with appropriate consideration of sunlight, ventilation, gardens, etc.,

3. integration of the social and formal design qualities of the neighbourhood whilst providing for mixed use of the public and private spaces and buildings, along with a range of architectural proposals.

The design method involved several stages; first the definition of the neighbourhood for the consideration of individual buildings and the spaces between them, each stage involving an increasing number of teams of architects to a total of 35 at the end of 1989.

About 2,500 dwellings were to be built, as well as shops, offices and hotels making in total 530,000 m^2 of built floor area not including underground car parks. This will result in a gross density of 0.68 m^2. Buildings occupy 26% of the land, the rest is public pace split between streets (26%), parks (36%) and the shoreline promenade (12%).

2. View of the sunken garden, one of a series of features along the shore-line park.
3. Axonometric view of the urban centre of the Olympic Village.

4. View along the Avinguda de Carles I looking towards the Mediterranean Sea showing how the Olympic Village fits to the nineteenth-century Cerdà plan.

Square in Mendebaldea, Pamplona
1986-92

The motive of the Pamplona City Council in constructing a public square in the middle of an area of new development was to impose a precise urban form on what was seen as a disorderly chaotic part of the city. The scheme imposes an overall architectural framework and, by this means, seeks to coordinate the contributions of different architects each of whom is involved in developing private buildings around the square. This presented difficulties in terms of harmonizing the individual development and architectural concerns. The project applied principles which have a long tradition in the history of the European city, namely, the creation of squares and streets as basic urban building blocks with special attention to paving and the façades and less emphasis on the differentiation of building types and expression of private uses.

The object was one of organizing the volumes and façades, the exact definition of these elements in order to establish a strong urban space as a focus, while at the same time allowing each architect a degree of freedom to develop their projects as they wished behind the public space and façade of the square.

The highrise blocks and towers in the vicinity of the square posed a particularly difficult problem; this was how to establish a satisfactory relationship between them and the new buildings surrounding the square. This was resolved by constructing a second outer ring surrounding the square itself of higher buildings to serve as a transition. In this way, the central square maintained the dimensions and visual characteristics of a more traditional urban space without violating the scale and character of the new Pamplona.

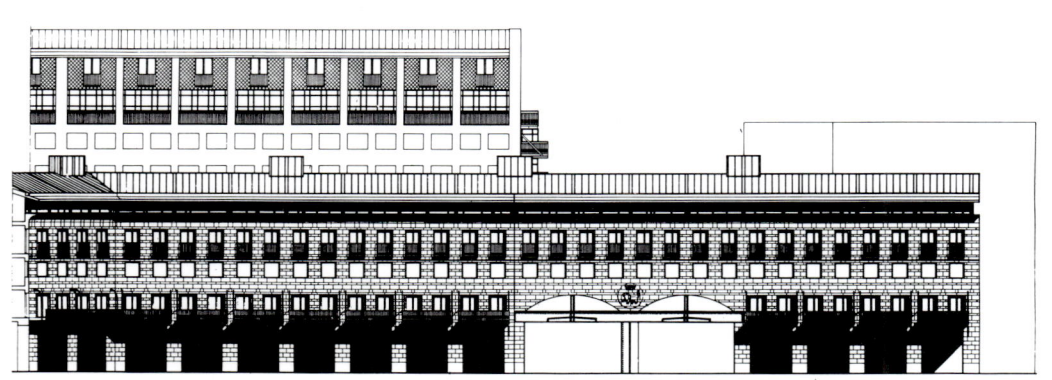

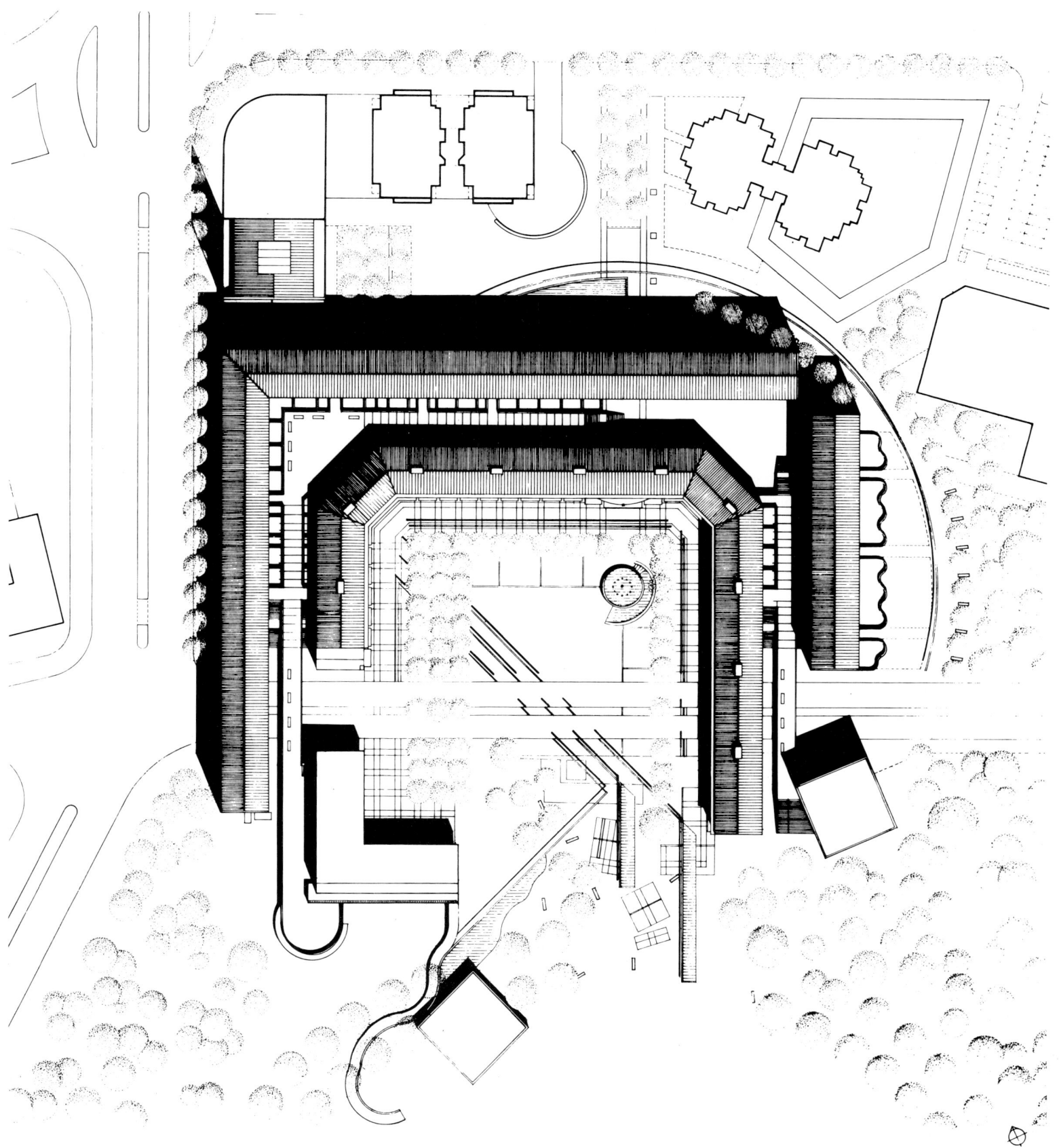

1. Elevation of the façade behind which the other architects and developers attached their buildings.
2. Façade detail.
3. Site plan showing the grouping of the two rings open to the south and containing the new public space.

»Un Progetto per Siena«, Piazza Matteotti and Piazza Gramsci, Siena
International competition, 1st prize
1988

The project was initiated by a two-stage International Competition. A requirement was the provision of new accommodation for the Chamber of Commerce and Europe's oldest bank, the Monte dei Paschi of Siena on a site between two squares next to the entrance to the historic city. It is located at the beginning of a route that culminates in the famous Piazza del Campo. The critical task posed by the competition was to somehow design a public space between and including the two squares so as to allow it to function as an urban filter for the old city, at the same time relating the two squares and the new buildings which replaced the existing forty-year-old »dam-like« Chamber of Commerce, while retaining the old Palazzo Ciacci. This was asking a great deal.

MBM were successful in competition with such celebrated names as Giancarlo De Carlo, Oswald Mathias Ungers, Siza Vieira, Natalini, Ralph Erskine, Peter Eisenman, Pagliara, Gregotti Associati, Giorgio Grassi. Their design created a maximum of public space and kept the existing floor levels of the Palazzo Ciacci. The new building was lengthened at the same time preserving the roof line below the eaves of the adjoining Palazzo. The connection of the new building to the palace was accomplished by means of ramps above street level and by other connections below it.

The new office building has two façades: a rigid brick façade on the south to match the formality of the »modern« blocks on the opposite side of the road; and an articulated timber-and-glass façade on the north side to reflect the collection of Sienese houses as well as to assist the pedestrian movement between the two squares. The unfinished east wall of the neighbouring palace is hidden by a circular auditorium and contract hall for the Chamber of Commerce.

The Piazza Matteotti was left undisturbed to avoid interrupting the continuity of its traditional weekly market. Most of the contracts between farmers and distributors which are initiated in the Piazza or the bar (which is to be relocated on the ground floor at the bow of the new building) are later concluded in the nearby contract hall.

Another important aspect is the bus station. It was located on the ground floor of the new building to enable the Piazza Gramsci, presently congested by buses, to once again function as a public space serving the city.

1. General plan showing the urban context of the new public spaces.

2. Perspective view of the low building that forms
the main entrance to the old city.
3. Perspective view showing the relation of the new
buildings to the Palazzo Ciacci.

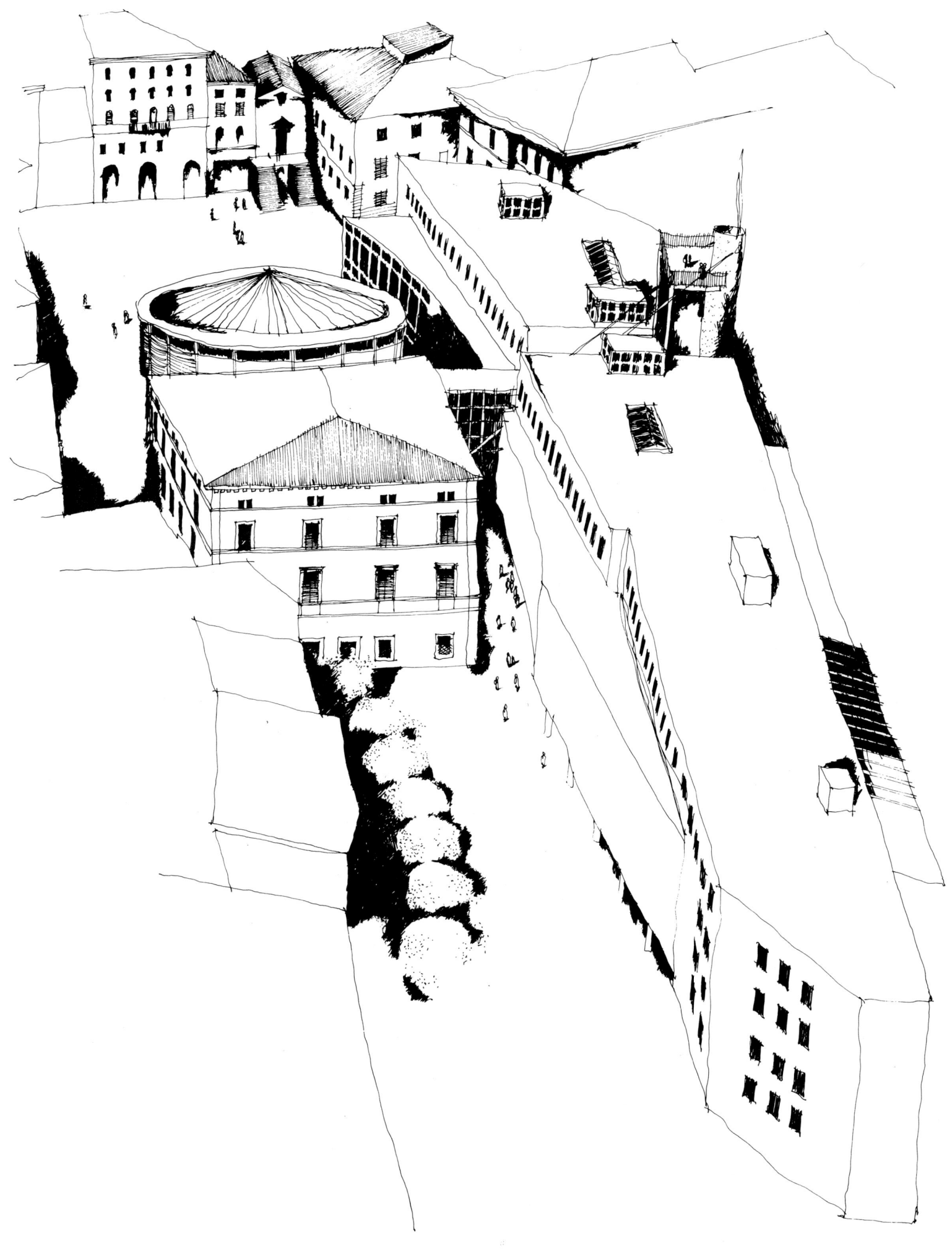

»Opération Sextius-Mirabeau«, Aix-en-Provence

International competition, 1st prize
1990
In collaboration with F. Guy/R. Inglesakis (Atelier 9), Marseille, and J. P. Siame,
Aix-en-Provence

Founded by Augustus Caesar as a Roman colony, Aix-en-Provence lies just north of Marseilles. A former provincial capital and a University since 1409, it is famous for its hot mineral springs, notably the sextius, and the Cours Mirabeau, a splendid tree-lined avenue that links the old city to the eighteenth- and nineteenth-century grid extension of the city to the south.

The Cours Mirabeau, La Rotonde, once began in front of the main railway station terminal. This and the numerous railway lines have now been removed leaving a huge vacant space which has been filled in the interim by a car park and bus terminal. A railway line cuts across south of this and an internal link road is planned which stops short of the entrance to this dusty bowl. Beyond it, the new leafy suburban blocks of dwellings are inhabited by middle and professional classes displaced from the multi-racial port of Marseilles. For some decades, Aix has urgently needed to link the two parts of the city without losing its natural car park or sacrificing its busy network of high-quality specialist shops and restaurants.

The MBM, Atelier 9 and Siame submission won the International Competition in tough competition with such invited participants as Richard Meier, Gregotti Associati, Vasconi, Anselmi, Kurokawa, AUSIA, Richard Rogers, and Jean Nouvel.

The urban problem posed by Aix is typical of many European cities: how to recover land from the displacement of industry and railway terminals at the centre of old cities. The 1960s and 1970s often ignored the form and identity of the city in tackling such problems and the challenge was to learn from these mistakes and to ensure the urban fabric was not rent in a similar manner.

The urban design proposal for the off-centre Sextius-Mirabeau seeks to complete the urban fabric paying particular attention to the edges. This will include such things as the enclosure of La Rotonde, the conservation of the gardens sloping down to the south on the northern edge, and the transposition of the housing blocks on the west and their integration into the street pattern of the new neighbourhood. One option was the displacement of the Mirabeau axis and its replacement by a series of smaller urban rooms similar in their pattern to those of the old city. This added another edge to the Cours Mirabeau. The other option of lengthening the historically mature Mirabeau would have cheapened both the new and the old, without either benefitting much, and with the attendant risk of downplaying the centre whilst encouraging a regressive gesture towards strengthening what was considered as a heroic vocabulary symptomatic of autocracy. In the end, the centre was not moved but reinforced at its present location.

The public spaces have been strictly defined without, at the same time, seeking to freeze the architecture, and in such a manner as to permit the very natural process of rebuilding to occur flexibly to accommodate the unforeseen contributions from many sources. This poses a dilemma for the architects: that of delaying the definition of the final architectural result, to allow a certain latitude while giving clear instructions to serve as a guide for the later stages of building.

1. General plan of the winning design of the competition.

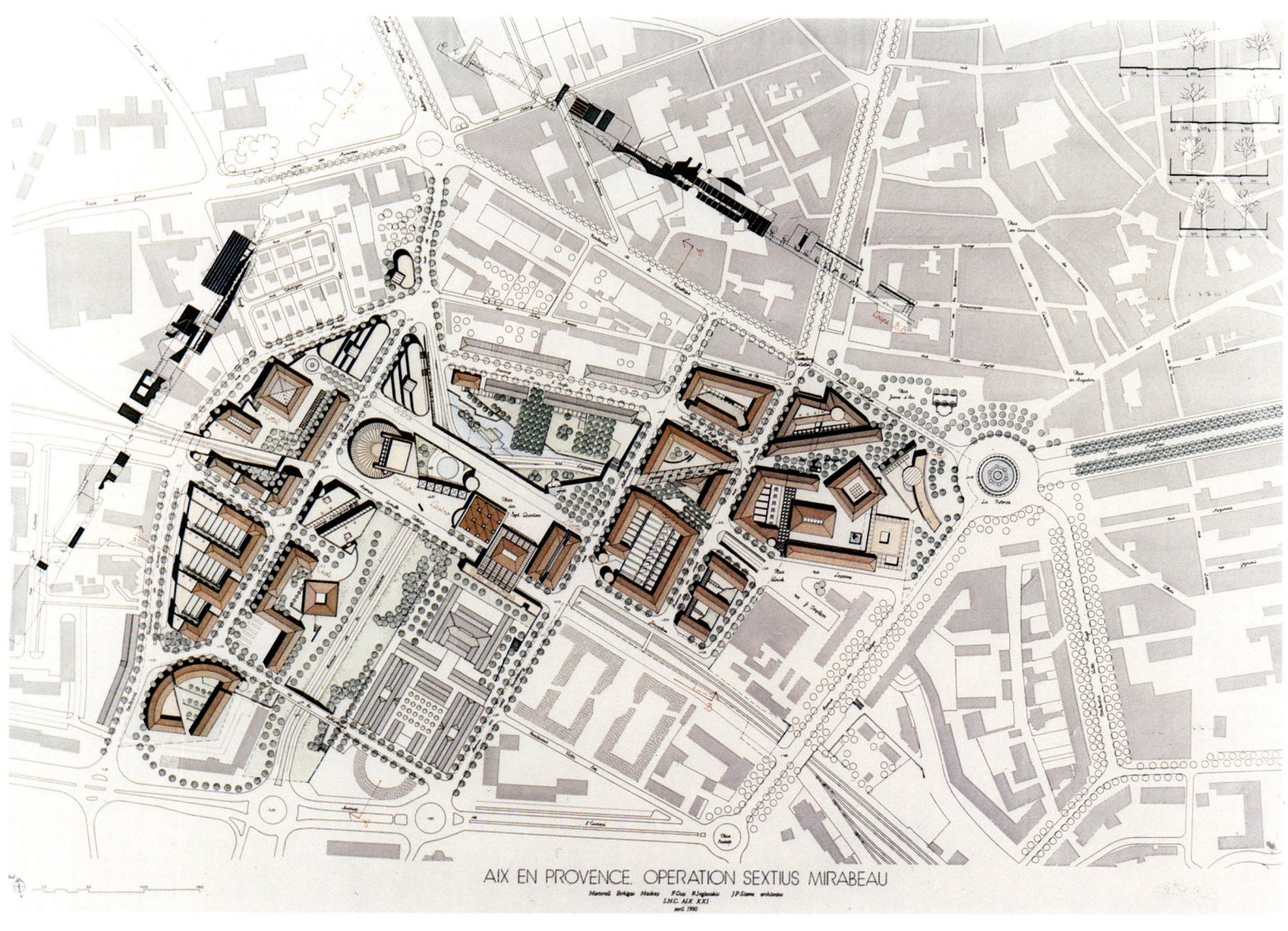

AIX EN PROVENCE. OPERATION SEXTIUS MIRABEAU

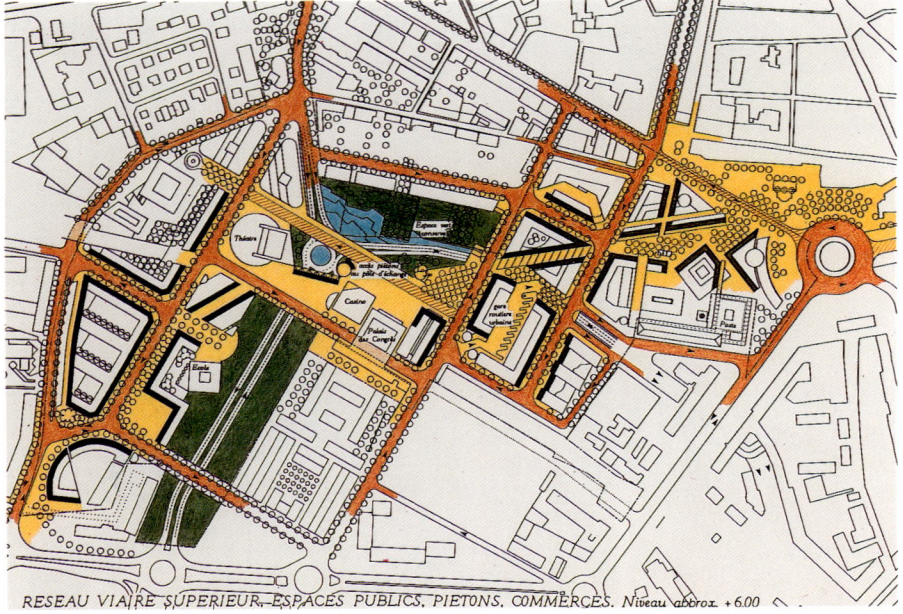

RESEAU VIAIRE SUPERIEUR, ESPACES PUBLICS, PIETONS, COMMERCES. *Niveau approx. +6.00*

2–4. Schemes of the street, the public spaces, the railway station, the car parking and the motorway connection.
5. Perspective of the pedestrian spine that will link the divided city.

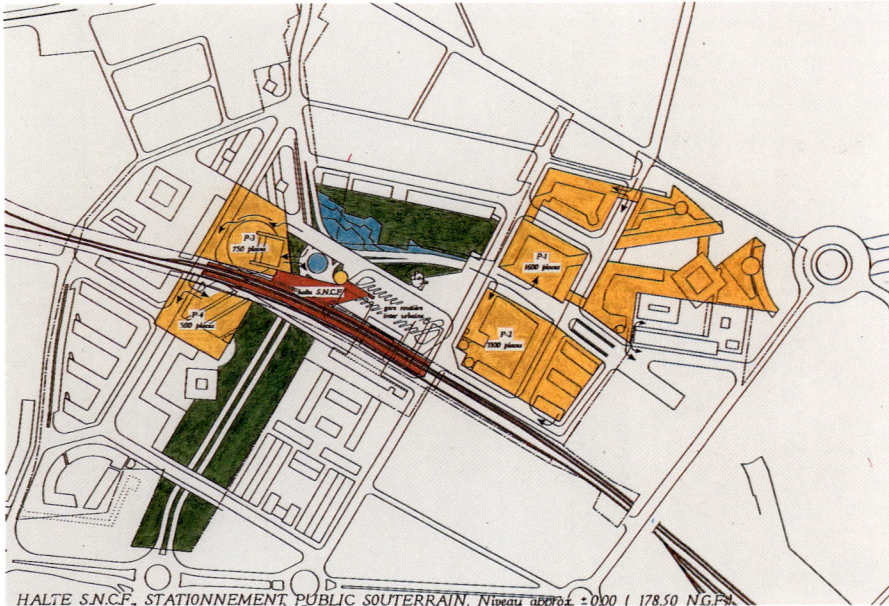

HALTE S.N.C.F. STATIONNEMENT PUBLIC SOUTERRAIN. *Niveau approx. ±0.00 (178.50 N.G.F.).*

RESEAU VIAIRE INFERIEUR. GARE ROUTIERE INTER URBAINE. *Niveau approx. -6.00.*

Sant Oleguer Sports and Leisure Park, Sabadell
1983-86

Sabadell is an industrial city near Barcelona which grew rapidly in the 1960s in a somewhat haphazard way that was typical of Spain in that decade. Industry and housing expanded quickly but without essential physical and social infrastructure. The new democratic municipal councils, aided by financial help from the autonomous government, sought to remedy this lack. In Sabadell, the huge working class population had few facilities for sport and leisure. A dilapidated running track in the seedy industrial wasteland in the valley of the heavily polluted river Ripoll which ran through the north of the city, provided a start for the new leisure centre.

The programme was intended to transform this industrial wasteland into a public park with an open-air swimming pool with picnic areas and to renovate the athletics track.

The social and formal success of the project hinged on the scale of the urban design. A circular pool 100 m in diameter, similar to that of Moscow, and a series of agricultural basins near Lleida supplied the basic framework of the new park. The pool is crossed by a tree-lined causeway which helps to integrate it into the overall structure of the park. This pool is bounded by a hard »beach« paved with concrete slabs containing drainage for overflow water and links up with the platform in which a porch housing the changing rooms and refreshment facilities is situated. The open space around the pool consists of lawns with trees for shade and is intended for sunbathing and picnics.

The pool can accommodate up to 5,000 people and has a minimum depth of 60 cm sloping gently to a maximum depth of 1,60 m. An island serves as a stage for open-air pop festivals and other entertainment events. In the evenings and in winter, the pool becomes a lake for wind surfing and boating.

An interesting social footnote is the fact that city street vandalism during school holidays has decreased by about 90 per cent since the opening of the leisure centre.

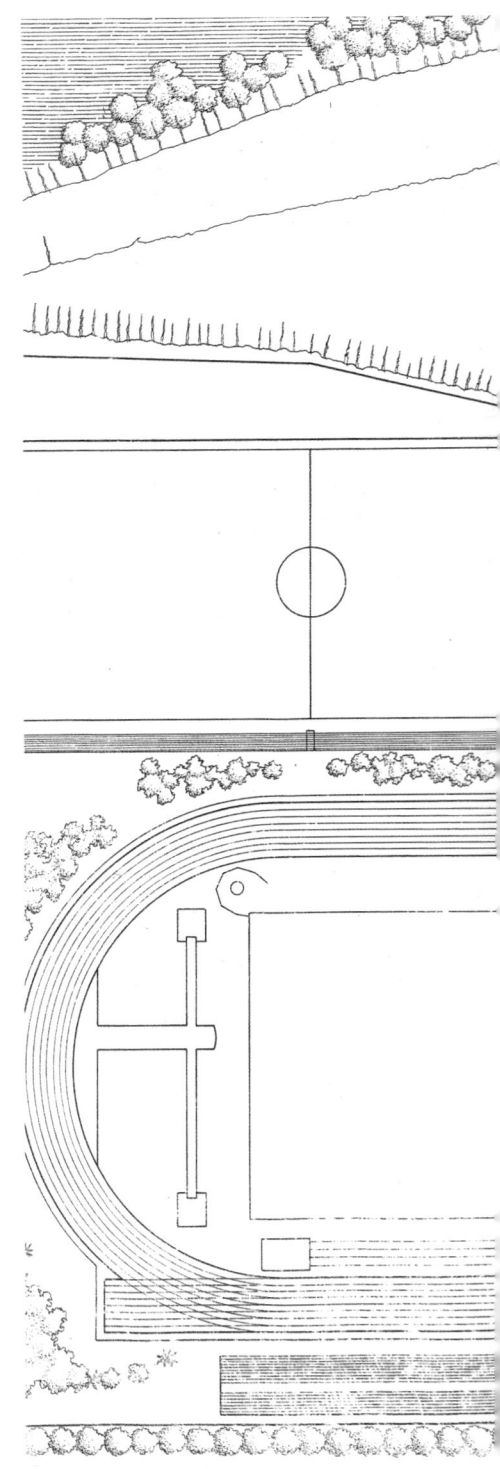

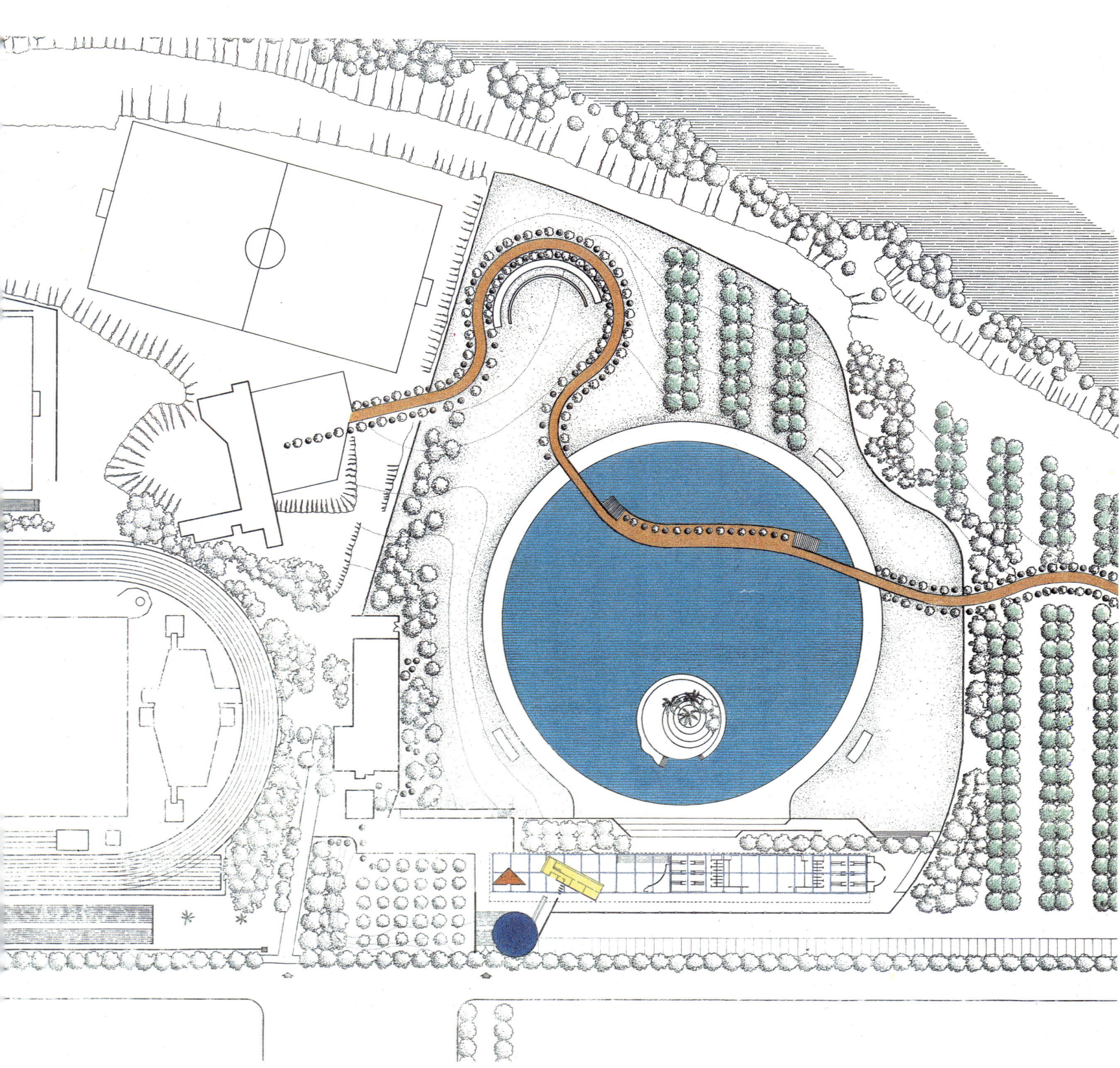

2. The tree-lined causeway that crosses the
swimming pool.
3. Swimming pool with the island that is also used
for music festivals.

Parque de la Creueta del Coll, Av. Mare de Déu del Coll, Barcelona
1981–87

The first sketch for this park was made in 1976 in response to a request from an activist and politically alert neighbourhood association which was concerned about the future use of the old quarry and derelict hill. On the one hand, the Municipal Parks Department proposed an ornamental garden, correct, but lacking any mediating social vision, and on the other, an active socialist group lobbied for a football ground. The conflict was shelved until the first democratic municipal elections were over and the new city administration was in a position to take stock of the situation and sort out some of the problems, as well as looking at the opportunities offered by the new decade.

By 1981 the issues were becoming clearer: the football playing field was relocated to another piece of derelict wasteland, and social use of the new park was now agreed upon by both the city and the neighbourhood association. The agreement developed further as the design progressed.

The project is on 16 hectares of park divided into two sectors, each with a distinct character of its own: the north slope, looking towards Tibidabo, was wasteland and was treated as a reafforestation site, provided with paths essential for laying out play areas, and clearings for picnic facilities; on the south slope, looking towards the sea, the crater left by the disused quarry provided a natural amphitheatre where a more urban set of uses could be provided in a park for promenades and festivals which also served as a source of identity for the neighbourhood itself. The various elements of the main space – such things as planting, paving, *pèrgola*, service buildings etc. – were related to each other by means of a large sweeping circular space which is interrupted by the hillside terraces and lake. This lake is used for swimming in summer and can accommodate some 1,000 people at a time. Two large sculptures adorn the space, one is a vertical piece by Ellsworth Kelly at the hinge of the entrance route, the other is a huge piece of concrete by Eduardo Chillida suspended just above the surface of the pool in the heart of the crater.

1. Aerial view of the park.

2. The bathing lake.
3. Sculpture »Eulogy to Water« by Eduardo Chillida
suspended from the rocks.

Notes

[1] Sant Climent de Taüll is a perfectly plain triapsidal wooden-roofed Catalan Romanesque-styled basilica without even a clerestory. The handsome square tower is traditionally Lombard. The church is famous for its paintings and is almost archaic for its date (1132).

[2] The preference for the hall church and wide vault can be seen as reflecting a certain Catalan reluctance to surrender to the full verticality of mature Gothic; towers are adjuncts rather than the crowning glory of the whole. Alastair Boyd, *The Essence of Catalonia: Barcelona and its Region,* London, 1988, p. 206.

[3] Both *seny* and *rauxa* are identified by Boyd, ibid., p. 276, as representing the two poles of the Catalan national consciousness.

[4] The sensuous side of Catalan architecture is immediately apparent in the Modernisme at the beginning of the century, and was accompanied by a certain ability to sustain fantasy. Oriol Bohigas recognized this side of Catalan expression in his study, published as *Proceso y erótica del diseño,* Barcelona, 1972. A second revised and augmented edition of the work was issued in 1979.

[5] These characteristics mesh well with the Catalan temperament. They were singled out by Boyd, op. cit. p. 197, as the dominant characteristics of the principal Catalan Romanesque churches.

[6] This observation comes from Simone Weil, *The need for roots: prelude to a declaration of duties towards mankind,* London, 1987, p. 156.

[7] The details of Oriol Bohigas' family background and the importance of his father who died when he was a young man, as well as his later successful professional career are contained in his autobiographical testament: *Combat d'Incerteses: Dietari de Records,* Barcelona, 1989.

[8] Bohigas is unusual in that he has managed to combine an active architectural career with important intellectual contributions as the co-editor of the magazine *Serra d'Or* and, parallel with this, an output of important books on Catalan architectural history. In *Arquitectura modernista* (1968) and *Reseña y catálogo de la arquitectura modernista* (1972) he examined Modernisme; architecture and urbanism during the Second Republic are examined in his *Arquitectura española de la Segunda República* (1970), and *Catalunya, Arquitectura i urbanisme durant la República* (1978).

[9] Lluís Domènech i Montaner, who was responsible for the nationalistic Palau de la Música (completed in 1908), played an important part in the formation of the Unió Catalanista of 1891. Josep Puig i Cadafalch, Domènech's young collaborator and seventeen years his junior, followed a similar path of architecture and politics when he took over the leadership of the Catalan Mancomunitat from 1917 to 1924 as its president on the death of Prat de la Riba, a position he held until its abolition in 1924. Gaudí was much more than an architect, being seen by many as a great patriot and a saint in his own lifetime. This mixing of architecture with politics only serves to emphasize the contribution of architecture as a vehicle for expressing Catalan national aspirations.

[10] Thus, Sibyl Moholy-Nagy in »In Barcelona, an architectural heritage is transformed into a modern tradition«, *The Architectural Forum,* July-August, 1965, described Martorell this way: »Josep Martorell is a gaunt taciturn type straight out of Cervantes. He is the thinker and innovator with the calm scepticism of an ancient people who have outwitted and outthought their oppressors.«

David Mackay is described in the same article as »...the mediator between the solitary intellect of Martorell and the expansive dynamism of Bohigas. He stands for architecture as the art of the possible«.

[11] Jujol's metalwork was essentially calligraphic, concrete writing with hatched bars contrasting with thin plate strips. See David Mackay, *Modern architecture in Barcelona 1854-1939,* Barcelona, Oxford, Berlin and New York, 1989, p. 87, 88.

[12] Ibid.

[13] Ibid.

[14] Ibid.

[15] Florensa's apparent ambivalence towards Modern Architecture in his lectures was remarked on by Josep Martorell in an interview with the author Feb. 15, 1990.

[16] This incident is recounted by Mackay, op. cit., p. 96.

[17] The acronym stood for Grup d'Artistes i Tècnics Catalans per al Progrés de l'Arquitectura Contemporànea, and was modelled on CIRPAC formed in 1928 which was subsequently known as CIAM at meetings held at the castle of La Sarraz in 1929.

[18] In all probability, Grup R stood for Realism with a regionalist bias. Charles Jencks exploited the deliberate vagueness of the group's name in an article entitled »MBM and the Barcelona School« commenting that »...in the event, Grup R was formed to swing the balance towards Regionalism (and away from Neo-Classicism), not because the R referred to these qualities (any more than Revolution, Red, Rationalist) but because Neo-Classicism was too *Pompier,* too much associated with the Franco Regime.« – Neo-Realism in the Italian cinema had its architectural counterpart which sought to express a new relationship between that country's culture and the realities of the day. This found expression in the work of Mario Ridolfi whose INA-Casa Tiburtino Quarter, Rome (1950), was a sort of manifesto of Neo-Realism. Other works in a similar vein were the »Case a torre« in the Viale Etiope by Ridolfi and the village of La Martella near Matera by Ludovico Quaroni, all realized in the 1950s. – For a different viewpoint to Jencks and discussion of the significance of the Barcelona School see also G.R. Cabrero, *Spagna Architettura 1965-1988,* Milan, 1989, pp. 15, 78.

[19] This possible connection was raised in a discussion of the author with Oriol Bohigas.

[20] In Italy, Neo-Realism in the cinema was definitely a reaction to the unreality of Fascist movie making during the war years under Mussolini known as »white telephone« films. See Ann Lloyd, *The Illustrated History of the Cinema,* London, 1986, p. 216-217. The great Italian director Roberto Rossellini defined Neo-Realism when he said: »For me it is above all a moral position from which to look at the world. It then became an aesthetic position, but at the beginning it was moral.«

[21] See Cabrero, op. cit., p. 15.

[22] Ibid., p. 73.

[23] See Kenneth John Conant, *Carolingian and Romanesque Architecture 800-1200,* Harmondsworth, 1974, p. 312.

[24] See Mackay, op. cit., p. 16.

[25] Catalonia took Naples in 1423 towards the end of a phase of vigorous military expansion in the Mediterranean which left it the greatest power in the region in the 14th and 15th centuries. Boyd, op. cit., p. 7.

[26] Many of the grander buildings feature an imposing staircase leading from the patio to the first-floor gallery with an arcade of pointed arches on clusters of slender columnettes. This motif is prevalent in the larger important dwellings in the old quarter of Palma on Mallorca.

[27] From discussions with the architectural staff of the MBM office specifically with reference to the verandas of the Can Bordoi House.

[28] See Le Corbusier, *Oeuvre complète, 1910-1929,* Zurich, 1935, referred to by Kenneth Frampton, *Modern architecture: a critical history,* London, 1980, p. 224.

[29] This work is illustrated in Bruno Zevi, »The Italian Rationalists«, in: Dennis Sharp, *The Rationalists,* London, 1978, p. 126, fig. 11.

[30] There is a further and much deeper similarity with MBM in Hertzberger's call for prototypes which make individual interpretations of the collective patterns, which possess the potential to be interpreted to suit individual needs. Hertzberger's 1974 Centraal Beheer Building at Apeldoorn, Holland, provides a further parallel with the formulation of MBM's ideas on urbanism in the Olympic Village at Nova Icària with its irregular clustering of working platforms set within a regular orthogonal tartan grid comprising floors, columns, light slots, and service ducts. Indeed, Hertzberger introduced Islamic patterns such as the »bazaar« or »patio« and an introverted spatial scheme which are not all that different from the Mansana housing by MBM in its general approach.

[31] The church confessional screen is also called a *gelosia,* a factor which must be taken into account when considering the identification of the *gelosia* with privacy and secrecy – with hidden inner matters.

[32] The period of ascendancy of Catalonia in the 14th and 15th centuries began with the conquest of Mallorca in 1229, to be followed by the invasion of Sicily, Athens, Neopatria, Corsica, Sardinia, and reached its climax with the fall of Naples. Boyd, op. cit., p. 7.

[33] The Catalan language is derived from vulgar Latin and belongs to the same group of western languages as Occitan, French, Castilian, Portuguese and Galician, so it is not surprising to find this linguistic relationship being reflected in architectural preferences. For example, a typical feature of the Romanesque is the Lombard band, which entered the region from North Italy via Provence and Perpignan. For an examination of the relationship of MBM with Milanese architecture and Italian influences in general see Joseph Rykwert, »On the Architecture of Martorell/Bohigas/Mackay«, *A + U* (Tokyo), 225 (June 1989), p. 74.

[34] David Mackay, »First of April 1989«, *A + U* (Tokyo), 225 (June 1989), p. 68.

[35] For an analysis of the role of selected typologies in Aalto's work see Demetri Porphyrios, *Sources of Modern Eclecticism,* London, 1982. See chapter III: »The Retrieval of Memory«, p. 25 ff., especially.

[36] Wittkower analyzed eleven of Palladio's villas. This was published in Rudolf Wittkower, *Architectural Principles in the Age of Humanism,* London, 1973, p. 71 ff. See p. 73 and fig. 8 especially.

[37] Peter Blake, *Frank Lloyd Wright: Architecture and Space,* Harmondsworth, 1960, pp. 115-118. Blake examines the spiral theme in Wright from an unbuilt planetarium project for Gordon Strong, done in 1925, to the later Guggenheim Museum proposal.

[38] See Cabrero, op. cit., p. 68.

[39] Barbara Lane, *Architecture and Politics in Germany 1918-1945,* Cambridge, Mass., 1968, p. 216.

[40] See Cabrero, op. cit., p. 68. Cabrero noted: »When the dictator died the obligation for architects to give testimony disappeared. And thus, also, the ideas that unified Catalan architecture, rendering them homogeneous evaporated also.«

[41] Ibid., p. 20.

[42] Ibid., p. 73.

[43] Noted by the author in an interview with Bohigas, Feb. 21, 1990.

[44] From the same interview.

[45] See Oriol Bohigas, *Planning and Urban Design in Barcelona 1981/82,* Ajuntament de Barcelona, Area of Urbanism and Public Works, Barcelona, 1987, pp. 11, 12.

[46] The metastasis analogy applied to urban renewal is set out in Oriol Bohigas, »Strategic Metastasis«, in: *Barcelona: Spaces and Sculptures (1982-1986),* Barcelona, 1987, pp. 11, 12.

[47] Lynch defined the district as »...the relatively large city areas which the observer can mentally go inside of, and which have some common character.« From Kevin Lynch, *The Image of the City,* Cambridge, Mass., 1960, p. 66.

[48] From the Introduction to *Barcelona: Spaces and Sculptures (1982-1986),* loc. cit.

[49] Robert Hughes, »The Spaces and Sculptures«, ibid., p. 25.

[50] Ignasi de Solà-Morales, »Matters of Style«, ibid., p. 17.

[51] These currents are summarized by Kenneth Frampton in »The Renewal of Barcelona: An Appreciation«, ibid., p. 20.

[52] The contribution of architecture to the developing urbanism of Barcelona is spelled out by Oriol Bohigas in »Architecture in the emerging metropolis«, in: M. Raeburn (ed.), *Homage to Barcelona: The City and its art 1888-1936,* London, 1986, p. 101.

[53] The intended structure of the Cerdà »eixample« and what transpired in later developments and attempts to regulate it are described by Oriol Bohigas in: *Reconstrucción de Barcelona,* Barcelona, 1986. See Chapter 4, El Ensanche, pp. 55-68.

[54] Ibid., p. 11.

[55] A detailed account of the theoretical premises and urban design intentions of the new Olympic Village and seafront park are set forth in: *Transformation of a seafront: Barcelona. The Olympic Village, 1992,* Barcelona, 1988.

[56] Ibid., p. 34.

[57] Ibid., p. 34.

[58] Sir Ove Arup and Jack Zunz, *Sydney Opera House,* Reprint Series 1, Sydney, 1988. See in particular »The Roof Structure – early development«, pp. 7-14.

[59] By Josep Tarradellas, head of the Catalan Government in exile and first president of the restored Generalitat after Franco's death. Quoted by Boyd., op. cit., p. 10.

[60] From George Orwell, *Homage to Catalonia,* Harmondsworth, 1989, p. 10.

[61] Ibid., p. 111.

[62] David Mackay, op. cit., p. 99, comments that the 1929 exhibition had no impact on the young Rationalist group, in spite of displaying two pavilions by Mies van der Rohe.

[63] The tabernacle archetype was illustrated by Le Corbusier in *Vers Une Architecture* (1923) in the essay on regulating lines. Possibly, the Spanish tradition of the *toldo* may also be a factor in the design of the Casa Canovelles.

[64] See John Shearman, *Mannerism,* Harmondsworth, 1967, pp. 15-22. Shearman equates Mannerism with facility and ease of invention which he regards as positive virtues.

[65] Notably Arnold Hauser in his two-volume study *Mannerism: The Crisis of the Renaissance and the Origin of Modern Art,* London, 1965.

[66] A similar device can be found in the Casal De Sant Jordi House (1929-31) by Francesc Folguera, in which V-shaped bay-window bays are formed on the corner splay and return to interrupt the flatness of the three façades.

[67] Giuseppe Terragni's Novocumum Flats, Como (1927/28), spring to mind in this connection.

[68] This early progressive stance in the planning of educational facilities in Barcelona is discussed by David Mackay, op. cit., p. 79-80.

[69] »The school as the city« idea was explored by Shadrock Woods in »The education Bazaar«, *Harvard Educational Review: Architecture and Education,* 9 (4, 1969), pp. 116-125.

[70] The Munkegard School at Gentofte, Copenhagen (1956), by Arne Jacobsen proved to be extremely influential in later years as a model structure that offered both an ordered framework for learning, while permitting and making available opportunities for individual development within this same framework.

[71] Quoted from the guide *What is Montserrat,* Barcelona, 1989, p. 14.

[72] I have described the »third generation« of architects in the monograph *Third Generation: The Changing Meaning of Architecture,* London and New York, 1972. The »third generation« includes the likes of Jørn Utzon, James Stirling, Frei Otto, Kisho Kurokawa, I.M. Pei, Harry Seidler, architects now nearing the end of their careers with some forty years of solid practice behind them. To varying degrees, they have tended to maintain links with Modernism, reinterpreting and extending it rather than turning to Post-Modernism as the alternative. The first mention of the »third generation« was made by Sigfried Giedion in the fifth edition of his *Space, Time and Architecture* in 1966.

Some Local Architectural Terms

Balcó This is an opening in the main façade facing the street which is typified by a small balustraded platform (balcony) but which does not have a roof for protection from the weather. Occasionally, a flexible mat is draped over the balustrade from the head of the window for sun protection which provides additional privacy for the room behind it while allowing side views down the street.

Corredor Especially the interior which serves as a passage and connecting way between rooms. The equi-valent of the English hallway.

Galeria A *corredor* or long passage, for the most part situated in the interior surrounding a *pati* or at the rear of the dwelling. It usually has glazing enclosing it with a roof and overlooks the garden or a patio/courtyard. It may also refer to a *corredor* or principal passageway in a large building with many rooms off it. Unlike the *balcó,* the *galeria* is protected from the weather and offers a solarium-like environment in winter protected from the wind but exposed to the sun.

Gelosia The Spanish term is *celosia,* from the French *jalousie* which referred to a slotted blind; Venetian shutter; Venetian blind, etc. The Catalan term *gelosia* refers to the small square gridded lattice work used to screen one part of a room from the other or disposed on the outside of buildings to shade the interior, windows, openings or hide services. The term also applies to the confessional screen in churches.

Glorieta This may refer to a small square in a garden, or it may apply to a little covered square which is the confluence of several streets or boulevards. It is also used to designate a pavilion or small covered structure in the garden generally closed in by a screen of columns or lattice grille work with climbing plants. There is a strong suggestion that it is circular in shape.

Mansana This is a building occupying a large city block such as was envisaged by the Catalan civil engineer Ildefons Cerdà in his visionary 1859 plan for the city. Cerdà's plan consisted of a square grid 133 m x 133 m (three blocks every 400 m) with 20 m wide streets.

Pati (Patio) A court space enclosed by either walls or within a building. A yard surrounded by houses and communicating with the street by means of a formal entry. A confined yard opening off a street. It is principally used to describe any enclosed internal space open to the sky which is used to provide additional daylight and ventilation to the surrounding rooms of a building. Commonly, the windows, balconies, galleries of buildings overlook it.

Pèrgola An arbour, covered walk, formed by training climbing plants over a trellis framework. It is usually formed in two parallel rows or lines of columns supporting an open timber roof (as a vine arbour). In practice, it is constructed to ornament the garden and to further embellish the terrace.

Persiana Blinds or awnings used to shade the balcony. Wrought iron frames were provided for this purpose to support the *persiana* awning, and a rail above the door or window head provided a tie.

Porxo A covered, open-air space, limited with columns or pillars and adjoining the façade of the ground floor of a building.

Rotonda A building or circular room covered by a dome.

Terrassa A flat platform for sitting or walking which is sometimes attached to the dwelling and serves as an extension of the living area. The term is the equivalent of the English veranda.

Toldo Canvas awnings.

Tribuna An enclosed balcony. A covered space enclosed by glazing and erected over the platform of a balcony. In effect, an enclosed balcony.

Biographies

Josep Martorell

Born 1925 in Barcelona.
1951: Title of architect, Escola T.S. d'Arquitectura, Barcelona. Went into partnership with Oriol Bohigas. Founder member of »Grup R«. Assistant in the Technical Department of the Provincial Commission for Urbanism of Barcelona until 1956.
1963: Title of Doctor in Architecture, Escola T.S. d'Arquitectura, Barcelona.
1968: President of the Cultural Commission of the Col.legi Oficial d'Arquitectes de Catalunya until 1970.
1970: Spokesman for the Commission for Urbanism and Public Services for Barcelona and other municipalities until 1974.
1979: Member of the Provincial Commission for Urbanism of Barcelona.
1980: President of the Executive Committee of the »Congrés d'Arquitectura de Catalunya 1980-81«.
1981: Member of the Architectural Heritage Commission, Barcelona.
1987: Head Director of Urbanism and Architecture of »Vila Olímpica, S.A.« until 1989.
1992: President of the XIX Congress of the U.I.A. Barcelona, 1996.

Published books: *La Immigració a Catalunya* (collab.), Barcelona, Edicions de Materials, 1968. – *Guia d'arquitectura de Menorca. 1977,* Publicacions del Col.legi d'Arquitectes de Catalunya, Barcelona, La Gaya Ciencia, 1980. – *Transformación de un frente marítimo. Barcelona. La Villa Olímpica 1992. Transformation of a seafront. Barcelona. The Olympic Village 1992,* Barcelona, Gustavo Gili, 1988. – *La Villa Olímpica. Barcelona 92. Arquitectura. Parques. Puerto deportivo. The Olympic Village. Barcelona 92. Architecture. Parks. Leisure Port,* Barcelona, Gustavo Gili, 1991.

Oriol Bohigas

Born 1925 in Barcelona
1951: Title of architect, Escola T.S. d'Arquitectura, Barcelona. Went into partnership with Josep Martorell. Founder member of »Grup R«.
1963: Title of Doctor in Architecture, Escola T.S. d'Arquitectura, Barcelona.
1964: Senior lecturer in the Escola T.S. d'Arquitectura, Barcelona, until 1966.
1971: Chair of composition at the Escola T.S. d'Arquitectura, Barcelona (1971 onwards).
1974: Member of the board of directors of the magazine *Arquitecturas bis*, Barcelona.
1975: Member of the board of directors of *Lotus International*, Milan.
1977: Head of the Escola T.S. d'Arquitectura, Barcelona, until 1980.
1980: Director of Planning, City Council of Barcelona, until 1984.
1981: President of »Fundació Miró«, Barcelona, until 1988. Member of the Accademia Nazionale di San Luca, Rome.
1986: Gold Medal for Artistic Merit from the city of Barcelona.
1988: Medal of Urbanism from the Fondation Académie d'Architecture de Paris.
1989: Sikkens Award, Rotterdam.
1990: Gold Medal for Architecture awarded by the Consejo Superior de los Colegios de Arquitectos de España, Madrid.

1991: Creu de Sant Jordi awarded by the Generalitat de Catalunya, Barcelona. Councillor of Culture of the City Council, Barcelona.
1992: Doctor honoris causa of the Technical University of Darmstadt.

Published books: *Barcelona entre el Pla Cerdà i el barraquisme,* Barcelona, Edicions 62, 1963. – *Arquitectura Modernista,* Barcelona, Lumen, 1968; Italian edition: *Architettura Modernista, Gaudí e il movimento catalano,* Torino, Einaudi, 1969. – *Les escoles tècniques superiors i l'estructura professional,* Barcelona, Nova Terra, 1968; Spanish edition: *Las escuelas técnicas superiores y la estructura profesional,* Barcelona, Nova Terra, 1970. – *Contra una arquitectura adjetivada,* Barcelona, Seix y Barral, 1969. – *La arquitectura española de la Segunda República,* Barcelona, Tusquets, 1970; Italian edition: *Architettura spagnola della Seconda Repubblica,* Bari, Dedalo, 1978. – *Polèmica d'arquitectura catalana,* Barcelona, Edicions 62, 1970. – *Reseña y catálogo de la arquitectura modernista,* Barcelona, Lumen, 1972 (second edition 1983). – *Proceso y erótica del diseño,* Barcelona, La Gaya Ciencia, 1972 (second edition 1978). – *Once arquitectos,* Barcelona, La Gaya Ciencia, 1976. – *Catalunya. Arquitectura i urbanisme durant la República,* Barcelona, Dopesa, 1978. – *Reconstrucció de Barcelona,* Barcelona, Edicions 62, 1984; Spanish edition: *Reconstrucción de Barcelona,* Madrid, Ediciones del MOPU, 1986. – *Transformación de un frente marítimo. Barcelona. La Villa Olímpica 1992. Transformation of a seafront. Barcelona. The Olympic Village 1992,* Barcelona, Gustavo Gili, 1988. – *Combat d'incerteses. Dietari de records,* Barcelona, Edicions 62, 1989; Spanish edition: *Desde los años inciertos,* Barcelona, Anagrama, 1991. – *La Villa Olímpica. Barcelona 92. Arquitectura. Parques. Puerto deportivo. The Olympic Village. Barcelona 92. Architecture. Parks. Leisure Port,* Barcelona, Gustavo Gili, 1991.

David Mackay

Born 1933 in Eastborne, Sussex, England.
1949: R.I.B.A. Essay Prize.
1958: Honors Diploma in Architecture, Northern Polytechnic, London.
1959: Member of the Royal Institute of British Architects.
1960: R.I.B.A. Andrew Prentice Prize for the study of Spanish Architecture.
1962: Went into partnership with Josep Martorell and Oriol Bohigas.
1964: Contributing editor of *World Architecture* until 1967.
1966: Title of architect, Escola T.S. d'Arquitectura, Barcelona.
1979: Consultor of the *Contemporary Architects* encyclopedia, New York.
1981: Director of »Foreign Studies Program« of the Catholic University of America, Barcelona. 1981, 1982, 1984, 1985, 1986. Professor, Washington University, St. Louis, USA.
1986: Distinguished guest professor, School of Architecture, Wisconsin University, Milwaukee, USA.
1990: Berlin-Zentrum Seminar, Dessau.
1991: Member of the Stadtforum to study the reconstruction of Berlin.
1992: Member of The Urban Advisory commitee for the Senate of Berlin.

Published books: *Contradictions in living environment,* London, Crosby Lockwood and Son Ltd., 1971; Spanish edition: *Contradicciones en el entorno habitado,* Barcelona, Gustavo Gili, 1972. – *Wohnungsbau im Wandel,* Stuttgart, Verlag Gerd Hatje, 1977; English edition: *Multiple family housing,* New York, Architectural Book Publishing Co., 1977; Spanish edition: *Viviendas plurifamiliares,* Barcelona, Gustavo Gili, 1979. – *La casa unifamiliar. The modern house,* Barcelona, Gustavo Gili, 1984; English edition: *The modern house,* New York, Hastings House Publishers Inc., 1984; German edition: *Einfamilienhäuser,* Stuttgart, Verlag Gerd Hatje, 1984. – *Modern Architecture in Barcelona. 1854-1939,* Sheffield, The Anglo-Catalan Society, 1985; Catalan edition: *L'arquitectura moderna a Barcelona. 1854-1939,* Barcelona, Edicions 62, 1989, English editions: Oxford, BSP Professional Books, 1989; Berlin, Ernst & Sohn, 1989; New York, Rizzoli, 1989. – *Transformación de un frente marítimo. Barcelona. La Villa Olímpica 1992. Transformation of a seafront. Barcelona. The Olympic Village 1992,* Barcelona, Gustavo Gili, 1988. – *La Villa Olímpica. Barcelona 92. Arquitectura. Parques. Puerto deportivo. The Olympic Village. Barcelona 92. Architecture. Parks. Leisure Port,* Barcelona, Gustavo Gili, 1991.

Albert Puigdomènech

Born 1944 in Barcelona.
1969: Title of architect, Escola T.S. d'Arquitectura, Barcelona.
1970: Vice-secretary of the Col.legi Oficial d'Arquitectes de Catalunya until 1972.
1971: Regular contributor to the architecture and urbanism section of the Barcelona newspaper *Tele-Exprés* until 1972.
1972: Director of the Urbanistic Information Office of the Col.legi Oficial d'Arquitectes de Catalunya until 1973.
1976: Urbanistic advisor for the Gavà Town Council, Barcelona, until 1978.
1979: Urbanistic advisor for the Canet de Mar and Vilassar de Dalt Town Councils, Barcelona.
1980: Director of Services for Urban Design and Management to the Barcelona City Council until 1983.
1982: Member of the Provincial Commission for Urbanism of Barcelona.
1983: Town-planning advisor for the Ciutadella Town Council, Menorca, until 1985.
1985: Went into partnership with Josep Martorell, Oriol Bohigas, and David Mackay.

Published books: *Transformación de un frente marítimo. Barcelona. La Villa Olímpica 1992. Transformation of a seafront. Barcelona. The Olympic Village 1992,* Barcelona, Gustavo Gili, 1988. – *La Villa Olímpica. Barcelona 92. Arquitectura. Parques. Puerto deportivo. The Olympic Village. Barcelona 92. Architecture. Parks. Leisure Port,* Barcelona, Gustavo Gili, 1991.

Collaborators 1954–1992

José A. Acebillo, Albert Aguirre, Javier Alba, Rosa Albet, Thierry Andersen, Pilar Anglada, Liliana Antoniucci, Lluís Archs, Joan Arnalot, Josefa Aymerich

Carles Babot, Jaume Bach, Carles Bàguena, Francisca Balbontín, José M. Baquero, Alfredo H. Barbosa, Carola Barchi, Angel Barco, Antonio Barco, Rosa Bartolí, Josep Ll. Bellés, Montse Beltran, Alejandro Bermúdez, Joaquim Blanc, Ferran Blancafort, Ramón Blay, Josep Bohigas, Maria Bohigas, Pere Bohigas, Jordi Boldú, Fina Bonell, Lia Bonzanigo, Jordi Borén, Anna Bosch, Elena Bosch, Marta Bosch, Victor Bosch, Ramón Bufí, Núria Buigas

Mario Calavera, Xita Camps, Katia Canha, Enric Cantero, Oriol Capdevila, Jordi Carbonell, Francesc Cardeña, Robert Carvajal, Rosendo Casanovas, Alex Casas, Josep M. Castells, Carme Casterá, Marta Cervelló, M. Teresa Codina, Jordi Colomina, Josep M. Comas, A. A. Compagnucci, Clara Cornudella, Josep M. Cots, Xavier Cots, Josep Croses, Carles Culasso

Núria Dalmases, Lluís Dalmau, Núria Darbra, Glausia Dias, Amàlia Diéguez, Carme Domènech, Jordi Domènech, Lluís Domènech, Pia Domènech, Niclas Dünebake

Maro Efthymiadou, Joan Escat, Horacio Espeche, Miquel Espinet, Albert Estany, Marite Evaristo

Patrizia Falcone, Agnès Farré, Marta Finzterwal, Montserrat Fons, Francesc Fortuny, Jaume Freixa, Dolors Furés

Hector Gath, Reiner Ganz, Jordi Garcés, Joan García, Joan J. García, Josep Gaspar, Francesc Gelizo, M. Joana Gibanel, Rafael Gispert, Pau Granados, Rosa Granados, Artur Grau, Sebastian Gribbling, Francesc Gual, Josep Guasch, M. Teresa Guimerà

Annabelle Henderson, Vera Hofbaverova, Tomàs Homs, Alfons Hostan

Glòria Ibáñez, Pedro V. Ibáñez, Anne Imbert, Ivar Ivarsoy

Agustí Jarque, Pilar Jarque, Steve Jensen, Andreu Jurado

Anna M. Labayen, Angeles León, Claudia Libermann, Claudio Libeskind, Patti Liu, Jaime Loayza, Carles Lumeras, Mercè Llopis

Mark Mackay, Martha Mackay, Monica Mackay, Sònia Mackay, Duccio Malagamba, Christoph Mann, Josep Marqués, Pere Martín, M. Carme Martín, Adolf Martínez, Anna M. Martínez, Josefa Martínez, Tania C. Martins, Laia Martorell, Josep Mascaró, Xavier Massísimo, Alan Mee, Carme Megías, Joan Mestre, Jordi Mestre, Josep M. Miralles, Toni Miserachs, Joan A. Montfort, Anna Montoliu, Francesc Montseny, Pere Mora, Antoni Moragas, Susan Mortimer, Francesc Mullerat

Kazuo Nakajima, Clare Nelson, Ines Novak

Manuel Ocaña, Jordi Oliva, Carles Olmo

Montserrat Padrós, Joan A. Paez, Hortensia Palou, Agustí Pallejà, Rafael Panadés, Marta Parpal, Lluís

Pau, Antoni Pérez, Joaquim Pérez, Victor Pérez, Annukka Pietilä, Jaume Piñol, David Plantada, Enric Poblet, Carol Portabella, Joaquim Prats, Josep M. Pujol

M. Carme Quesada

Pau Ramis, Toni Ramis, Anna Ravell, Jaume Riba, Carme Ribadulla, Enric Ribadulla, Marta Ribalta, M.D. Rocamora, Joan Rodón, Arantxa Rodrigo, Carmen Rodriguez, Jeanne Roig, Laura Roig, Josep M. Roldán, Lluís Romaní, Judit Romeu, Maria Romeu, Oriol Romeu, Asun Rubio

Chander Sabherwal, Pedro Sánchez, Marc Sant, Nicolau Sant, Pachi Santos, Carmina Sanvicens, Enric Satué, Ferràn Segarra, Eulàlia Serra, Josep M. Simó, Josep L. Sisternas, Roser Solanic, Dolors Solé, Joan Solé, Galo Soler, Enric Sòria, Assumpta Sòria, Enric Steegmann, José Stravalachi

Manuel Tàpia, Joaquim Teixidor, Ignasi Tiana, Marc Tintoré, Montserrat Tomàs, Josep M. Torra, Margarita Torrente, Jordi Torres, Rosa Trilla

Antoni Ubach, Josep Urdeix

Pilar Val, Josep Vallès, Miquel Verdaguer, Carme Vernis, Núria Vich, Josep Vila, Maria Vila, Mònica Vila, Marta Vilaseca, Blanca Vives

Thomas Winkelbauer

Albert Zabala, Joan Zaballos, Xavier Zubillaga

Selection of Works and Projects

Roger de Flor Housing, Roger de Flor 215, Barcelona, 1954-58
Guardiola House, Argentona, 1954/55
Maragall Housing, P. Maragall 243, Barcelona, 1954-59
Instituto Laboral, Sabiñánigo, Huesca, 1955-58
Mutua Metalúrgica de Seguros Clinic, Av. Diagonal 394, Barcelona, 1955-59
Baró de Viver School, Pol. Baró de Viver, Barcelona, 1956-61
Escorial Housing, Escorial 50, Barcelona, 1955-62
Timbaler del Bruc School, Riera d'Horta, Barcelona, 1957/58
CEAC Publishing House, Aragó 472, Barcelona, 1957-59
Redemptor Church, Av. Mare de Deu de Montserrat 34-40, Barcelona, 1957-68
Pallars City Block, Pallars 299-317, Barcelona, 1958/59
Calvet Housing, Calvet 71, Barcelona, 1958-61
Piher-Badalona Factory, Riera Cañadó s/n, Badalona, 1959-64
Camèlies Housing, Camèlies 50-58, Barcelona, 1959-64
Luján House, Palau de Plegamans, 1959-62
Max Cahner House, Iradier 32, Barcelona, 1959-62
Meridiana Housing, Av. Meridiana 312-316, Barcelona, 1959-65
Navas de Tolosa Housing, Navas de Tolosa 296, Barcelona, 1960-63
Secretari Coloma Housing, Secretari Coloma 79-89, Barcelona, 1960-65
Sant Sebastià del Verdum Church, Viladrosa, Barcelona, 1960-68
Orpi House, El Figaró, 1961/62
Col.legí Oficial d'Arquitectes de Catalunya Offices, Pl. Nova 5, Barcelona, 1961/62
Holiday Centre for Young Children, Mas Silvestre, Canyamars, 1961-65
Casa del Pati Housing, Rda. del Guinardó 44, Barcelona, 1961-64
Milans del Bosch Housing, Sant Adrià 196, Barcelona, 1962-65
Via Augusta Housing, Via Augusta 168, Barcelona, 1957-64
La Vanguardia Workshops, Offices and Flats, Tallers 52-54, Barcelona, 1962-65
Can Bordoi House, Llinars del Vallès, 1962-65
Garbí School, Esplugues de Llobregat, 1962-78
Europalma Apartments, Costa de la Calma, Mallorca, 1963/64
Pere IV Workshops, Pere IV 162, Barcelona, 1963-65
Xiol Housing, Torrebadal 23-25, Badalona, 1963-65
Borrell Housing, Borrell 87-89, Barcelona, 1963-66
Europalma Houses, Costa de la Calma, Mallorca, 1963-65
Sant Martí Housing, Pol. Sant Martí, Barcelona, 1963-66
Piher-Navarra Factory, Tudela, Navarra, 1964-66
Gama Housing, Via Laietana 16-18, Badalona, 1964/65
Dr. Carulla Housing, Dr. Carulla 53, Barcelona, 1964 to 1967
Xaudiera Housing, Entença 99-101/Aragó 20-22, Barcelona, 1964-70
Destino Publishing House, Riera Cañadó sln, Badalona, 1965-67
Sagrada Familia Church, Igualada, 1965-69
Santa Agueda Apartments, Benicassim, Castelló, 1966/67
Montaña House, L'Ametlla del Vallès, 1966-69

Casp Housing, Casp 114, Barcelona, 1966-69
Sant Jordi School, Pineda, 1967-69
Flats for teachers, Pineda, 1967-69
Buscarons Housing, Buscarons 16, Barcelona, 1967-69
Roca Flats, Av. Angel Sallent, Terrassa, 1967-72
Heredero House, Tredòs, Vall d'Aràn, 1967/68
Dr. Moragas Housing, Av. Dr. Moragas 1, Sta. Maria de Barberà, 1967-71
Piher-Granollers Factory, Av. Sant Julià s/n, Granollers, 1968-71
Serras Shop, Av. A. Clavé 28, Granollers, 1968-72
Alegre de Dalt Housing, Alegre de Dalt 32, Barcelona, 1968-70
Augusta Clinic, Madrazo 8-10, Barcelona, 1968-75
Flats for teachers, Vilanova i La Geltrú, 1969, project
Piher-Badalona II Factory, Riera Cañadó s/n, Badalona, 1969-71
Giró Factory, Av. Navarra s/n, Badalona, 1969-72
Haïssa Factory, Av. Martí Pujol 273, Badalona, 1969-72
Viladecans Crescent Housing, Sol, Viladecans, 1969-73
La Salut City Block, Sant Feliu de Llobregat, 1969-73
Bonanova Flats, P. Bonanova 92, Barcelona, 1970-73
Iluro Building, S. Antoni 82-88, Mataró, 1971-74
París Housing, Rocafort 244-246, Barcelona, 1971-73
Pals Golf Houses, Platja de Pals, Girona, 1971-73
Tharrats House, Valseca 39, Barcelona, 1971-73
Casa de la Torre Housing, Mossèn C. Verdaguer, Sta. Perpètua de Mogoda, 1971-75
Martí House, Sant Jordi d'Alfama, 1972-74
Twin houses, Rectoria 36-38, Barcelona, 1972-74
Thau School, Ctra. d'Esplugues 49-53, Barcelona, 1972-74
Regàs House, Llofriu, 1973, project
Misser House, Llinars del Vallès, 1973-75
Vall Roig Housing, Cerdanyola, 1974
La Costa Housing, La Costa 59-63, Barcelona, 1974-77
El Hacho Tourist Complex, Manilva, Málaga, 1974, project
Martí l'Humà City Block, Martí l'Humà, Sabadell, 1974-79
Jericó Housing, Jericó, Barcelona, 1974-78
Riudellots Housing, Riudellots de la Selva, 1975, project
Xipell Nursery School and Convent, Ciutadella, Menorca, 1975-78
Otero House, La Garriga, 1975-77
Almirall House, La Garriga, 1975-77
Ossi-Caponata Housing, Ossi 45-53, Barcelona, 1975-77
Amil House, Sant Vicenç de Montalt, 1975-78
Biennale di Venezia - Spanish Art Exhibition, Venice, 1976
Extension of the Col.legi Oficial d'Arquitectes and restructuration of Plaça Nova, Pl. Nova, Barcelona, 1976-80, project
Colegio de Arquitectos, Sevilla, 1976, competition project
Balmes Housing, Balmes 281, Barcelona, 1976-79
Eduard Conde Housing, Eduard Conde 50, Barcelona 1976-79
Offices and Bank Building, Rbla. de Mataró, Mataró, 1976-80
Costa i Llobera School, Can Caralleu, Barcelona, 1976-79
Canovelles House, Canovelles, 1977-81
Faculty for Teachers' Training, Universitat Autònoma de Barcelona, Bellaterra, 1977-80

Banco de España Extension, Marqués de Cubas 1, Madrid, 1979, Competition project
Gammans Housing, St. Andreu de la Barca, 1979-81
La Maquinista City Block, La Barceloneta, Barcelona, 1979-88
Parque de España, Rosario, Argentina, 1980, project
Jordà Housing, Jordà 14, Barcelona, 1980-83
Egress Canopy of the Sanctuary of the Virgin of Montserrat, Montserrat Monastery, 1980-83
Friedrichstadt City Block, Berlin, 1981, competition project
Parque Sarmiento, Córdoba, Argentina, 1981, project
Parque de la Creueta del Coll, Av. Mare de Déu del Coll, Barcelona, 1981-87
Catalunya School and Institute, Sant Adrià del Besòs, Barcelona, 1981-88
Pere de Montcada Library, La Sènia, 1981-83
Refurbishment of the Can Sumarro Farm House as a Library, C. Barcelona 138. L'Hospitalet de Llobregat, Barcelona, 1982-84
»Catalunya en la España Moderna 1714-1983« exhibition, Centro Cultural de la Villa de Madrid, Madrid, 1983
Mestres Montanya School, Barrio Palou, Granollers, 1983-86
Sant Oleguer Sports and Leisure Centre, Sabadell, 1983-86
Park of Zona de Ponent, Granollers, 1981-89
New office building extension, Sociedad Nestlé A.E.P.A., Esplugues de Llobregat, 1983-87
Mollet City Block, Mollet, 1983-87
Public library, Ciutat Badia, Barcelona, 1983-87
Secondary institute, Sant Adrià del Besòs, Barcelona, 1983-88
Cornice promenade of Maó Harbour, Maó, Menorca, 1983-89
Tourist village, Cala Canutells, Menorca, 1984-86
Poliorama Theatre, La Rambla, Barcelona, 1984/85
Historic centre, Amiens, 1984, competition project
»Homage to Barcelona. The city and its arts. 1888 to 1936« exhibition, Hayward Gallery, London, 1984/85
Villa Escarrer, Son Vida, Palma de Mallorca, 1985-88
Can Ferrero City Block, Av. Zona Franca, Barcelona, 1985-89
Olympic Village, Barcelona, 1985-92
Gateway House Kochstraße 75, Berlin, 1985-90
Gateway Houses Kochstraße 73, 74, Berlin, 1985, under construction
Gable House Kochstraße 65, Berlin, 1985-91
»Joan Miró escultor« exhibition, Centro de Arte Reina Sofía, Madrid, 1986/87
Expo '92 precincts, Sevilla, 1986, competition project
Hotel Claris, Pau Claris, Barcelona, 1986-92
Refurbishment of the lobby of the Hotel Melià Barcelona, Av. Sarrià, Barcelona, 1986-89
Offices building, Rbla. Catalunya 4, Barcelona, 1986, under construction
Caja de Múrcia y Cartagena, refurbishment of an ancient building, Cartagena, Múrcia, 1986-91
Square in Mendebaldea, Pamplona, 1986-92
Un bagno pubblico nel centro di Napoli, Naples, 1986, competition project
Torino. La città rifugio della Natura, Triennale di Milano, 1987
Hotel Melià Puerto Vallarta, Puerto Vallarta, Mexico, 1987-90
Archaeological museum, Tarragona, 1987, project
Spanish ambassador residence, Bonn, 1987, project
Restoration and refurbishment of the parish church of Santa Eulàlia d'Encamp, Encamp, Andorra, 1987 to 1989

»100 Anys de Fires« exhibition, Fira de Barcelona, 1987/88
Un progetto per Siena, Piazza Matteotti and Piazza Gramsci, Siena, 1988, competition project
Napoli Soterranea, Naples, 1988, project
Primary School, Salt, Girona, 1988-91
Vila Olímpica, S. A., Parc del Litoral, Poblenou, Barcelona, 1988-92
Vila Olímpica, S. A., Olympic Port, Poblenou, Barcelona, 1988-92
Nova Icàra, S. A., Can Folch Housing, Poblenou, Barcelona, 1988-92
Urban plan for the Barracks Area, Girona, 1988, under construction
Pavilion of the Future, Expo '92, Sevilla, 1988-92
Banri Corporation Tokyo Commercial Building, La Rambla, Barcelona, 1989, under construction
Birmingham Heartlands Ltd., Star Site, Birmingham, 1989, competition project
Vila Olímpica, S. A., Harbourmaster's House, Olympic Port, Barcelona, 1989-91
Vila Olímpica, S. A., Sailing School, Olympic Port, Barcelona, 1989-91
Opération Sextius Mirabeau, Aix-en-Provence, 1990, competition project
»Mostra Internacional de Disseny« exhibition, Fira de Barcelona, 1990
Consultation Clichy-Berges de Seine, Clichy, Paris, 1990, competition project
The area round the TGV Station of Le Creusot-Monceau, Le Creusot-Monceau, 1990, project
Suresnes L'Ecluse, consultation pour l'aménagement de la zac de l'écluse, Suresnes, 1990, competion project
Aménagement du Littoral, Commune de La Ciotat, 1990, competition project
Brau und Brunnen Company, office building, Berlin, 1991, competition project
Opération Bassin Berard, Nîmes, 1991, competition project
Preliminary study for the implantation of the Universitat Pompeu Fabra in the historic centre of Barcelona, Barcelona, 1991, project
Aménagement de l'axe historique de Paris à l'Quest de la Grande Arche de la Défense, Paris, 1991, competition project
Project for the reconstruction of the historic centre of Berlin, 1991, project
Parc de détente et de loisir du Lac de Lourdes, Lourdes, 1991, competition project

Awards and Prizes

Foment de les Arts Decoratives (FAD) award to the best building in Barcelona in the years 1959, 1962, 1966, 1979, 1984
ADI/FAD award »Delta de Plata« for industrial design, 1966
First prize in the competition of preliminary plans for a residential unit. Banco Garriga Nogués, Barcelona, 1975
ADI/FAD award »Delta de Oro« for industrial design, 1976
Two first prizes. Prototype schools competition. Ministry of Education, Madrid, 1979
First prize in the competition of the »Internationale Bauausstellung Berlin 1984« for the project »Kochstrasse/Friedrichstrasse in the Südliche Friedrichstadt« IBA, Berlin, 1981
First prize in »Premio Formica 84« for the best project for the library »Can Sumarro« in Barcelona, 1984
First prize in the international competition »Un progetto per Siena« of ideas for the planning of the urban, architectural and functional development of an area in the historical centre of Siena, 1990
First prize in the international competition »Opération Sextius-Mirabeau« for the urban planning of the Sextius-Mirabeau in the centre of Aix-en-Provence, 1990 (in collaboration with Atelier 9: F. Guy/R. Inglesakis and J. P. Siame)
First prize in the international competition for the urban planning of $2^1/_2$ km of the coast of La Ciotat, 1991 (in collaboration with Atelier 9: Guy/Daher)
First prize in the international competition »Opération Bassin Berard« for the planning of a part of the historic centre of Nîmes, 1991
Second prize »ex-aequo« (with the project of the architect R. Castró) in the international competition »L'axe historique de Paris à l'Quest de la Grande Arche de la Défense«, Paris, 1991 (in collaboration with J. P. Buffi, P. Ayguavives and G. Bouchez)
First prize in the competition »Parc de détente et de loisir du lac de Lourdes«, 1991
Foment de les Arts Decoratives (FAD) award to the best urban space in Barcelona in the year 1991.
Gold medal »Barcelona 92« awarded by the Ajuntament de Barcelona, 1992

Selected Bibliography

Books

Juan Daniel Fullaondo, *J. Martorell, O. Bohigas, D. Mackay. Arquitectura 1951-1972,* Madrid, Barcelona, Alfaguara, 1974.
Ch. Jencks, H. Piñón, *Martorell, Bohigas, Mackay: arquitectura 1953-1978,* Madrid, Xarait, 1979.
K. Frampton, *Martorell, Bohigas, Mackay: 30 anni di architettura 1954-1984,* Milan, Electa Editrice, 1984; Spanish edition: *Martorell-Bohigas-Mackay: 30 años de arquitectura 1954-1984,* Madrid, Xarait Ediciones, 1984; French edition: *Martorell-Bohigas-Mackay: 30 ans d'architecture 1954-1984.* Paris, Electa Moniteur, 1985.
Martorell, Bohigas, Mackay, Puigdomènech, *Transformación de un frente marítimo. Barcelona. La Villa Olímpica 1992. Transformation of a seafront. Barcelona. The Olympic Village 1992.* Barcelona, Gustavo Gili, 1988.
Martorell/Bohigas/Mackay. Der Baublock 1958 bis 1988, Berlin, Galeria Aedes, 1988.
Martorell, Bohigas, Mackay, Puigdomènech, *La Villa Olímpica. Barcelona 92. Arquitectura. Parques. Puerto Deportivo. The Olympic Village. Barcelona 92. Architecture. Parks. Leisure Port,* Barcelona, Gustavo Gili, 1991.

Magazines

»Josep Martorell, Oriol Bohigas, David Mackay, Lluís Pau. Interiores Diseños«, *On,* 49, Barcelona, April 1984.
»Martorell/Bohigas/Mackay«, *El Croquis,* 34, Madrid, May-July 1988.
»Martorell/Bohigas/Mackay«, *A+U,* 225, Tokyo, June 1989.
»Martorell-Bohigas-Mackay. La Manzana«, *Documentos de Arquitectura,* 9, Almeria, June 1989.
»Oriol Bohigas. Medalla de Oro de la Arquitectura 1990«, *Arquitectos,* 119, Consejo Superior de los Colegios de Arquitectos de España. Madrid, December 1990.

Sources of Illustrations

Fernando Alda 30, 174 (3–5), 175
Oriol Bohigas 110
Lluís Casals 17 (15), 27 (34), 60, 62 (3, 4), 63 (5, 7),
65, 67 (4, 5), 68 (6, 7), 69 (8, 9), 114 (5), 115 (4, 6, 7),
121, 123 (4, 5), 145 (2, 3), 147 (6, 7), 150, 151 (4–6), 161,
162, 164 (6, 7), 165, 210, 211, 214, 215
Francesc Català-Roca 10 (5), 11, 15 (10), 18 (16, 17),
19, 20 (20, 21), 21 (23, 24), 38, 39, 40, 44, 45 (2, 3),
47, 49 (3), 51, 77, 79, 83, 84, 92, 95, 99, 107, 127, 129
(4, 5), 130, 131, 132 (4, 5), 133, 134, 136, 138, 139 (4, 5),
141, 143, 156, 157, 158 (1, 2)
CB Foto 15 (11), 26 (31, 32), 52, 53 (2), 55 (7), 56, 59,
108, 111, 135 (8, 9), 149
Philip Drew 13 (7), 16 (13)
FRIS Fotografia 9, 25, 29, (37)
Stefan Koppelkamm 117, 118, 119
Lourdes Legorreta 167, 168 (2, 3), 170 (5, 6), 171 (7, 8)
David Mackay 49 (2)
Duccio Malagamba Cover, 16 (12), 18 (18), 37, 41, 43,
53 (3), 55 (6), 58 (3, 4), 87, 89 90, 91 (6), 98, 101, 103,
105, 113, 183 (1, 2), 184 (3, 4)
Oriol Maspons, Julio Ubiña 20 (22), 75, 76 (3)
Xavier Miserachs 8, 213
Paisajes Españoles 144
Enrique Pimulier, José Luis Larrión 198
Raimon Ramis 31, 81, 181
M. Roselló/Editorial G. Gili S. A. 17 (14)
Deidi van Shaewen 80 (3, 4)
Hisao Suzuki 97, 140
TAVISA 177, 196 (2), 197